14-95

TELEVISION AND GENDER REPRESENTATION

TELEVISION AND GENDER REPRESENTATION

Barrie Gunter

John Libbey

LONDON · PARIS · ROME

British Library Cataloguing in Publication Data

Gunter, Barry
  Television and Gender Representation
  I. Title   II. Series
  Acamedia Research Monograph: 14

ISBN 0 86196 478 0
ISSN: 0956 9057

Series Editor: Manuel Alvarado

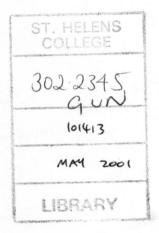
Published by

John Libbey & Company Ltd, 13 Smiths Yard, Summerley Street,
London SW18 4HR, England
Telephone: +44 (0)181-947 2777: Fax +44 (0)181-947 2664
John Libbey Eurotext Ltd, 127 avenue de la République, 92120 Montrouge, France.
John Libbey - C.I.C. s.r.l., via Lazzaro Spallanzani 11, 00161 Rome, Italy

iv

CONTENTS

1 INTRODUCTION

A fundamental aspect of human social development involves learning to behave in ways deemed socially and culturally to be appropriate for one's own sex. This socio-cultural normalizing of displayed, acceptable characteristics and behavioural roles for males and females has been found to develop among children at an early age (Fauls and Smith, 1956) and may influence a child's choice of activities as early as nursery school (Fagot and Patterson, 1969). Spence, Helmreich and Stapp (1975) demonstrated that stereotyped beliefs were significant factors affecting how people perceived themselves and have an effect particularly on levels of personal self-esteem.

Gender-role socialization has been a focus of scholars in numerous disciplines including sociology, psychology, anthropology and communications. In each discipline the term has a slightly different connotation. Psychologists tend to look at socialization as a form of personal learning, development or adjustment. Sociologists, on the other hand, use the term to refer to the social processes by which an individual is introduced to the society's or group's culture, and anthropologists regard socialization as in culturation.

Roles, according to sociological definition, are the expectations attached to social positions, and gender-role expectations are the behaviours, attitudes, emotions and personality traits appropriate for each sex (Boudreau *et al*, 1986 p. 8). These expectations depend on what Berger and Luckman (1966) term socially constructed reality, a definition of reality that members of a society learn.

The processes that contribute to this definition of reality are institutionalization, patterns of interactions based on rules, laws, customs and rituals that become habits; legitimation, which justifies and explains why things are done the way they are; and internalization, which occurs where individuals accept the group's norm as their own (Boudreau *et al*, 1986, pp. 9–10)

According to this perspective, a social definition of what is male and what is female is transmitted to the young. Society defines what is male and what is female. In social learning theory, the dominant explanation of gender-role socialization, children are thought to learn sex roles through observation as well as through rewards and punishments. They have the opportunity to watch members of their own sex in order to discover how

1

they are supposed to behave and feel. Models of the opposite sex can provide direction for what is to be avoided (Maccoby and Jacklin, 1974).

A common thread running through various disciplines' definitions of gender-role socialization is the notion that socialization is a social process representing the way that people learn about their culture and acquire some of its values, beliefs, perspectives and social norms. In short, socialization is the way in which an individual comes to adopt the behaviour and values of a group.

Traditionally, the major responsibility for socialization has been the domain of parents, peers, schools and churches. Numerous studies have also identified that the mass media may play an important role in the socialization process for both children and adults (Berry and Mitchell-Kerman, 1982; Roberts and Bachen, 1981; Roberts and Maccoby, 1985). The actual processes of media socialization, however, are different from those used by more traditional agents of socialization.

All known societies assign certain traits and roles for males and others to females. In western society, for instance, aggressiveness, competitiveness, independence, and self-confidence were long considered to be traditional *masculine* traits; neatness, tactfulness, gentleness, and talkativeness were considered to be traditional *feminine* traits (Broverman *et al*, 1972). In terms of role differences, women have historically been cast as homemakers with responsibility for child care, and men as the providers or breadwinners. While such traits and roles are no longer as strongly associated with members of a specific sex, they are nevertheless still prevalent. Many advertisers still appeal to such gender-linked roles, and consumer tastes are frequently influenced by gender role factors.

Children learn at an early age which personality traits are linked to their own gender (Bem, 1981). By virtue of our gender we learn the appropriate ways to behave in accordance with society's definition of masculinity and femininity.

Gender-role inventories have been developed to determine the degree to which individuals adhere to society's definitions of masculinity and femininity (Bem, 1974; Spence, 1974). According to Bem (1974) our culture has arbitrarily clustered a diverse collection of personality attributes into two mutually exclusive categories – masculinity and femininity – prescribed as more desirable for one or the other sex. Individuals, however, differ in the extent to which they adhere to these idealized standards of masculinity and femininity, with sex-typed individuals adhering more strongly to the traditional standards.

In the psychological literature, gender differences have been studied from many perspectives. One of the major gender differences is the achievement – affiliation orientation where males are supposed to have a higher level of achievement orientation (Anastasi, 1961; Bakan, 1966; McClelland, 1975; Maccoby and Jacklin, 1974).

Achievement orientation involves the drive to accomplish external goals, to achieve success, and being assertive, independent and self-centred. Affiliation orientation involves concern for other people's feelings, seeking approval from others, creating nurturing relationships with others, and maintaining interpersonal harmony.

A number of gender differences in aptitude and personality traits have been reliably established. Males tend to excel in speed and coordination of bodily movements, spatial orientation and other spatial aptitudes, mechanical comprehension and arithmetic reasoning. Females tend to exceed males in manual dexterity, perceptual speed and accuracy, memory, numerical computation, verbal fluency, and other tests involving the mechanics of language.

In terms of intellectual capability, females tend to do well in verbal skills, communication, speech and literature (Bakan, 1966). Males by implication tend to do well in quantitative aspects of learning skills. Males are also much less likely to indulge in self-disclosure to others. Consequently, the incidence of suicide is much higher among men than among women (Bakan, 1966).

In most forms of aggression tests men score higher than women (Bakan, 1966). Further evidence has shown that violence features more prominently in the fantasy and real lives of males than females (Pollack and Gilligan, 1983; Benton *et al*, 1983; Maccoby and Jacklin, 1974). Women tend to repress their anger and hostility, inhibit their aggressive impulses and develop anxieties about aggression (Maccoby and Jacklin, 1974; Feshbach, 1969). Men display more physical and verbal aggression (Sears *et al*, 1965).

Males tend to score higher on most forms of aggression, females tend to score higher on many aspects of interpersonal relations. Girls, for instance, are more sensitive to the nuances of relationships and reactions of others towards one another and towards themselves in interpersonal contexts (Garai and Scheinfeld, 1963).

Gender differences have also been observed in relation to how men and women construct relationships between themselves and others (Bakan, 1966; Carlson, 1971; Guttman, 1965; McClennand, 1975; Witkin, 1979). Males and females perceive relationships differently. While males perceive threat from situations of affiliation for fear of entrapment, females perceive relationships as protective from the danger of isolation (Pollack and Gilligan, 1982).

Traditionally, the role of women in our society has primarily centred on nurturing and family life. In fact, for a long time, motherhood was the only acceptable role for women (Friedan, 1963). In the 1970s and 1980s the proportion of working women grew dramatically. Concurrently, women were evaluating their roles in society. Many women began to perceive alternatives to the traditional role including choices to pursue non-traditional careers and non-traditional relationships. Many women, in addition to caring for their families, began striving for independence, equality, and success in the workplace.

Thus, some researchers have defined two general role types for women. The 'traditional' role is typified by a focus on family life and bringing up children. The 'modern' role exhibits a sharing of family commitments with a professional life or career. The degree to which a woman adheres to traditional female roles is defined as gender-role identity (Bem, 1974; Spence, Helmrich and Strapp, 1974).

With the emergence of the women's rights movement, gender-role stereotyping has been identified as a source of restrictive practices which limit the number and range of roles, opportunities and prospects open to women socially and more especially in professional and occupational spheres. One particularly prominent line of argument is that the acceptance of women into certain professional roles is restricted to a significant degree by prevailing stereotypes and images of women in society.

The observation of male and female models in the child's environment has been postulated as a major source of gender-role information (Kohlberg, 1966; Mischel, 1970). The developing child has two principal sources of models – the home and school environments and the mass (chiefly audio-visual) media.

For some writers, gender has been regarded as one of the crucial mechanisms in structuring an individual's cultural experiences and outlook on life in general (Fiske, 1987; Morley, 1986). For feminist media theorists, the media are seen as principal instruments in conveying stereotypical, patriarchal and hegemonic values about women and femininity. The mass media are instruments of (male-dominated) social control. According to liberal feminists, the media transmit deeply sexist values and beliefs down from one generation to the next (Tuchman, 1978). Radical feminists perceive an even more sinister role of the media, which engender and serve the needs of an essentially patriarchal society, in which women's experiences and views of the world are suppressed (Mattelart, 1986). Socialist feminists align sexism with the economic domination of men in society, and perceive the media as perpetrating and maintaining a value system in which men control the key centres of capitalism.

The media – especially television – can contribute to children's gender-role socialization by providing models for observation. Many researchers have looked at television's part in gender-role socialization, asking such questions as: what are the role models to which children are being exposed on television and what behaviours are being reinforced as culturally acceptable?

Research that has examined the way the sexes are portrayed on television has noted a pronounced stereotyping of women in adult daytime, peak-time and children's programming and in advertisements (see Butler and Paisley, 1980 Cathey-Calvert, 1983; Durkin, 1985a). This has led writers interested in the elimination of gender stereotypes to request an enforced balance in the portrayal of social and occupational roles which have traditionally been presented as exclusively or predominantly associated with one or other sex (Busby, 1975).

According to the conclusions of this work, stereotyping has been characterized by two principal features: first, there is a gross under-representation of women in action-drama shows in terms of actual numbers relative to the presence of men; something which has been referred to by one writer as the 'symbolic annihilation of women' (Tuchman, 1978). Secondly, even when women do appear, they tend to be portrayed only in a very narrow range of roles. In television's fictional life, women tend to be most often found in the home, and much less often at work. Television has also been accused of portraying women as incompetent, especially when they appear in anything other than marital or familial roles. American researchers have observed that this is reflected particularly in the extent to which female characters in American peak-time television are on the receiving end of violent attacks. One major series of US research studies has indicated that whenever women in television drama programmes are involved in violence, they are more likely than men to be helpless victims (Gerbner, 1972; Gerbner and Gross, 1976; Signorielli, 1984). Thus, Tuchman (1978) has argued that television plots symbolically denigrate women, so that even when they are portrayed in leading roles and outside the home, they are surrounded and continually rescued by male colleagues.

For many years, under-representation of women was noted not only on television's fictional programming, but also in news broadcasts. Researchers in the United States in the 1970s observed that white males were the predominantly featured newsmakers (US Commission on Civil Rights, 1977). There was also a disproportionate lack of treatment of issues related to women. In Europe, at around the same time, women were found to lack the visibility afforded men in news broadcasts (Kuchenhoff, 1975; Koerber, 1977). Even by the mid-1980s, despite differences between countries, most European newsrooms were still predominantly staffed by men (Thoveron, 1987).

The serious implication of this apparent tendency towards disproportionate representation of genders and gender-role stereotyping on television lies with the possible impact this content may have on the public's beliefs about men and women. The greatest concern is for the effects on young children at the stage when they are just beginning to learn gender-appropriate attitudes and behaviours. Several studies have indicated that a heavy diet of television viewing at an early age is associated with exaggerated stereotyping of gender-role beliefs among boys and girls (Beuf, 1974; Frueh and McGhee, 1975; McGhee and Frueh 1980; Morgan, 1980). This and other research will be examined in this book to see what evidence there is for an influence of television on people's beliefs about the sexes.

In going beyond content analysis studies of gender representation on screen, however, research into audience perceptions of televised gender-role portrayals and the effects these portrayals might have on public gender-role conceptions, has not unequivocally reinforced the inferred influences of television derived from content analysis studies. Boys and girls may pay more attention to same-sex characters on television (Slaby and Frey, 1975) and indicate closer identification with actors of their own gender (Miller and Reeves, 1976). Closer examination of these results, however, indicates that children are far from preoc-cupied with television role models (Durkin, 1985). Nevertheless, culturally-socialized gender-role stereotypes, wherever they originate, can produce distorted memory for what has been seen on television (Drabman, Robertson, Patterson, Jarvie, Hammer and Cordua, 1982).

Concern about gender depictions on television is further fuelled by the finding that viewers' perceptions reveal that not only is the traditional male role predominant, but also that many male characters display extreme masculine traits, far greater than any that would normally be found among men in real life. Female roles, in contrast, have been observed to be more diversified in terms of psychological androgyny. Female role deviations in the direction of masculine attributes have been found to be acceptable because these qualities are highly valued, but male displays of feminine characteristics are found less acceptable (Peevers, 1979).

In examining evidence for effects of televised gender-role or gender-trait sterotyping, the review of research presented in this book will reveal a mixed array of empirical findings. A body of research has emerged from the United States which has suggested that heavy exposure to television is associated with holding stronger gender sterotypes. There are important questions of methodology which need to be addressed, with much of this work, however, in order to establish the degree of confidence it is possible to have in the findings to date.

A particularly worrying aspect of gender portrayals in audio-visual mass media has emerged in the context of displays of sexual behaviour. Explicit media portrayals of human sexual activity have become more commonplace over the past 20 years. Of particular concern here are certain forms of pornographic material which feature degrading images of women which may convey unhealthy impressions about female sexuality and wider aspects of the female gender. Portrayals of aggressive sexual behaviour, depicting rape, usually of female victims, have been found to produce distorted beliefs about women among young males (see Donnerstein, Linz and Penrod, 1987).

Finally, the issue of television as a force for counter-stereotyping is addressed. Portrayals of males and females which run counter to traditional role depictions present alternative views about gender potentials. While the evidence so far has been limited, there are promising signs that exposure to televised counter-stereotyped characterizations can produce reductions in gender-role stereotypes held by individuals. Television alone, however, appears to be limited in its power to achieve such an outcome, and works best when reinforced by other channels of learning such as follow-up discussion and written exercises (Johnson and Ettema, 1982). Television could probably be expected to come into its own more significantly if greater balance is achieved between the way each gender is depicted across its programming and advertising in general.

I
PORTRAYAL
OF GENDER
ON
TELEVISION

2 GENDER ROLE PORTRAYALS IN PROGRAMMES

Research into the portrayal of the sexes in television programmes over four decades has indicated that the medium is guilty of perpetrating various stereotyped impressions of men and more especially of women. This finding has underscored a degree of concern about the possible influences of television portrayals on what people think about the sexes. Monitoring projects since the mid-1950s have indicated, for example, that the portrayal of men and women on television drama is monotonously stereotypic. The accumulated evidence from numerous content analyses has strongly suggested that portrayals of women on peak-time television tend to be unfavourable and lack balance relative to depictions of men both in terms of the frequency with which female characters appear and in the nature of the roles to which they are allocated. We shall look first of all at evidence on the *frequency* and *nature* of appearances by women in adult television fiction. Then, we will take a look at similar evidence for children's programmes, before finally turning to research on gender-role portrayals in television news and educational programmes and music videos.

Adult fiction programmes

Most content analyses have focused on soap-operas and action-drama series broadcast at peak-viewing times, although there have been a few studies of daytime programmes, quiz shows and news and public affairs programmes. One of the major issues throughout this research has concerned the frequency with which women are shown on television. Typically, the major finding is that women are seen much less often than men, though there are variations across programme types. Even during the formative years of popular television in the United States, for example, several investigators in that country noted a gross under-representation of women as major characters in programmes (Head, 1956; Smythe, 1954).

Head analysed thirteen weeks of prime-time programming from the major American television networks in 1952, while Smythe examined programmes broadcast during one week by seven television channels in New York over three consecutive years (1951, 1952 and 1953). Both studies revealed that only one-third of leading characters were female. Subsequently, similar general patterns of the numerical prevalence of male and female characters on American network television were recorded by a number of independent workers in this field during the 1960s, 1970s and into the beginning of the 1980s.

Many content analytic studies since have indicated that not only does television portray women less often than men, but more especially women are seen much less frequently in central dramatic roles. In an analysis of US prime-time network dramatic programming aired during the 1969 to 1972 season, Tedesco (1974) found that on average only 28 per cent of all major roles were played by women. Several further studies during the first half of the 1970s corroborated this finding. In a study of a sample of output from the local television station during 1972, Cantor (1973) reported a 70:30 ratio of male to female fictional characters. Similar ratios were reported by Turow (1974) and Miles (1975). In a subsequent content analysis which covered both dramatic and other types of television programming, O'Kelly and Bloomquest (1976) found a lesser, though still pronounced, two-thirds to one-third numerical bias in favour of males. Rather more promising news for women emerged from a study of female appearances on US television spanning nearly ten years of output. Seggar, Hafen and Hannonen-Gladden (1981) monitored dramas, movies and situation comedies broadcast during five-week periods in 1971, 1973, 1975 and 1980. In terms of actual numbers of appearances and percentages of all portrayals, the presence of women on television drama increased across the decade. Around one in five portrayals were female in 1971 compared to nearly one in three by 1980. Furthermore, increased female presence was most marked in major roles.

The most extensive long-term analysis of television drama content was that routinely conducted each year and from the mid 1960s to the mid 1980s on prime-time American network television output by Gerbner and his colleagues. From 1967 to 1972 Gerbner (1972; Gerbner and Gross, 1976) noted that women accounted for only one-quarter of all leading characters. From the same research group, more recently, Signorielli (1984) reported that from 1969 to 1981 women were generally outnumbered by men by about three to one and that actual year-to-year fluctuations were very slight.

Female presence and programme type

Whilst television generally appears to be characterized by a gross under-representation of females, the visibility of women on television does seem to vary across programme types. Whilst men certainly dominate in terms of frequency of occurrence throughout most kinds of programmes, the numerical imbalance between male and female characters was observed in some studies to be far less pronounced in, for example, soap-operas and situation comedies than in action-adventure programmes (e.g. crime-detective series and westerns).

Women in serious and humorous drama

Drama is one of the predominant forms of programming on television. It represents a major component of television schedules during peak-time and across the day. A substantial body of research has accumulated on the representation of women and men in televised drama. In examining drama programmes distinctions can be made between different sub-types. Principally, in the research literature, serious drama is distinguished from humourous drama (e.g. situation comedies) and for serious drama, series can be distinguished from serials. In the case of 'series' each episode comprises a discrete and complete storyline, while with 'serials', the story continues across episodes.

In dramatic American television content as a whole during the mid-1970s, Miles (1975) noted that 39 per cent of major characters were women. However, when action-adventure programmes were analysed in isolation, the disparity between the sexes was much greater; only 15 per cent of leading characters were women. Meanwhile in situation comedies, nearly equal proportions of male and female characters were recorded. O'Kelly and Bloomquist (1976) found a numerical bias in favour of males on drama and other types of programmes (66.5 per cent males versus 33.5 per cent females).

This pattern of differential presence of the sexes according to programme type was reinforced by the observations of Miller and Reeves (1976). This content analysis of one week's prime-time television drama output on the American networks indicated that males outnumbered females in both major and supporting roles, but that female characters more closely approached males in frequency of appearance in family dramas (soap operas) and situation comedies.

With regard to situation comedy programming, American data have produced varying estimates of the relative numerical bias of men to women. Miles (1975) and Miller and Reeves (1976) reported much reduced numerical imbalances in favour of men, whilst in her longitudinal content analysis stretching from the end of the 1960s to the early 1980s, Signorielli (1984) found that even in situation comedies men generally outnumbered women by two to one. A similar ratio was observed for American comedy programmes by Barcus (1983). Elsewhere, Weibel (1977) had observed that males outnumbered females slightly in comedy, 2 to 1 in family drama and 8 to 1 in action-adventure drama.

Numerically and on balance, the research indicates that women in televised fiction seem to get the best deal in soap operas. Such programmes are populated almost equally by women and men (Katzman, 1972; Downing, 1974; Turner, 1974). Downing reported that 50 per cent of the characters in soap operas she studied were female. Whilst they seem to be more visible in soaps, however, many writers have argued that even here the range of roles female characters are given tends to be very narrow and emphasize certain stereotyped characteristics of the female sex (Butler and Paisley, 1980; Tuchman, 1978).

The overall impression, however, has been that the traditional woman has life just a little easier in soaps and is seen in a more positive light compared with action-drama. She often triumphs, whereas the liberated or modern woman is punished or has a harder time (Cantor and Pingree, 1983).

More recently, Davis (1990) content analysed one week's US television network schedules during spring 1987, focusing on comedy, action-adventure and drama. Little change in the pattern of sex-role portrayals was noted from observations made in the 1950s (Head, 1954) and the 1970s (Tedesco, 1974). Females were most prominent in comedy shows (43 per cent of characters), but less so in drama (36 per cent) and action-adventure (29 per cent). Davis argued that one reason for this under-representation of women on mainstream television programmes may be that considerable creative control is wielded by men in the television industry. Men write, produce and direct best from the male point of view and are less comfortable writing for women.

Characteristics of women and adult programmes

In examining the portrayals of the sexes in television drama, some writers have identified recurrent characteristics or stereotypes as revealed by content analysis research. Ceulemans and Fauconnier (1979) put forward seven characteristics as typifying gender-role portrayals in drama, which had originally been tested by McNeil (1975). These were:

- Female characters are fewer in number and less central to the plot;

- Marriage and parenthood are considered more important to a woman's than to a man's life;

- Television portrays the traditional division of labour in marriage;

- Employed women are shown in traditionally female occupations, as subordinates to men with little status or power;

- TV-women are more personally- and less professionally-oriented than TV-men;

- Female characters are more passive than male characters;

- Television dramatic programming ignores the existence of the women's movement (p. 18).

Focusing on the attributes of women on television therefore, it seems that gender-role stereotyping women is woven more deeply into the fabric of television programming than the obvious numerical discrepancy between the sexes suggests. Following frequency counts of the distribution of women in different types of role in television drama, a number of basic and recurring characteristics of female portrayals have been identified. 'Propositions' about the nature of a woman's role in life have been formulated which have been assumed to represent messages directly conveyed by television to the public about women. It has been further argued that such 'propositions' are learned by television audiences, thus cultivating a distorted common public consciousness about men and women in reality (Paisley and Butler, 1980; Tuchman, Daniels and Benet, 1978). Gender stereotyping on television has been identified to occur in relation to the kinds of roles in which women and men are portrayed and in connection with the personality attributes they typically display. Stereotyping therefore divides neatly into two types: *gender-role* stereotyping and *gender-trait* stereotyping.

Gender role stereotyping

Societal attitudes towards which roles are most appropriate for women have been undergoing great changes. In particular, there have been changes in beliefs about the value of the family, the manner in which child care can best be implemented, the role of marriage in people's lives today, and the possibility of self-fulfilment through work.

Changes have occurred in the traditional housewife role which have given many women more time and cultivated needs for outside stimulation and more money. Modern domestic appliances, manufactured goods and prepared foods among other things, save on time and labour. Also, women are having fewer children and often delay having any for the first few years of marriage – so they spend fewer years occupied with child care. Nevertheless, this is apparently not the image of the contemporary woman portrayed by television.

Implicit in the gender-role portrayals of much of television drama is the suggestion that marriage and parent-hood are of greater significance to a woman's life than to a man's life. Television's fictional world apparently places greater emphasis on establishing the marital status of its female characters. In an analysis of programme samples over a four-year period, Tedesco (1974) reported that marital status could be identified and coded for 51 per cent of female characters, but for only 32 per cent of male characters. At about the same time, Downing (1974) reported another content analytic study which corroborated Tedesco's findings. Once again, marital status was (at least according to this particular researcher) portrayed as more crucial in the lives of women than of men in the world of television drama. Whether a character was married or single was identified more often for women (85 per cent) than for men (73 per cent). McNeil (1975) noted that women's marital and parental status were far more often clearly indicated than in the case of men.

Seggar (1975) also found a significant difference in the portrayal of marital status of males and females performing major roles in 1974 television drama on US network television. A further study reported by the US Commission on Civil Rights (1977) examined both marital and parental roles for male and female characters in network prime-time dramatic programming in the 1969-1972 period. Less than one-third of all males were portrayed as husbands, while almost half of all female characters were depicted as wives. Neither male nor female adults were frequently portrayed as parents. Women, however, were more often shown as mothers than men appeared as fathers.

A further point on this theme is the apparent confinement of women on television to a home life dominated by family and personal relationships and interests. Studies of dramatic television content have indicated that not only are female characters usually depicted in domestic settings but that they also seem to be much more concerned about family and personal matters than men, *outside* the home as well as in it. McNeil (1975), for example, showed that personal relationships associated with romance or family problems accounted for 74 per cent of female interactions but only 18 per cent of male interactions. On the other hand, professional or work-orientated interactions constituted only 15 per cent of women's versus 35 per cent of men's relationships on television drama programmes.

Research on US television in the mid-1970s found that of the overall male television population, almost three-quarters were gainfully employed, while fewer than half of the female characters held jobs. Among married characters, the disparity was even greater. Few married women, and fewer mothers were portrayed as employed. Working wives typically appeared in comedies, but their employment status was never substantially portrayed (McNeil, 1975).

Additional support for the personal or familial orientation of women's relationships on television comes from the general finding that women are numerically better represented in soap operas and situation comedies whose settings are predominantly domestic. In soap operas, women appear in almost equal numbers with men and female characters are usually more central to the plot in these programmes than they are in action/adventure programmes. In addition to their higher visibility, soap opera females often hold respected positions in the family and immediate social environment (Downing, 1974). But whilst, on the surface, this suggests greater balance in the depiction of women and men, many of the characteristics of the daytime serial females continue to reflect the conventional images of women found in action-drama content. Following a content analysis of 300 episodes from fifteen television serials, Downing (1974) revealed a persistence of gender-segregated role divisions in which women were concerned mostly with their physical appearance and marital relationships, while the world of work was still largely the preserve of males.

The major action in most soap operas and situation comedies consists of conversation, the nature of which centres on romance, familial and other interpersonal relationships, and problems with these relationships – once again reflecting the traditional female stereotypes (Katzman, 1972). Thus, in these programmes even when women are shown outside the home environment (e.g. at work), their conversations tend to revolve around domestic matters. Gender-stereotyping of occupational roles in television drama in the United States was highlighted in several studies during the early 1970s. Although the actual percentage distribution of the sexes in work contexts on television varied from one study to another, the overall pattern was one of under-representation of female characters in employment relative to male characters *and* compared with the participation of women in the labour force in the real world. Downing (1974) reported that in the sample of prime-time television output she examined, 58 per cent of men were shown in professional occupations against just 19 per cent of women.

Turow (1974) further demonstrated that the fact that women appear in almost equal numbers with men, and that female characters are more central in soap operas as compared to evening drama does not guarantee the absence of gender stereotypes. As the next section on gender-trait stereotyping will show, behavioural and personality attributes of television characters display gender basis regardless of the extent to which male and female characters appear on screen.

McNeil (1975) found that not only were women portrayed proportionately more often than men in marital roles, but also that the percentage of characters who were employed differed significantly according to gender. Almost 75 per cent of the male television population were depicted as gainfully employed, while less than 50 per cent of female characters held jobs. Among married characters, the disparity was even greater. Few married women, and fewer mothers were portrayed as employed. Working wives and mothers generally appeared in comedy shows, where their work status was rarely elaborated. According to McNeil, in the few instances when television women held high-prestige positions, they played less important roles and their work activities were not central to the plot. Female characters generally worked under close supervision and had far less authority than men.

Overall, it has been observed, even in recent years, in the United States that occupational portrayals on television are varied, but stereotyped. Women's employment possibilities are somewhat limited, with clerical work the most common job (Steenland, 1990). According to some commentators, television does not recognize adequately that women can successfully mix marriage, homemaking and raising children with careers. Rather, programmes in which married women work outside the home (e.g. Claire Huxtable in *The Cosby Show*) often focus on the character's home-related role rather than her work position. At the same time, there is a view that the world of television does not adequately acknowledge the importance of homemaking and raising children (Signorielli, 1993).

Gender-trait stereotyping

A prominent stereotype of women in our culture is that they are more emotional than men. The emotional woman is believed to become flustered in the most minor crises; she is seen as sensitive, often fearful and anxious, and generally dependent on male help and support in all kinds of personal and professional situations. With respect to television, some writers have argued that portrayals convey an impression of the 'emotional' women that is often inaccurate and unfair. Indeed in more general terms, it seems that there has been a significant gender-bias in the way behaviours have been labelled emotional (Sherman, 1971). Emotionality tends to refer most often to those reactions – fearfulness, anxiety, moodiness and neuroticism – which are typically associated with women, but less often to overt responses – aggression and dominance – which are regarded as masculine traits.

We have already seen that evidence from content analysis research has been interpreted predominantly to support the argument that television drama tends to confine women to the home and family where their lives are dominated by personal relationships. While men are frequently faced with problems related to the outside world and work, women are shown by television to be much more involved in family and romantic conflicts in which their 'characteristic' emotionality is highlighted (McNeil, 1975). Following an analysis of US peak-time television programme samples over three television seasons from 1975 to 1978, Greenberg, Richards and Henderson (1980) reported that women were portrayed as needing emotional support more often than men. Men, on the other hand, more often needed physical support of various kinds. Together, these findings indicated a generalized gender-stereotyping pattern in which male television characters were orientated more towards physical needs, while female characters were orientated towards emotional needs.

Is there evidence that females are in fact more emotional in these particular ways? The answer seems to depend on the type of measure of emotional responsiveness that is used. With regard to fearfulness, females have been found to be somewhat more emotional when rating scale measures are used (e.g. Spiegler and Liebert, 1970; Wilson, 1966, 1967), but observational studies of gender differences in response to a frightening stimulus in young children have not produced consistent results (Bronson, 1970; Maccoby and Jacklin, 1973; Stern and Bender, 1974). Overall though there does seem to be a general tendency for females to display more emotionality than males, at least after early childhood. But there is a further problem of interpretation, particularly of investigations of anxiety and fearfulness using paper-and-pencil tests. As males are socialized to hide their emotions, whereas females are expected openly to admit and display their feelings, it is therefore possible that gender-differences arise as a result of males being less willing to report their anxieties and fears than females (Frieze *et al*, 1978). In fact, a few studies have indicated support for this hypothesis (Spiegler and Liebert, 1970; Wilson, 1967). In these studies people who reported few fears or anxieties were also likely to score high on a measure of social desirability – the tendency to respond in culturally-approved ways. Much less ambiguity is presented in the way women are characterized and portrayed on television however.

Another particularly important issue that is frequently highlighted by critics of the way television portrays gender is that relating to the dominance of men and the subordination of women. Analysis of the demographics of men and women and of behavioural sequences involving interactions between male and female characters have indicated that television could possibly cultivate the belief that men are naturally more competent and more powerful than women.

Focusing chiefly on demographic indicators of dominance, Lemon (1978) described an *intersex measure* – a method of analysis of gender-role portrayals on television drama which divided two-party interactions between men and women into those dominated by men, those dominated by women and those where men and women were portrayed as equals. A second and interrelated measure devised by the same author was called the *percentage of total appearances measure* which contrasted the number of times someone of a particular gender was portrayed as dominant, dominated, or equal with the total number of times members of that gender participated in such dyadic interactions.

Lemon found that one of the most important defining attributes of power and competence was occupational status. Men tended to be portrayed more often than women in high-prestige occupations – and they also gave more orders. However, even during interactions between the genders where professional status was irrelevant, men still generally dominated women. There were variations in the pattern of domination-subordination between different programme genres. On her intersex measure, Lemon found that men dominated women in 23 per cent of situation-comedy interactions, were dominated by women in 13 per cent of interactions, and were portrayed as the equals of women in 65 per cent of interactions. This pattern was more pronounced in crime-dramas, however, where men were dominant 47 per cent of the time, were dominated six per cent of the time and were equals with women the remaining 47 per cent of the time.

One problem with this study which clouds the meaning of its findings is that Lemon was not clear on her definition of dominance in interpersonal interaction. Was the dominance of one character over another usually a function of the demographic (i.e. occupational or other social) position to which each was respectively allocated, or was it more often a function of the behavioural sequences which occurred between males and females and the outcomes of their behaviours for each of them?

Other researchers have been more precise in their definition of measurement of dominance between the genders, sometimes analysing several different categories of behaviour to show differential patterns of power and competence among males and females in television drama. Among those behaviours analysed are order-giving and receiving, advice-giving and receiving; support-seeking and the ability to make plans and carry them through. Evidence on support-seeking has been discussed already under the emotionality of women on television, but male superiority is perhaps demonstrated even more clearly by patterns of order and advice giving and receiving among the genders.

Turow (1974) studied patterns of advice giving and receiving and order-giving and receiving between men and women in a sample of twelve hours of daytime programming and twelve hours of prime-time programming consisting mainly of soap operas and other dramatic television content. Turow reported that men gave orders or advice in 70 per cent of all episodes of advice or order giving. Results of this analysis were interpreted to show that in the world of television drama, characters are apparently selected, occupations assigned and plots developed in such a way as to minimize the chances of women displaying superior knowledge or abilities to men. Furthermore, even when female characters were given such opportunities, the advice or order-giving tended to be concerned with traditionally female topics.

Manes and Melnyk (1974) carried out two studies in which they examined the models of female achievement available to television viewers. These studies surveyed television's portrayal both of achievement behaviour and its social consequences for the female achiever. The first study compared female models at four levels of achievement and showed that only those models at the lowest level of achievement were depicted as having successful social relations with men. The message thus offered is that women who are ambitious in a professional sense may have to forfeit a happy social and private life.

In their second study, Manes and Melnyk compared the marital status of male and female job holders on television. Compared with male job holders, females were depicted as less likely to be married, less likely to be successfully married, and more likely to be unsuccessfully or unhappily married. Content counts revealed that female characters who held jobs were ten times as likely to be unsuccessful in marriage as were housewives. The authors suggest, from their findings, that female achievers portrayed on television are depicted in a way that does not encourage female viewers to imitate their behaviour and in fact serves to inhibit achievement – oriented behaviour in female viewers. As with so many analyses of this sort, however, an assumption is made that the meanings read into television portrayals by the researchers are similarly apprehended by the viewers. But this may not necessarily be true. Indeed, whilst television drama portrayals of women who are both successful in a career and happy in their home life may be less commonplace on the screen than portrayals in which success is achieved in only one sphere, the former may be more outstanding in the minds of viewers and provide more salient models for emulation.

Another example of the relative competence of the sexes on television is to be found in the extent to which male and female characters seem to be in control of events in their lives. One of the most extensively researched variables in the psychological literature on competence is 'attribution of causality'. According to this concept, people can be broadly categorized into those who believe they have a great deal of personal control over determining life's outcomes and those who believe that their lives are controlled primarily by forces external to themselves which they cannot influence. De Charms (1976) introduced the terms 'origin-like' (feeling of having personal control over events) and 'pawn-like' (feeling of not having personal control over events) to distinguish these two types of individual. Subsequently, Hodges, Brandt and Line (1981) conducted a study in which they catalogued the frequencies with which male and female characters in peak-time family shows, violent-action shows, and daytime serials made statements which according to a scheme developed by de Charms could be classified either as 'origin-like' or 'pawn-like'.

Hodges and colleagues found that in violent action shows and in family shows, female characters made substantially fewer origin statements than did males. Gender differences were especially pronounced in violent action shows where females made twice as many 'pawn-like' as 'origin-like' statements, while the pattern for males was of the same degree but in the opposite direction. According to the authors, from the perspective of social learning theory which would predict that viewers are likely to be influenced in their own behaviours by the behaviours of television characters similar to themselves, female viewers would be most likely to identify with the model themselves after female television actors. They argue therefore that the less favourable depiction of women than men in violent action shows for which at least half of US viewers are female, might lead to a lowering of female self-esteem. Unfortunately they provide no empirical evidence bearing directly on this hypothetical assumption. As we shall see in a later discussion of viewers' perceptions of the sexes, distinctions are often made between the world of television and the real world and it would be wrong to assume that viewers passively accept all that is presented to them on the screen.

Two further studies of gender-trait stereotyping concentrated on the younger and older ends of the age spectrum. Pierce (1989) carried out a content analysis of child characters on prime-time US television and compared young male and female characters in terms of a number of traits. This analysis revealed that while boys and girls were significantly different on just four out of thirteen character traits (boys were considered more active, aggressive, rational and unhappy than girls), they differed more clearly in the types of activities in which they participated. Girls tended more often to talk on the telephone, read and help with housework, and boys were shown more often playing sports, going places and making mischief.

Another content analysis study of the US television networks prime-time programming covering one week in autumn, 1987 and a second week in summer, 1988, examined the way elderly men and women were portrayed. Even among elderly characters on television, females were found to be significantly underrepresented (Vernon, Williams, Phillips and Wilson, 1990).

Comparisons of elderly men and women showed patterns of traditional stereotypes, with men more likely to be depicted positively on seven out of nine 'desirable' traits and women more likely to be depicted negatively on six out of seven 'undesirable' traits which showed a gender difference. However, the proportional differences for specific characteristics typically were neither large nor statistically significant, suggesting that there has been some change in television's portrayal of the elderly during the 1980s.

Men had higher percentages who were classified by coders as 'active', 'creative', 'flexible', 'healthy', 'highly intelligent', 'socially involved', and 'wealthy'. Women had lower percentages judged to be 'attractive' and 'pleasant'. On undesirable traits, women were judged to be presented more often as 'rigid' and 'unpleasant'. All these differences were small and statistically non-significant.

Another observation was that the girlfriends and wives of older middle-aged men were approximately 10 to 15 years younger than their partner. The researchers concluded that one implication of this pattern was perpetuation of the idea that women must remain youthful in appearance, while men are allowed to show signs of aging. Elsewhere it has been observed that what status women have is based on their sexuality and that inevitable physical symptoms of aging make women sexually unattractive much earlier than men, while men are valued more 'in terms of personality, intelligence and earning power than physical appearance' (Bell, 1970, p. 75).

Research outside the United States has corroborated many American findings. Research on drama programmes broadcast on German television understandably supported American evidence, given that almost half of German television at the time was imported, mainly, in the case of drama, from the United States (Kuchenhoff, 1975). Females were underrepresented and seldom appeared as central figures. Males overwhelmingly occupied the dominant, active and central character roles. The portrayal of women as housewife/mother was one of two dominant female images. However, it was quantitatively subordinate to the image of the young, single, independent, beautiful and sexy woman. Although the researchers interpreted this finding as conflicting with the general contention that television depicts women predominantly in domestic and maternal roles, the divergence from other research data was small and was most probably attributable mostly to coding and classification procedures.

Of all the female dramatic characters on German television, 35 per cent were married, 45 per cent single and 13 per cent widowed. Young women, aged 19 to 35, were mostly single (73 per cent). Although active and liberal in their relationships with men, young female characters nevertheless exhibited an orientation towards marriage as their eventual goal. Although many of the women monitored in drama programmes on German television were identified as having jobs, they were seldom depicted at work. Half the working women held traditionally female jobs, and few worked in management or as professionals. Married women were less likely to be employed than single women. A study of British television in the 1970s revealed that in light entertainment programming, active, adventurous, victorious men dominated over victimized, supportive, laughable or merely token females (Koerber, 1977). Television drama, on the other hand, showed a shift in favour of women. Koerber noted that more programmes were written by women, featured women and as a result provided a female perspective of women's lives.

Another recent British study of the portrayal of the sexes in television programmes found that men appeared more than twice as often as women (70 per cent of all people monitored were men, 30 per cent were women). The proportions of women and men varied significantly across different programme types. The difference ratio was smallest in the case of children's programmes, where 53 per cent of people were men and 47 per cent were women. The widest margins of difference in favour of men occurred for sports programmes (11:1) and national news (4:1). The position of women improved markedly when level of appearance was taken into account. A higher proportion of women (22 per cent) than of men (16 per cent) were classified as making a major contribution to programmes, even though there were significantly fewer females seen on screen as a whole (Cumberbatch, Maguire and Woods, 1994).

Signs of shifting profiles

Not all researchers have held to the view that television has been unchanging in its stereotyping of the sexes down the years. Although some writers observed even during the mid to late 1980s that women on television generally lacked power in the workplace (Pribram, 1988), some evidence has emerged that television is beginning to reflect the changing roles of women in the way it portrays them.

The number of female characters depends upon programme genre. Women have been found to make up at least half of the characters in situation comedies and serial dramas on US network television, but are practically invisible in most action-adventure programmes (Steenland, 1990). There are signs that women's roles have improved with more women presented in 'typically male' occupations. Women have also been observed to be portrayed as affluent and as rarely having problems with child care, harassment or sex discrimination (Huston et al, 1992).

A small study of 13 programmes on the US television networks in 1977 in which women had leading roles concluded that women were being depicted 'more fairly than in the past' and television was helping to 'adjust the public image of the American woman' (Haskell,

1979). Contemporary women, the study concluded, were portrayed as moving into non-traditional occupations, heading households, and interacting with men at different levels than in the past.

Another study, based on one full week of prime-time television shows in 1978, reported that programme content put less emphasis on the negative consequences of professional success for women (Weigel and Loomis, 1981).

Subsequently, Reep and Dambrot (1987) selected six prime-time US network shows during the 1985-86 season which featured single, professional women sharing the lead with a male partner in a working relationship for content analysis – *Hotel, Hunter, Moonlighting, Remington Steele, Scarecrow and Mrs King*, and *Who's the Boss*.

The study revealed a less stereotypical portrayal of working women than in the past and a serious attempt to present realistically the problems of professional women. The programmes analysed showed that women can be competent in demanding careers, and men can work successfully with women who hold higher professional status. These women are not consumed with domestic interests; rather they concentrate on their careers and are often shown problem solving and decision making. The researchers argued that the fact that four of the six women tended to be more serious than their male partners may reflect the pressures to succeed in careers and the expectation that women must work harder than men to be successful.

These women were to some extent shown as being less successful in their personal lives, however. They were less than perfect mothers and generally lacked romance in their lives. The theory that many capable young women fail to achieve professional success because it can lead to loneliness and a less than satisfactory private life receives some support here. Although these female television characters were shown as having the ability to hold their own professionally, the programmes in which they appeared were nevertheless continuing to say that marriage, motherhood and having a career might conflict.

Finally, Atkin (1991) noted greater prevalence of network television series in the United States which featured single women in lead roles. This pattern was earlier observed during the mid-1970s and in both instances represented a reaction to periods of increased competitiveness among networks or, in the late 1980s, between the networks and cable channels. Such periods of greater competition motivate experimentation with fresh programme formats. Series such as *Rhoda, Designing Women, Kate and Allie*, and *Murphy Brown* exemplified this movement in the 1980s.

Children's programmes

In so far as television may have a socializing influence on the beliefs, attitudes and behaviour of its audience, investigation of the content profiles of children's programmes and the gender-role concepts they may communicate to young viewers is of more than a little interest. A series of American content-analytic studies conducted during the early and mid-1970s indicated that children's programming on US network television tended to be more sexist than adult programming.

One general impression, again deriving from research carried out primarily in the United States, is that women have been short changed and under-represented on children's programmes. In the case of cartoons, for instance, studies have consistently revealed that men outnumber women by four or five to one (Signorielli, 1991) and that women are presented in very stereotyped roles (Levinson, 1975; Streicher, 1974).

Gender-role portrayals were also found not to differ in programmes that were toy-based compared to those that were not toy-based (Eaton and Daminick, 1991). Public television programmes for children, although better on some dimensions, still fell short in relation to gender representation (Dohrmann, 1975; Matelski, 1985).

Early evidence for the lack of balance in gender-role portrayals on American television came from Levinson (1973) who reported that male characters outnumbered female characters by three to one in Saturday morning children's cartoons on the three major US networks. Even three out of four of the animal characters were identified as males. In another study of US network children's programmes, O'Kelly (1974) found that males heavily outnumbered females by 85 per cent to 15 per cent, and that adult male characters appeared more frequently on the screen than did adult females. Males also enjoyed a much broader range of occupations than females, with females most often portrayed in marital or familial roles. This last finding was repeated in other studies of children's programme's during this period. Cantor (1973) observed that male characters were more likely to have occupations than female characters in these programmes. Busby (1975) meanwhile found that women were depicted in only a narrow range of occupations. According to Busby, the occupational portrayal in children's television did not reflect the actual employment situation of women in terms of quantity and range of occupations, while it closely resembled the real-life employment of men. Another study by O'Kelly and Bloomquist (1976) also revealed the portrayal of women in traditionally female occupations.

The physical portrayal of women observed in children's programmes, as indicated elsewhere in television by American researchers, emphasized youth and attractiveness. Women on television, whether single or married, were invariably slim and attractive. Not only did female characters appear as very attractive, they were also portrayed as very concerned with the way they looked (Long and Simon, 1974).

The other great concerns of the women portrayed in children's programmes were their homes and their families. Female characters were more likely to be married than were male characters, but even though more prevalent in the marital context, they were not dominant in it. The status of married women observed in children's and family shows assessed by Long and Simon (1974) was one of deference to and dependency on their husbands. Women were no more likely to be portrayed in authority at home than at work. This was so even though, as observed elsewhere, married women tended to be attractive and youthful whilst their partners tended quite often to have gone to seed physically (Busby, 1974). Marital status was associated with the attractiveness of television characters, according to some observers of American television in the 1970s and this applied to men as much as it did to women. Busby (1974) noted that prominent women in children's television were sleek, agile and attractive regardless of marital status. Marriage did, however, seem to influence the physique of men in a different way. Married males were invariably overweight with poorly defined physiques, as opposed to the physically attractive single men and women. The conclusion consistently reached by content-analytic researchers during the early seventies was that television represents women and men in a highly stereotyped manner, and if it influences children's gender-role perceptions at all it probably reinforces the status quo.

Further American studies of children's programmes conducted throughout the latter half of the 1970s and into the early 1980s revealed few changes in the way women were portrayed. An analysis of 20 hours of Saturday morning children's programming on the US networks by Nolan, Galst and White (1977) indicated that males still outnumbered females by three to one. Subsequently, Barcus (1978) analysed 899 characters from weekday and weekend children's programmes and found the same ratio of male characters to female characters. At weekends, the margin of difference was four to one in favour of males. This imbalance was found to be characteristic of all types of fictional and entertainment programming. More recently, Barcus (1983) replicated the above ratios following an analysis of an even larger sample of over 1100 television characters from children's programmes.

In another study Sternglanz and Serbin (1974) directed their attention to the consequences of a wide range of behaviours involving male-female interactions in cartoon programmes. The outcomes of male-instigated and female-instigated actions differed significantly; males were more often treated with positive (or rewarding) outcomes for their actions, whilst females tended to experience neutral or negative outcomes. Elaborating on this finding Sternglanz and Serbin suggested that children would be 'taught' different lessons by these portrayals according to whether they identified with male or female characters.

The behavioural sequences analysed from these cartoons involved making and carrying out plans. Young girls who identified with female characters, who were generally unsuccessful in their achievements, would be shown that it is inappropriate for a woman to make plans and carry them out because more likely than not she will be punished for doing so.

Later studies of children's programme content have continued to record gender-role stereotyping in the way women and men are portrayed. In particular, in the context of occupations and careers, men continue, so it seems, to enjoy more variety and greater success at work. Schechtman (1978) assessed the distribution of male versus female occupational portrayals in terms of occupational prestige on six television shows which had been most frequently mentioned by pre-school children as ones they watched – *Batman, Bugs Bunny, The Flintstones, Happy Days, Road Runner* and *Sesame Street*. Schechtman divided occupations into four ranges of occupational prestige – high, medium, low and very low – and explored patterns of distribution of occupational portrayals. From this analysis, he concluded that television, as a source of incidental learning about the world of work, offers the child a male-dominated picture of the occupational world. Women were generally portrayed in inferior occupational roles and in proportions not representing real world numbers. Men out-numbered women in all occupational prestige categories. No women at all were portrayed in the high level occupational prestige category.

Schechtman did not restrict his research purely to an analysis of television content however. He went on to assess possible relationships between television portrayals and the career awareness of pre-school children. He found that 95 per cent of the children he questioned named an occupational choice for adulthood. Furthermore, there was a strong relationship between the occupational choice prestige levels of boys and girls and the occupational prestige level of their favourite television character's occupation.

In recent British research, Cumberbatch, Maguire and Woods (1994) reported that men and women were fairly evenly represented in children's programming. Just under half of all the people catalogued were men (53 per cent) and just under half (47 per cent) were women. Slightly more of the men (60 per cent) than the women (50 per cent) played major parts, while more of the women made a minor contribution (32 per cent compared with 8 per cent of men).

There were variations in the distributions of women and men across different types of children's programmes. In factual programmes for children, more women than men were major presenters (63 per cent versus 44 per cent). This was largely due to the regular occurrence of two particular female presenters in the popular, long-running children's magazine, *Blue Peter*. In children's fictional programming a greater proportion of men (69 per cent) than women (43 per cent) played major roles.

Educational programmes

Some television programmes aimed at children and young people have been designed to serve educational purposes. A number of these programmes have been highly rated for their quality and progressiveness, and have achieved international popularity. However, in their early days, even these broadcasts were found to include outdated, stereotyped portrayals of the sexes, reflecting those commonly observed in mainstream commercial television.

Dohrman (1975) found that males – human, animal and non-human – were numerically dominant in children's educational television programmes. They made up three-quarters of the television population. Males further exclusively occupied the lead role of moderator and the majority of major parts, as well as most off-camera voice-overs. Not only was the ratio of males to females seriously out of proportion, but the behavioural modes assigned to males versus females also differed significantly. Analysis of the behaviours exhibited by children's television characters revealed an overall strong relationship between male gender and active mastery, and between female gender and passive dependency.

Breaking down characters according to age, Dohrman revealed that adult males were most visible, followed by male children and female adults who had almost equal degrees of visibility. Female children had the lowest frequency of appearance. Women's overall share of characters was 24 per cent.

According to Dohrman, exposure to the persistent dominance and power of male television models, both adults and children, socializes the boy viewer into accepting and valuing man's dominant position in society. The girl viewer, who is consistently confronted with female models performing secondary roles and submitting to male power, learns to accept women's diminished societal rank. The presence of such gender-role stereotyping in educational programmes was thought to be a matter of particular concern given the authority attached to these programmes.

News programmes

The representation of women in television news programmes has been investigated in terms of the appearances made by women as newscasters, reporters and subjects of the news. Research largely derives from North America and Western Europe, carried out during the 1970s, 1980s and 1990s.

An analysis of a sample of evening news programmes broadcast on NBC, BCS and ABC in 1974–75 revealed that white males predominated in newsmaker roles with a share of 78.7 per cent of the total (US Commission on Civil Rights, 1977). In comparison with ethnic and racial minority people, both male and female, white women fared better, occupying nearly 10 per cent of newsmaker roles. Non-white females rarely featured in the news (3.5 per cent), while nearly eight per cent of the newsmakers were non-white males.

The limited availability of women as spokespersons was also reported by the Women's Advisory Council (WNBC News Monitoring, 1976). Its report concluded that women tended to be either invisible or the silent presence in news programmes. Nearly complete omission in news programmes of women, their views, abilities and accomplishments, was the most common criticism of all the monitors who participated in a study of newscasts on a network-affiliated station in Sacramento (AAVW, 1974). The Women's Advisory Council to KDKA-TV, Pittsburgh (1975) compared female visibility on network and local news. Local news programmes represented women relatively more frequently (23 per cent) than network – produced shows (15.5 per cent).

The capacity in which women made the news was examined in three US studies during the 1970s, but used differing methodologies which rendered direct comparisons between them difficult. Women considered newsworthy by WNBC-TV were mostly criminals, victims, entertainers, or relatives of famous men (WAC, 1976). A document produced by the US Commission on Civil Rights (1977) reported a predominance of white female news makers appearing as wives and mothers. The AAUW survey (1974) concluded that television news programmes generally presented two stereotyped images of women: the helpless victim and the opinion-less, supportive wife/mother.

Another pattern in the representation of women in news broadcasts noted in the United States was the disproportionate treatment of issues related to women in comparison with other news topics. Canter (1973) concluded that women are not considered news on the basis that, out of 21 news categories, women's rights and women's changing role were least emphasized. less than one per cent of news broadcasting time was devoted to women's issues. Elsewhere, the US Commission on Civil Rights (1977) reported that only 1.3 per cent of the news stories in the sample they examined dealt with women's issues. No news reports focused on individual women's achievements or accomplishments.

In a German study, Kuchenhoff (1975) found that women were not very visible either as news reporters or as news-makers. Women's share of news-maker roles amounted to 5.2 per cent on ARD and to 6.6 per cent on ZDF. In addition, 5.9 per cent (ARD) and 3.1 per cent (ZDF) respectively of correspondents were female. The appearance of women was further restricted to traditionally female spheres such as health and family-oriented news stories. The male position of authority in television news, which focused heavily on politics, was an accurate reflection of the male dominance in public life, according to Kuchenhoff.

In Britain, Koerber (1977) examined female participation in reportage and presentation of news programmes. Findings based on a week's monitoring of news and public affairs programmes on BBC and ITV, indicated a gross underrepresentation of women in these roles.

A study of the representation of women in news and current affairs programmes on Finnish television found an even balance of male and female reporters and journalists in a Swedish language news programme, but a predominance of male journalists in a second main news programme. All the senior duty editors in the Swedish-language programme were women, while in the main evening news they were all men. Of the news items presented in the Swedish-language programme, almost half (45 per cent) were by women, while in the main evening news the corresponding figure was less than a third (28 per cent). The breakdown between the sexes of those interviewed and those doing the interviewing showed that although women also carried out interviewing work, the interviewees were almost without exception men; of 79 people interviewed only two were women (Holopaimen, Kalkkinen, Rantanen, Sarkkinen and Osterlund, 1984).

In a further study by the same group of Finnish current affairs programmes, in which a sample of 24 programmes was monitored, it was once again found that women were interviewed markedly less often than men. Generally, men were more readily interviewed than women on the strength of their profession or position, while women appeared more often as members of the public or as rank and file members of some group.

A cross-national study of television programmes broadcast in ten European countries encompassed an investigation of female representation in news in each country (Thoveron, 1987). This research examined female appearances on screen as news professionals and as featured news items. Out of a total of 221 news personnel, women were found to represent 14.5 per cent of journalists staffing the news rooms whose output was observed (see Table 2.1). Around one in five news items (21 per cent) were presented by a woman.

Table 2.1. News broadcasters by gender

Country	Total no of broadcasters	Number	
		Men	Women
French-speaking Belgium	16	13	3
Dutch-speaking Belgium	11	10	1
Denmark	18	15	3
France	28	23	7
Germany	9	9	0
Greece	28	24	4
Ireland	29	26	3
Italy	28	25	3
Luxembourg	10	10	0
Netherlands	12	11	1
United Kingdom	31	24	7
EEC TOTAL	221	189 (= 85.5%)	32 (= 14.5%)

Source: Thoveron, 1987

There were variations between countries. Women were more numerous as news broadcasters in France (25 per cent), the United Kingdom (12.6 per cent) and French-speaking Belgium (18.8 per cent). Thoveron (1987) advises caution in interpreting the data for individual countries, however, because of sample limitation.

Out of the 32 women broadcasters identified by the researchers, 15 (49.9 per cent) were presenters, 11 (34.4 per cent) were journalists, and 6 (18.7 per cent) were reporters. The women presenters covered the whole range of news topics with no signs of discrimination. On the other hand, the journalists dealt with 18 'soft' subjects (news in brief, weather events, station announcements) and 10 'hard' subjects (politics, the economy). The reporters handled five serious subjects and one light. Of voices heard off camera, 82.3 per cent were male and 17.7 per cent were female.

Turning to the occurrence of women as subjects of the news, Thoveron (1987) found that this was a rarity. Only 17 news items (1.4 per cent) dealt specifically with women's issues. When such items did occur, they came late in the broadcasts, rather than ever being in the forefront of the news.

Out of 374 people interviewed in the news broadcasts analysed, 315 were men (84.2 per cent) and 59 were women (15.8 per cent), a ratio of five to one. Interviews with women were proportionately more frequent in Italy (78.6 per cent of the total), Denmark (23.4 per cent), the Netherlands (22.2 per cent) and Luxenbourg (21.3 per cent). Out of men and women interviewed in the street, 53.8 per cent were women, while 10 per cent of artistes, celebrities and experts and nine per cent of the political personalities interviewed were women.

A study of factual programmes on British television included national and regional news, current affairs and a variety of other 'informational' programmes (Cumberbatch, Maguire and Woods, 1994). In national news programmes, out of 1,003 people who appeared, the majority (82 per cent) were men, while fewer than one in five were women (18 per cent). Despite this wide ratio of disadvantage overall, women appeared more often than men in the role of major presenter (13 per cent versus 5 per cent). Men were more likely to be minor presenters than women (21 per cent and 13 per cent respectively). Equal proportions of both women and men appeared as interviewees (74 per cent of men and 75 per cent of women). A similar pattern emerged in other factual programmes.

Just under one in three women interviewed in national news programmes were either representatives of an organization (24 per cent) or 'experts' (6 per cent). Nine per cent were politicians. Nearly half (48 per cent), however, were members of the general public. In regional news programmes, there was a greater likelihood that female interviewees were either victims (16 per cent) or relatives of people involved in a news story (15 per cent).

The subjects on which female interviewees were most likely to be consulted were health (18 per cent of female interviewees in national news, regional news and current affairs) and personal insights (14 per cent).

Music videos

In the past 10 years, music videos have become an important television genre for youngsters, particularly adolescents. Women, however, are very under-represented in videos (Brown and Campbell, 1986; Caplan, 1985) and some stereotyped gender roles occur (Vincent, 1989).

Sherman and Dominick (1986) found that women were presented as submissive, passive, physically attractive, and sensual and were often used as decorative objects, particularly in concept videos. Men, on the other hand, were in control of relationships. Other male images in videos include gang members, thugs, and gangsters whereas female images include night-club performers, temptresses, servants, and goddesses (Aufderheide, 1986).

Sherman and Dominick (1986) analysed music videos from three sources: MTV (available on cable only at that time), WTBS's *Night Tracks* (carried on cable and broadcast over the air) and NBC's *Friday Night Videos* (broadcast over the air). A total of 366 prime-time (12.30–2.00 am Saturday morning) music videos were recorded. Focusing upon 'concept' videos, in which more than 50 per cent of screen time was devoted to a story, dramatization or narrative and not to performance, character portrayals were analysed to reveal a number of gender differences. Men outnumbered women two to one: 75 per cent of solo acts and 82 per cent of groups were male. More significant, however, were differences in the way male and female characters were depicted.

Violence occurred in nearly 57 per cent of the concept videos studied. Videos with violence averaged 2.86 separate aggressive acts each. Men accounted for nearly three quarters (73 per cent) of aggressors and a similar proportion of victims of violence (77 per cent). Men were three times more likely than women to get hurt or killed. Only one in ten women were visibly affected by video violence. Also, violence targeted toward men was presented more realistically than acts of aggression carried out against women.

The 'risk ratio' in music videos for males – that is, the ratio of male victims to male aggressors – was similar to that in conventional programming. The ratios for females, however, were reversed. In music television, females involved in violence were more likely to be aggressors than victims, perhaps substantiating the observation that the predatory female is a popular music television stereotype.

As well as aggressive imagery, visual presentation of sexual intimacy appeared in more than three-quarters of music videos analysed (76 per cent). A clear male orientation was seen in the way females were portrayed in videos in a sexual context. Half of all women who appeared were dressed provocatively. Women were also significantly more likely than men to be portrayed as upper class. In many cases, women were presented as upper-class sex objects for lower class males with visions of sexual conquest.

Brown and Campbell (1986) reported an analysis of music videos which examined gender and race portrayals. They recorded material from MTV and the Black Entertainment Channel. MTV was dominated by white male singers or bands led by white males (83 per cent of all videos on this channel). White female singers or band leaders were featured in only 11 per cent of the videos recorded from MTV. Black males and females were seen even less often. On *Video Soul* (Black Entertainment Channel) white males still featured in over half of all music videos (58 per cent), with around one in ten (9 per cent) featuring white female leads. Black artists were more prominent, but males (20 per cent) far outnumbered females (6 per cent).

Females, both black and white, were less likely than males to be portrayed as professional people. Counter to stereotype though, black males were almost as likely as white males to be portrayed as professionals. Most of these blacks (all but 17 per cent), however, appeared in videos shown only on *Video Soul*.

Much of the action in music videos analysed by Brown and Campbell involved solitary activities. These most usually involved a character looking at another person without response and walking without apparent purpose. These activities were most likely to be displayed by white females. The women (especially black women) in these videos were also more likely to be shown dancing than singing or playing a musical instrument. According to the researchers:

> This configuration of gender differences is a subtle indication of persistent stereotypes of women as less active, less goal-directed, and less worthy of attention (p. 101).

Vincent, Davis and Boruskowski (1987) reported a further analysis of the presentation of women and men in music videos. They focused upon videos aired on MTV and recorded

30 hours of programming, comprising 300 individual videos. Videos were eliminated if they were live performances without a storyline or when they lacked a female character. This left 110 music videos for analysis.

A scale of sexism was applied to each video which provided four levels of analysis concerning the way women were portrayed. These levels were as follows:

> Level I: 'Condescending'. The woman is portrayed as being less than a person, a two-dimensional image. Includes the dumb blond, the sex object and the whimpering victim. This level of portrayal [could] include an aggressive, sexual role ...

> Level II: 'Keep Her Place'. Some strengths, skills and capacities of women are acknowledged, but tradition also dictates 'womanly' roles ... emphasis on subservience in romantic or secondary relations.

> Level III: 'Contradicting'. Emphasizes a dual role where a woman plays a traditional, subservient role while also displaying a certain degree of independence .. Anything she does outside of domesticity is viewed a 'something extra' ... domesticity/nurturance dimension is of foremost importance.

> Level IV: 'Fully Equal'. Treated as a person (possibly a professional) with no mention of her private life. Does not remind us that domesticity and nurturance are non-negotiably the woman's work as well. Women are viewed non-stereotypically (Vincent *et al*, 1987, p. 752).

The results indicated that sexism was fairly high in televised music videos. This was clearly manifested in the finding that 57 per cent of the videos were rated Level I, and 74 per cent were judged to portray women in one of the top two sexist categories. Furthermore, there was no significant lessening of the degree to which women were stereotyped in videos featuring all-female or mixed female–male musicians.

In the videos examined by Vincent *et al* it was common for women to be used exclusively as decorative objects. In these productions, women were often portrayed as background decoration in scant and highly seductive clothing. There was a fairly high level of violence in music videos (with 34 per cent containing some violence). Ten per cent of videos monitored portrayed violence directed toward women.

A follow-up study was reported 18 months later by Vincent (1989) which looked for changes in the level of sexism in music videos and in the nature of female portrayals and intimate behaviour between men and women featured in videos. Vincent found that sexism remained fairly high in music videos, though there was a 22 per cent decline in videos rated Level I. This change was largely counter-balanced by a 173 per cent increase in Level IV videos. The presence of women in music videos made a difference to the nature of female portrayals. However, there were notable increases in Level IV ratings even for videos featuring only male musicians. Despite this shift, exclusively male performer videos remained easily the most likely to receive a Level I rating for their portrayal of female characters in the supporting narrative storyline.

There was no change in the extent to which women were used exclusively as decorative objects, even though Level IV ratings had increased overall. These decorative women were often clad in highly seductive clothing. Small increases were noted for nudity and lingerie, but no changes in other seductive attire. Finally, levels of intimate behaviour exhibited little change, but levels of violence, including violence directed toward women, showed a slight increase. As Vincent concludes:

> In the period when the rock music industry was being criticized for its orientation to sex, drugs and violence, we found that females were still portrayed as submissive, passive and physically attractive .... These videos can too easily provide young people with questionable behaviour models (p. 160).

Concluding remarks

For 40 years research into the on-screen depiction and representation of males and females has, for the most part, observed that television gives preferential treatment to males more often than to females. During the 1950s, 1960s, 1970s and 1980s, an accumulating body of evidence derived from content analysis of television programming indicated that males tended to outnumber females and were treated generally to more 'favourable' roles in narrative drama and to greater prominence and authority in factual programmes. This pattern was true of television especially in North America and Western Europe.

The numerical presence on males and females was found to vary with the type of programme under consideration. Females have tended to be more prominent in serialized, romantic dramas (soap operas), for instance, than in action drama series. Even in soaps, however, the range of roles occupied by women was generally found to be narrower than those filled by men.

Females have tended therefore to be stereotyped in the way television has traditionally portrayed them. This stereotyping has been typified not only by the range of roles played by female actors and but also in terms of the personality traits shown to characterize women. Men have tended to be shown more often as dominant, powerful, independent and achievement-oriented. Women are more often presented as being submissive, weak, dependent and affiliation-oriented. Male characters are more rational, while female characters are more emotional. These characteristics have been noted across a variety of programme genres including educational programmes, children's programmes and comedy programmes, as well as in serious drama.

During the 1980s and 1990s, some signs have been observed that stereotyping of the sexes is beginning to ease. More female characters are being featured in leading roles, exhibiting independence, achievement, career success and an almost masculine-type potency. Numerically, such portrayals have not yet attained parity with male portrayals, but represent an important shift which is high profile insofar as it has occurred in respect of popular, peak-time television programming.

Counter-balancing this shift, more recent times have witnessed the emergence of new entertainment channels carrying new forms of gender stereotyping. Perhaps the most significant of these new developments, given its popularity with young people, is the music video. Dedicated music video channels such as MTV provide a constant stream of material which has been found to contain repetitive and highly stereotyped portrayals of women. Here, seductively dressed women are featured as decorative objects and occasional targets of hostile masculine behaviour. Despite the increasing prevalence of popular female artists, these images of women have shown little sign of diminishing.

3 GENDER ROLE PORTRAYALS IN ADVERTISEMENTS

Advertising has been a focal point of concern in respect of sex-role portrayals in mass media. Many advertisements are targeted specifically at women, manipulating the female image in such a way as to persuade women to buy.

The role of women in television advertisements has become an important area of research in the past two decades. Many types of studies have been conducted, ranging from exploratory research to investigations conducted to provide evidence for use in the courts. In the United States, Silverstein and Silverstein (1974) noted that litigation in the courts and petitions to the Federal Communications Commission were increasingly being employed in the hopes of implementing changes in the portrayal of women in television programming and commercials.

Major criticisms included the observation that strong links were typically made between attractiveness and women (Downs and Harrison, 1985). Research conducted over more than 20 years revealed that a woman's voice is rarely used as a voice over and that only men are generally presented as authoritative, even for products used primarily by women (Brettl and Cantor, 1988; Dominick and Roach, 1971; Lovdal, 1989; W.J. O'Donnell and K.J. O'Donnell, 1978).

Initial criticism of the way the sexes were portrayed in advertisements centred on the unequal distribution of men and women, with men generally outnumbering women. Even when established that the distribution of men and women was fairly evenly matched, there were still concerns about the nature of gender-role portrayals in advertisements. Advertisements were regarded as showing an inaccurate and narrow view of women's roles in society. It was felt that women were too often shown in domestic roles and dependent on men.

The conclusions drawn from content analysis research can be divided into two general categories. The first category comprises those studies saying that women are portrayed in a negative, stereotypical manner. Verna (1975, p.301) concluded that 'the roles in which women have been portrayed in the media are neither flattering nor representative of the female workforce'. The second category consists of those studies which see women as gaining substantial ground on their male counterparts and breaking out of the negative stereotypical mould.

Although the focus of this chapter is upon gender-role representations in television advertisements, stereotyping has been observed to occur in advertising appearing in magazines. Courtney and Locheretz (1971) found that only three per cent of women were portrayed in working roles in magazine advertisements compared with 45 per cent of men. A follow-up analysis by Wagner and Banos (1973) found that the percentage of women in working roles had increased to 21 per cent. Sexton and Berman (1974) compared the content of advertisements appearing between 1950 and 1971 and concluded that there had been some increase in the depiction of women in working roles but that these occupations were still very stereotypic in nature. Venkateson and Losco (1976) found that traditional housewife's role and sex object role portrayals of women had declined over the same period.

Weinberger's (1977) content analysis for the period between 1972 and 1978 revealed an 8.8 per cent in the proportion of females shown in occupational roles while between 1958 and 1978 the decline was 0.8 per cent. The depiction of women in professional occupations was not found between 1958 and 1970, while in 1972 it rose to four per cent but declined to just over two per cent in 1978. Portrayal of women in non-working roles in family and recreational situations declined in favour of decorative (inactive) roles, which increased from 47.5 per cent in 1958 to 61.4 per cent in 1978, though in 1970 had declined to 31 per cent.

In a German study of print advertising in two weekly magazines, the German *Stern* and American *Time*, Brosius, Mundorf and Staab (1991) found that the presentation of men and women exhibited some changes over time. The most salient of these was a clear trend to present both men and women as being more submissive. The German magazine exhibited a decrease in the use of traditional female (housewife) roles in its advertising content over a period of 20 years from the late 1960s to late 1980s. The American magazine had apparently moved in this direction even earlier. In spite of this shift in female imagery, non-verbal signals in magazine advertising indicated male dominance and female submissiveness characteristics as prevalent throughout the whole period of analysis.

Advertisements directed at adults

In 1972 the *New York Times Magazine* published the first major content study of television commercials conducted by the National Organisation for Women (NOW). Over 1200 television commercials were content analysed over a period of one-and-a-half years by 100 NOW supporters in New York city (Hennessee and Nicholson, 1972). Over one-third of the advertisements monitored, claimed the authors, showed women as the domestic agents of men and as dependent on men. Nearly one-fifth showed women as sex objects and a similar proportion showed them as unintelligent. Over four out of ten commercials portrayed women as household functionaries. Often, women turned up in advertisements for food or cleaning products. NOW monitors also noted that women never seemed to tell men what to do; in television commercials men were constantly advising women.

Published for a general readership, exact details of the NOW methodology were not given, but it seems on the basis of the information that was supplied that the study may have been unreliable. There is some uncertainty surrounding the professionalism of the monitoring techniques employed, and some doubt must be cast on the homogeneity of the large number of coders in the ways they classified women in advertisements along subjective judgemental dimensions such as 'submissive', 'intelligent' and 'dependent'.

The first major academic study of female stereotyping in television commercials was conducted at around the same time. Dominick and Rauch (1972) sampled almost 1,000 television advertisements, again from network stations in New York City, during April, 1971. These researchers coded commercials for, among other things, the products being advertised, sex of voice-over, sex of prime purchaser, the role played by the women in the advertisement, and the apparent occupation of the female presented. The appearance of men in a selection of commercials was also monitored for comparisons between the sexes.

Once again, a pronounced pattern of gender-stereotyping was reported, with 75 per cent of all advertisements using females being for products generally found at home in the kitchen or bathroom. According to the authors, the television commercials they studied conveyed the message that a woman's place is in the home; 38 per cent of women in the sampled commercial population were shown inside the home versus only 14 per cent of men. The single largest occupation for females was housewife with over half so portrayed. Men were generally more often in authority roles within commercials. When women were shown outside the home in some sort of occupation, they were more often than not in a job subservient to men. Voice-overs were predominantly male; 87 per cent of coded commercials used a male voice, six per cent a female one and seven per cent a chorus. In addition, 60 per cent of the on-camera product representatives shown were male.

A couple of years later, Courtney and Whipple (1974) reported a longitudinal and comparative analysis of the portrayal of women in television advertisements drawing on four studies conducted over a two-year spell between April 1971 and February 1973. Included in their analysis were the findings of the NOW and Dominick and Rauch studies. Their major conclusions reinforced the earlier findings. Women were shown mainly as housewives and mothers, while men were shown in at least twice as many occupations. Almost 40 per cent of women were shown in domestic settings at home compared to about 15 per cent of men. Female product representatives were shown most often performing domestic duties, while males may have demonstrated product features but did not actually use the products. Men were responsible for the vast majority of voice-overs (85 per cent) and dominated as on-camera product representatives on prime-time television advertisements. Over the two years of the study, Courtney and Whipple noted, however, that the number of female product representatives did increase significantly, particularly on daytime television where they appeared as often as male representatives.

At around the same time, another study of the sexes in US television commercials was undertaken by McArthur and Resko (1975). While their principal findings reflect those of Dominick and Rauch, the interest in this study lies in its examination of authority roles in advertisements. Seventy per cent of men were presented as authorities, but only 30 per cent by virtue of product use. In all, 14 per cent of women were product authorities, 86 per cent were portrayed as product users. Men were also much more likely than women to provide an argument for the use of products. Confirming this pattern, Culley and Bennett 1975) concluded that:

> ... women are portrayed in most advertisements as being more concerned with personal appearances and household matters, and less concerned with durable good purchases and complex decisions (p. 168).

Similar findings to the above with respect to the occupational roles, voice-overs, product representation and product category associations of women in television advertisements were reported by Silverstein and Silverstein (1975). These researchers also found that although women sometimes gave advice in commercials for female and household products, men gave advice more often in every product category.

Throughout the mid-1970s, further American studies continued to find pronounced stereotyping in the way women were portrayed in television commercials. Focusing yet again on the relative portrayed expertise of males and females, Maracek, Piliavin and others (1978) reported a more even distribution of voice-over experts between the sexes across three years of monitoring (1972, 1973 and 1974). However, female voice-overs were associated with a fairly limited range of product categories – food, household, or feminine care products. Within these traditionally female product categories there was a marked increase in the extent to which the female was the last word of authority heard. Maracek *et al* concluded that the voice-over shows males not only demonstrating expertise but continuing to have the final word in commercials. This study also found that even though there was a slight increase in female voice-overs, the increase was only evident in commercials for 'women's products'.

During the second half of the decade, further studies indicated that while males and females appeared in equal numbers as product representatives, women still were predominantly found in commercials for domestic products and invariably appeared in the home. Men, on the other hand, dominated the non-domestic product categories and settings. The male also continued to be the voice of authority (O'Donnell and O'Donnell, 1978).

Thoveron (1987) analysed 480 television advertisements from eight European countries. Most of these were related to food and drink (40.3 per cent), and cleaning, hygiene and beauty products (27 per cent). In most of the countries, other than Ireland and to a lesser extent France, most of the actors were women (up to 68 per cent in Germany and Greece) (see Table 3.1).

Table 3.1. Distribution of males and females in television advertising across Europe

	Male (%)	Female (%)
Ireland	71.4	28.6
France	59.4	40.6
Italy	47.0	53.0
United Kingdom	45.0	55.0
Luxembourg	40.7	59.3
Netherlands	37.1	62.9
Germany	32.4	67.6
Greece	32.1	68.0
ALL	45.6	54.4

Source: Thoveron, 1987

People portrayed at work in European television advertisements were mostly men, while those shown in the home were mostly women. Women were at home in more than 43 per cent of their appearances and at work in 18 per cent of them. Most of the women at home were depicted as housewives or as mothers.

Some studies have noted a few slight and subtle changes in the portrayal of the sexes in television advertisements, though the old patterns of stereotyping still largely prevail. Schneider and Schneider (1979) reported trends in gender-role portrayals on television commercials from 1971 to 1976. They monitored a sample of approximately 300 commercials aired in Minneapolis-St Paul during October 1976 which they compared to Dominick and Rauch's (1971) sample. Over this time they observed certain changes in the patterns of gender-role portrayals, but also that stereotyping was still prevalent. There were differences in the demographic profile of television advertisements monitored by the Schneiders and those analysed by Dominick and Rauch. More older people were shown in the 1976 commercial sample, though there was still more emphasis on youth among women than among men. Married men and women were both under-represented in 1976 television advertisements compared to census population figures, but women were more often portrayed as married than men by 20 per cent. It was also found that fewer members of both sexes were portrayed as employed in 1976 compared with 1971, but the gap between men and women had narrowed. Although women were no more or less likely to be in out-of-home settings, more men were shown in the home in the latter half of the 1970s.

Ferrante, Haynes and Kingsley (1988) compared portrayals of women on American television advertisements in 1986 with findings reported for the early 1970s (Dominick and Rauch, 1972). This replication indicated that women were portrayed in a wider range of occupations and appeared more frequently in settings outside the home in 1986 than in 1972. Although women were still most often portrayed in the role of wife or mother figure, men were increasingly seen in the role of husband or father. The nature of women's occupations exhibited little change, but the total number portrayed in occupations increased significantly.

Rak and McMullen (1987) studied the degree of gender-role stereotyping on television advertisements on the three US television networks (ABC, NBC and CBS) and the two major Canadian networks (CTV and CBC) over a three-month period in 1983-84. Comparisons were made between daytime and prime-time advertisements using a content analysis and a verbal response mode (VRM) analysis.

The VRM classification procedure (after Stiles, 1978) requires that both the grammatical form and the communicative intent of each independent clause, non-restrictive dependent clause, element of a compound predicate, or term of acknowledgement or address be judged as one of eight verbal response modes – Advisement, Interpretation, Confirmation, Reflection, Discourse, Question, Edification, or Acknowledgement (see Table 3.2). Based on the principles which underlie the taxonomy, each of these eight basic modes is assumed to be a presentation of certain interpersonal role behaviours and is considered as (a) either presumptions or unassuming (i.e. as presuming knowledge of the person to whom one is speaking or not), (b) either directive or acquiescent (i.e. as imposing the speaker's will on the interaction or acceding to the other's viewpoint), and (c) either informative or attentive (i.e. as concerning the speaker's own knowledge and opinions or attending to the experience of the other person).

The results revealed interesting differences in the nature of interactions between male and female characters in day-time and prime-time television advertisements. Advertisements aired in the day-time portrayed the female more often as the authoritative homemaker, spouse, or parent who provides information to the neutral male narrator, interviewer, or professional, often about a household cleaning product. This male, who was neutral in the sense that he was neither an authority about nor a user of the product, typically directed the interaction by asking for information about the product from the female or by making statements which served as a cue for the female to provide more information. In contrast, although the male in the prime-time airings was still portrayed more often as the narrator, interviewer, or professional who directs the interaction, the female was cast more often in neutral roles, i.e. as performing activities that were not highly gender-stereotyped.

Rak and McMullen found a reasonable degree of consistency between the results of the content analysis and the VRM analysis. Both analyses revealed that gender-role stereotyping was still present in North American television advertisements, but that it was somewhat less pronounced in prime-time than in daytime transmissions. For daytime advertisements, the content analysis revealed a fairly stereotypic pattern of differences, with the male being portrayed more often in an autonomous role and the female in a dependent role than vice versa. While it was time that the female was also cast more often as the authority, she was the authority *only* in her role as a dependent within the plot of the advertisement. That is, in her role as a homemaker, wife, or mother, she was the authority on matters of household cleaning, beauty, and hygiene, but not on more substantive matters.

Table 3.2. Description of verbal response modes with their role dimension values

Verbal response mode	Form	Intent	Role dimension
Advisement (A)	Imperatives or second-person sentences with verbs of obligation, permission or prohibition	To guide behaviour, e.g. suggestions commands, advice	P, D, I
Interpretation (I)	Terms of evaluation or second-person sentences with verbs that imply an attribute or ability	To explain or label the experience of the other; eg judgements or evaluations	P, D, At
Confirmation (C)	First-person plural sentences where subject includes both the speaker and the other	To compare one's own experience with another's; eg agreements or disagreements	P, Ac, I
Reflection (R)	Second-person sentences with verbs that refer to actions or experiences of the other	To put another's experience into words; eg repetitions, restatements, clarifications	P, Ac, At
Disclosure (D)	First-person singular declaratives	To reveal thoughts, feelings, perceptions, and motives; eg subjective statements	U, D, I
Question (Q)	Inverted subject-verb order; interrogatives	To request information	U, D, At
Edification (E)	Third-person declaratives	To state objective information; eg facts	U, Ac, I
Acknowledgement (K)	Non-lexical or contentless utterances; terms of address and salutations	To convey receipt of or receptiveness to another's communication eg, 'mm-hmm'	U, Ac, At

Note: P = presumptuous, D = directive, I = informative, At = attentive, Ac = acquiescent, U = unassuming; Source: Rak and McMullen, 1987, p. 28. Reproduced with permission.

The pattern of VRM findings for daytime advertisements was also generally consistent with the stereotypic relationship of a dominant male and a submissive female. Somewhat less stereotyping emerged in prime-time advertisements with the finding of greater directiveness for males in the absence of differences between males and females for presumptuousness and informativeness.

The findings from the VRM analysis revealed some very specific features of the interpersonal relationship between interacting males and females. In daytime advertisements, there was a greater tendency for males to presume to understand the females' experience or frame of reference and to impose their point of view on the interaction and for the females' experience to be the topic of the interaction than *vice versa*.

Attractiveness stereotyping in adverts

Downs and Harrison (1985) examined frequencies of attractiveness – based messages on 4,294 American network TV commercials 7 days (8am – 10pm). Attractiveness statements appeared to be associated more with food and drink and personal care ads, and with female performers and male voice-overs. The findings illustrated that commercials link attractiveness and sexism. When female performers were televised on commercials, they were far more likely than male performers to be associated with attractiveness stereotypes. These data coincided very well with other evidence that showed while adults of both genders held attractiveness stereotypes. Males were even more likely than females to hold these stereotypes and expect the stereotypes to be more often associated with females than with males (e.g. Downs and Currie, 1983; Downs *et al*, 1982). In the Downs and Harrison study male voice-overs, considered the voice of authority by the industry, and actual female performers promoted attractiveness stereotypes. 'The commercial message becomes clear that attractiveness is more associated with women than with men and that men (via authoritative voice-overs) are forging this attractiveness – women link!' (p. 17).

Using a coding frame modelled very closely on that developed by American researchers McArthur and Resko (1975), Manstead and McCulloch (1981) conducted a study to examine the portrayal of men and women in a sample of British television advertisements. They analysed 170 commercials from peak-time television in the north-west ITV region in Britain over one week. The analysis revealed that men and women were portrayed in markedly different ways.

Women were more likely than men to be shown as product users. Women were shown more often than men in the home. Women were apparently displayed in dependent roles more often than men were. Finally, women provided no arguments in favour of the advertised products with which they appeared. In other words, the nature of the differences in gender-role portrayals was systematic and in accordance with traditional dender roles. Men were typically portrayed as having expertise and authority, as being objective and knowledgeable about reasons for buying particular products, as occupying roles which are autonomous, and as being concerned with the practical consequences of product purchase.

Manstead and McCulloch noted many similarities in the way the sexes were portrayed in commercials in Britain and America and one major difference in the way the use of arguments was portrayed among central figures. McArthur and Resko reported that 30 per cent of their female central figures used no argument at all, whereas Manstead and McCulloch found that 63 per cent of central female figures used no product argument.

Another difference concerned the relation between gender of the central figure and the types of rewards associated with particular products. McArthur and Resko found no reliable correlation between gender of product users and the rewards suggested by these consumers, whereas Manstead and McCulloch found that females were significantly more likely than males to be shown suggesting social approval and self-enhancement rewards, rather than practical or other rewards. These British researchers concluded that on balance the portrayal of adults is more gender-role stereotyped in British than in American commercials.

The style adopted by women in advertisements has been found to be linked with the type of product being advertised (Thoveron, 1987). In an analysis of television advertisements broadcast in eight European countries, the character of the female model was determined by the nature of the product. Elegant women (visibly made-up, interesting or modern appearance) and sophisticated women (heavily made-up, affected manners, sometimes in party clothes) advertised beauty and personal hygiene products, car, clothes and alcoholic drinks. Well-groomed women (visibly made-up appearance) advertised non-alcoholic drinks, sweets, cleaning products and home accessories. The more reserved women (invisible make-up, reserved air, no accessories) advertised products for babies and children, pharmacy items, food for humans or animals and women's magazines. Thus, the exact type of women's image portrayed bore a striking relationship to the image of the product being sold.

One of the primary criticisms of advertising is its exploitative use of the female body. The use of the female form as mere decoration or as an attention-getting device is perceived to diminish women's self-esteem and ignores other aspects of women's personality and their human potential. The effect of the sexual sell advertising or male-female relationships and on children's sense of values is perceived as potentially harmful.

Dispenza (1975) suggested that women are primarily used by advertisers to sell products to both women and men on the basis of their sexual appeal to men. Depending on the gender of the target group, the strategies vary. In female-oriented advertisements, women are invited to identify with the female product representative who is offered the ultimate reward, i.e. success with males, as a result of using the product. In male-oriented advertisements, male consumers are promised the portrayed female as the bonus that comes with the product.

Venkatesan and Losco (1975) found that the female roles most frequently represented over the 13-year period from 1959 to 1971 were women as sex-object and women as physically beautiful. The portrayal of women as sex object, although overall on the decline, was most pronounced in men's (53 per cent of the portrayed females) and general audience magazines (65 per cent). The changes in female portrayal occurring over the 13-year timespan were mostly attributable to the shift of emphasis in women's magazines, while only 12 per cent of the females in women's magazine advertisements were coded as sex objects, the emphasis had shifted to 'women as physically beautiful', the most frequently portrayed role category (61 per cent) in the women's press. Pingree, Hawkins, Butler and Paisley (1986) also noted a predominance of sex-object images of women in men's magazines.

The exploitation of women as sexual objects was observed to be receding in the United States by the mid-1970s (Culley and Bennett, 1976). Even so, the use of the female body for its sexual appeal has remained a well-established advertising practice, particularly in male-oriented media. The decrease in sex-object images of women has been further compensated by an increased emphasis on female physical beauty (Sexton and Haberman, 1974).

Are men more authoritative in advertising?

Part of ideology supporting traditional stereotypes in television commercials has been the advertiser's belief that the male voice is more authoritative and convincing than the female voice. This point was illustrated in the comment of a leading American advertising agency spokesman: (A) man knows what he's talking about (and) has automatic credibility on TV' (Marecek *et al*, 1978, p. 167). Equally damaging to women was the view that in successful advertising, 'men act, and women appear' (p. 167). The idea that men are active participants, knowledgeable, and authoritative, and women are not, is detrimental to the status of women.

Some television commercials, however, did provide an updated version of women. However, this version merely represented superficial changes in women's appearance and activity, but still contrived to operate within the same patriarchal and restrictive economic contexts of the post. The practice of using these images of superficially liberated women has in itself become one of the most productive, profitable and effective advertising campaigns (Scheibe, 1979; Warren, 1978).

Krill, Pesch, Pursey, Gilpin and Perloff (1981) reported a content analysis of over 1600 commercials aired or daytime and prime-time US network television, and examined changes in gender role portrayals since the mid-1970s. On daytime television, over 90 per cent of voice-overs were supplied by males. Female product representatives far outnumbered males in afternoon television commercials, but there was a distinct variation in the occupational settings of female and male characters. Over 80 per cent of female product representatives were shown in family or home occupations, while nearly 70 per cent of male product representatives were portrayed in business or management occupations.

During prime-time, 90 per cent of voice-overs were male, dominating all product types. Males and females were equally likely to be seen as product representatives in prime time, but the majority of women were still shown in the home and the majority of men in business settings. Television commercials persisted with images predominantly of the 'traditional' woman Krill *et al* concluded, though the margin of difference between professional women and professional men shown in advertisements was decreasing.

Scheibe (1983) completed a content analysis of character portrayals and values using a large representative sample of commercials drawn from a composite week in March 1981. Scheibe analysed 2,135 commercials containing more than 6,000 characters, coding each character's gender, age, occupation, 'concerns', and social power. Scheibe found the commercials in her sample to have a nearly equal gender distribution, with about 52 per cent of the characters being male and 48 per cent female. Even though this is still distorted from the real world (US census figures indicated that about 52 per cent of the population was female), it was a much more realistic presentation than that of TV programmes.

Not every product type presented such an egalitarian picture, however. The ratio of male to female characters varied widely by product type. Females made up the majority of characters only in commercials for cleaners, hygiene, feminine hygiene/beauty products, apparel, and toys. Males dominated 12 of the 22 product categories, and were most likely to appear in alcohol, car, leisure/travel and financial services adverts.

As with programme-product relationships, the distribution of male and female characters in TV adverts seemed to be determined by the target audience. Men advertised products shown during sports programmes that were primarily directed toward men, whereas women were more often found selling products designed for use by women during programmes with a large audience. Most characters in adverts were shown with no discernible or obvious occupational role. Of the 40 per cent who were shown as having an occupation, only 5 per cent were shown as 'homemakers' (almost all female), leaving 35 per cent of the characters (44.5 per cent of the males and 23.6 per cent of the females) portrayed as having some occupation outside the home. In marked contrast to earlier research, Scheibe (1983) found that female characters were shown more often in occupational roles outside of the home (23.6 per cent) than they were as homemakers (9.7 per cent).

Turning to concerns, Scheibe found that female characters exhibited more concerns, more product-related and personal, than did male characters. The largest gender differences occurred for concerns involving beauty, cleanliness, family, and pleasing others, all of which concerned female characters more than male characters. Males, on the other hand, were significantly more concerned only with achievement and having fun.

In order to investigate earlier claims that women were portrayed as 'powerless' or 'helpless', Scheibe coded the social power exhibited by each character (using French and Ravens', 1960, categories of social power). These included four categories of power: power of approval/reward; its antithesis, seeking approval or reward; expert power (based on knowledge or ability); and its antithesis, seeking expertise.

Surprisingly, Scheibe found few differences between male and female characters in the social power they exhibited. Males and females were equally likely to have power of approval, expert power, and to such approval, although female characters were more likely to seek expertise from others than male characters were. These similarities were also true when the characters were shown in occupational roles. In spouse or parent roles, however, significant sex differences did emerge. Female characters shown either as wives or mothers were much more likely to have expert power and to seek approval from others, whereas males shown as husbands and fathers were more likely to have power of approval. So, although there were differences in what males and females in commercials were 'concerned about' and what kinds of power they were shown having, there were many similarities as well. Males and females were shown have almost equal power in an occupational context. In a family context, females were more often shown as expert, whereas males more commonly had final approval.

A group of studies in the late 1980s confirmed this observation about the authoritative role in advertising occupied predominantly by men. Brettl and Cantor (1988) showed that females were more likely than males to advertise products that are used primarily in the home. Men tended to be depicted in higher status occupations and women significantly more likely to be depicted without an occupation. Gilly (1988) noted that men were more likely portrayed in independent roles in relation to women. Women were shown in a plethora of stereotyped roles including wife, mother, bride, waitress, actress, dancer and in a dearth of professional roles such as photographer, athlete, dentist and businesswoman.

Lovdal (1989) examined what occupation the visible product representatives of television advertisements were placed in and which sex was shown in more professional roles. This study represented a replication and extension of one published more than 10 years earlier (O'Donnell and O'Donnell, 1978). Results showed that women were product representatives of 55 per cent of the domestic products advertised compared with 86 per cent ten years earlier. For non-domestic products, men were product representatives in 72 per cent as compared to the previous 78 per cent. In the late 1980s, 44 per cent of commercials showed men in the domestic category and 28 per cent showed women in the non-domestic category.

In general, these studies found that male voice-overs continued to resound an authoritative tone and to give the idea that men are more convincing, credible and knowledgeable. In only nine per cent of commercials when a woman's voice was present, she was not speaking to the population at large, but to dogs, cats, babies, children and women dieters. Women only talked to those of inferior status and to other women concerning feminine hygiene, headaches and diets (Lovdal, 1989).

Furnham and Bitar (1993) further extended earlier content analysis studies of British television advertisements to reveal a high level of consistency in gender role portrayals over a period extending for more than ten years. Males predominated as central figures in product advertising, were more likely to appear as voice-overs and as authoritative figures and were most likely to be portrayed as interviewers, narrators or celebrities in occupational settings or in unspecified locations, while women were most likely to be depicted as dependent on others and portrayed in the home. With regard to the association of gender of central figures and product type, there was further indication of stereotyping that tended to be frequently associated with financial services such as banking and insurance, while women were mostly connected with adverts for food products or body products.

International comparisons

A number of relatively recent studies have begun to make direct comparisons between different countries in terms of how the sexes are portrayed in television advertising. These have revealed a number of interesting similarities and differences. Furnham and Voli (1989) studied gender-role portrayals in Italian television advertisements, classifying them in terms of gender, mode, credibility, role, location, reward, product price, argument, background, humour and comment, using a coding scheme closely modeled on that of Manstead and McCulloch (1981). Results showed that men and women in Italian television advertisements were portrayed in several significantly different ways. Women comprised just 36 per cent of central characters portrayed in the adverts studied, thus being less well represented than earlier comparable research had revealed for the USA by McArthur and Resko (1975), but exhibited a similar level of representation to Britain (Manstead and McCulloch, 1981). Males were likely to appear as voice-overs, and females were depicted on screen more frequently. Males were more often the central authority figures, and appeared more often in advertisements for expensive products, thus replicating the findings of Livingstone and Green (1986) again for Britain. Women were more likely than men to be shown against a background of children, while men were more likely to be shown against a background of women. Although females were depicted humorously, they tended not to be humorous to the same extent as men. Finally, men were more likely than women to offer and comment about the product being promoted.

Research in Australia has revealed a conflicting pattern of results concerning gender-role portrayals in Australia advertisements. Dowling (1980) conducted an exploratory analysis of the portrayal of women in 105 Australian advertisements and found that women were likely to be portrayed in decorative roles, accounting for 38 per cent of the total number of advertisements portraying women. Only nine per cent of advertisements showed women as occupying a career role. Only five per cent of women in these advertisements were classified as 'sex objects', a finding which flew in the face of claims that advertising continually exploited the female form in this way. This study was limited in two ways, however. First, no data were presented on the presentation of males in the advertisements. Second, the coders worked in a group rather than independently, leaving the reliability of the data open to criticism.

Gilly (1988) compared advertising sex role portrayals on US, Australian and Mexican television. Stereotyping was found in advertising in all three countries, but was manifest in different ways. Male voice were much more likely to be used than female voices in advertising voice overs, women were portrayed as young more often than men, and men were more likely to be portrayed in independent roles. There were differences among these countries on other variables, however. Overall, the Australian advertisements exhibited differences between men and women on the fewest of the variably examined. No significant differences were evident in Australian adverts in terms of the type of product advertised by males and females, whether they acted as spokesperson or in their credibility in that role. They were no differences either in the extent to which male or female characters were the recipients or providers of help or advice.

More differences in the portrayal of the sexes were found in American and Mexican adverts compared with the Australian adverts. There were gender differences in terms of product user (women were more likely to appear in adverts for men's products than vice versa), employment status (men were more likely than women to be portrayed as employed), and credibility of the spokesperson (men were portrayed more often as product

45

authorities and women as product users). In addition, in the US adverts female characters tended to receive advice and male characters tended to give it whereas in the Mexican adverts female characters received help and male characters gave it. The Mexican adverts reflected more traditional gender roles than the US adverts, but the difference was not that great.

Mazzella, Durkin, Cerini and Buralli (1992) have provided a more up-to-date analysis of male and female role portrayals in Australian television advertisements. Following earlier studies (McArthur and Resko, 1975; Manstead and McCulloch, 1981; Livingstone and Green, 1986; Gilly, 1988) central figures were classified by gender, mode of presentation, age, credibility, role-type, location, nature of argument about product, type of reward associated with product, product type and price.

This analysis indicated that men and women appearing in Australian television advertisements were portrayed in markedly different ways, reflecting traditional gender-role stereotypes. Men were overrepresented in advertisements, and portrayed as authoritative experts who provided objective and knowledgeable reasons for buying the advertised product. They were depicted in masculine settings and occupied roles which were independent of other people. Male figures were also concerned with the practical consequences of buying a product, and were likely to emphasize social and career advancement as a reward for purchasing a product. Conversely, women were typically shown as consumers of inexpensive products, particularly those associated with food and the body. They were not likely to provide a reason for buying a product, but emphasized the social rewards for product purchase. Female central figures also occupied roles which were defined in relation to other people, and were more frequently depicted in domestic settings than were men.

Comparisons with other studies covering television advertising in different parts of the world revealed certain similarities. There was a high proportion (91 per cent) of males providing voice-overs in accordance with previous reports of between 88 per cent and 94 per cent in the United States (Brettl and Cantor, 1988; Harris and Stobart, 1986; Lovdal, 1990) and Great Britain (Livingstone and Green, 1986; Manstead and McCulloch, 1981). The depiction of 62 per cent of female figures as young was also a typical feature of advertisements from the United States, Mexico and an earlier Australian analysis (Gilly, 1988).

Male figures' credibility ratings confirmed previous US findings (McArthur and Resko, 1975; Rak and McMullen, 1987) and British findings (Livingstone and Green, 1986; Manstead and McCulloch, 1981). Women typically occupied roles which were defined in relation to other people, whereas men were more often portrayed as being autonomous, again reinforcing US results (McArthur and Resko, 1975; Harris and Stobart, 1986; Rak and McMullen, 1987) and British findings (Livingstone and Green, 1986; Manstead and McCulloch, 1981).

Advertisements directed at children

There are a small number of published US studies concerning gender-role portrayals in television advertisements directed at children. As with advertisements directed at adult audiences, advertisements on children's television have been found to contain a preponderance of male characters (Doolittle and Pepper, 1975; Riffe, Goldson, Sexton and Yang-Chou, 1989).

Gender-typing in children's advertisements has also been observed at the structural level with male-oriented advertisements containing more cuts, loud music and boisterous activity, whereas female-oriented advertisements contain more fades and dissolves, soft music and quiet play (Welch, Huston-Stein, Wright and Plehal, 1979).

Two American studies during the early 1970s found that this was certainly true of advertisements broadcast during Saturday morning's children's programmes. Winick, Williamson, Chuzmir and Winick (1973) found that 58 per cent of children's advertisements contained boys, while only 36 per cent had females. Thirty-five per cent contained males only, 19 per cent females only, and the rest featured both sexes. Chulay and Francis (1974) also found that girls in children's advertisements were most likely to be shown in advertisements for food, games, and dolls, while boys were mainly in advertisements for games, toy cars and toy planes. Boys were also more likely to be shown playing outdoors, while girls more usually played inside the home. The imaginary roles girls and boys took on in the games they played were also identified as highly stereotyped. Girls often played house-wife or mother figures, while boys were soldiers, pilots or racing drivers. The authors suggest that children's advertisements present girls only in traditional stereotyped roles, and that this might lead to a narrowing of ideas about women amongst youngsters especially with respect to their being successful in the business world.

McArthur and Eisen (1976), analysed 161 advertisements broadcast during children's programmes on US television. Of the central characters in these advertisements, 80 per cent were male and 20 per cent were female. The imbalance of males to females found here was much more marked than that reported by McArthur and Resko (1975) for adult-oriented advertisements. These results were supported by a study of televised toy advertisements during the 1977 and 1978 Christmas holiday season in the US (Feldstein and Feldstein, 1982). Not only were there more male-oriented than female-oriented advertisements, but on average there were also more boys and girls per advertisement.

Welch *et al* (1979) examined the *form* of children's commercials, analysing the pace, amount of action, visual and auditory techniques of advertisements directed at boys and girls respectively, as well as commercials intended for children of either sex. They found marked differences according to the gender of the intended market. Advertisements selling boys' toys showed the products involved in more activity than was found in either of the other types of advertisements. Commercials directed at girls had more 'fades' and 'dissolves' and were accompanied by more soft background music. The sound effects in the boys' advertisements tended to be loud and dramatic. As Welch et al (1979) point out, it is not just the content of children's advertisements which present different frequencies of males and females and portray stereotyped behaviour, but the forms and style of the commercials also offer different emphasis seemingly oriented around gender lines.

Macklin and Kolbe (1984) analysed the content of 64 children's television commercials, focusing on gender-role stereotyping. Advertisements were rated by six trained judges. Nearly 61 per cent of the ads had both sexes present; however, 63.9 per cent of the 'dominant characters' within advertisements were male. Male voice-overs were present in 69 per cent of the commercials for 'neutral' products.

In an analysis of 2,135 U.S. commercials broadcast in March 1981, there was a nearly equal number of males and females, although this varied by product type. Females made up the majority of characters in commercials for cleaners, hygiene and beauty products, apparel, and toys (Scheibe, 1983).

The portrayal of gender in children's television advertising has changed, according to research by Kolbe (1990). Children's Saturday morning television advertising in the USA for the years 1973 to 1988 were examined. The major findings were that (1) males remained the dominant presence in commercials, (2) females increased their presence in voice-overs and major roles, and (3) male and female advertising soundtracks and activity levels were comparable in tenor. While equality between the sexes was not fully in evidence, there were signs between 1973 and 1988 that advertisers had made strides toward greater gender equality.

Kline and Pentecost (1990) analysed 150 toy commercials broadcast in the US in 1986-87. Doll play predominated among toy commercials aimed exclusively at girls, accounting for 84 per cent of these ads. In contrast, only 45 per cent of the boys' ads featured doll play, mostly with action-figure dolls. Character toys were starting to break down the stereotype that doll play is for girls only. Still, the authors stated that 'profound genderization' nevertheless persists in toy commercials.

A British study by Smith and Bennett (1990) examined 75 children's television commercials from late October to the week before Christmas 1988. Boys were more often shown engaging in competitive play while girls' play was associated with sharing. Girls were more often shown in passive roles. There was an overwhelming majority of male voice-overs (75 per cent), compared to female voice-overs (26 per cent). Regarding gender stereotypes Smith and Bennett wrote, 'whatever gender imbalance there may still be in children's TV programmes, in these adverts there was exactly equal representation of males and females.'

Different production techniques seem to be employed in commercials directed to boys and girls. A clever study by Huston, Greer, Wright, Welch and Ross (1984) examined commercials using techniques, such as action, music, and editing, commonly found in advertisements typical of products for boys or for girls. Children aged 5 to 12 were shown specially-produced 'pseudo-commercials' for neutral objects in which these techniques were varied. The children were asked to judge whether each 'commercial' was better suited to advertise a girls' or boys' product. Children recognized the gender-typed connotations of commercial techniques: loud music, fast pacing and editing were seen as 'masculine,' and soft music and slower pacing were judged to be 'feminine'.

Schwartz and Markham (1985) asked university students to rate 48 categories of toys in terms of 'sex appropriateness,' that is, whether they were boys' or girls' toys. They then examined 392 pictures of children with toys in 12 toy catalogues and 538 pictures of children on toy packages. These were coded according to the gender appropriateness of the toy and the gender of children shown. Schwartz and Markham found that boys were shown playing with stereotypically masculine toys and girls with stereotypically feminine toys in catalogues and on toy packages. According to the authors, these finding suggest that toy ads reinforce conventional gender role definitions.

Boys and girls are often shown playing in different ways with their toys in advertisements. Kline and Pentecost (1990) observe that toy commercials portray girls *interacting* with toys, that is, adopting a separate identity that interacts with that of the toy. For instance, in an advertisement for 'My Little Pony', girls did not become ponies, but rather assumed identities or roles in relation to the ponies. Boys were most often shown *identifying* with toys, that is, taking on the characters of the toy as their own.

Riffe, Goldsen, Sexton and Yang-Chou (1988) reported a study of female and male portrayals in children's television advertisements. Commercials were analysed from Saturday morning US network television in February 1987 to reveal that these messages were populated mainly by males. Three times as many advertisements (29 per cent) used only human male characters as used only human females (9 per cent). Nearly one in four of the adverts used only animated characters. When animated-only spots were excluded, nearly 38 per cent of the human-only commercials used only males, while just over 11 per cent had only females. Overall, females were represented in 62 per cent of the adverts. Previous comparable estimates of total female representation were 51 per cent in 1971 and 60 per cent in 1973 (Barcus, 1971), suggesting that female representation may have increased over the intervening 15 years.

Product was related significantly to gender. Nearly 69 per cent of males, compared with 57 per cent of females, were shown in adverts for consumables, with a male-to-female ratio of 3-to-2 in snack food commercials, the most frequently advertised product category in the sample. There was no evidence of any gender difference tendency to be shown in home. Gender *was* related to setting, but the percentage of males shown in home settings was higher than the percentage of females. Males, however, were more likely to be shown in outdoor settings, and less likely to appear in non-home realistic settings.

Concluding remarks

Research into the portrayal and use of the sexes in advertising has revealed widespread stereotyping in terms of gender roles and gender traits. As with programme-related portrayals, males and females have been found to be differentially favoured in television advertising. Content analysis research, conducted predominantly in North America and

Western Europe, has consistently shown that females are disadvantaged not so much numerically but in terms of the nature of their appearances in commercials.

Early critics of advertising pointed specifically at the unequal distribution of males and females in television commercials. Men generally outnumbered women. However, what came to be regarded as even more serious was the allegedly narrow and inaccurate view of women's roles in society projected by advertising. This pattern was believed to characterize advertisements aimed at adults and children and to do so in different parts of the world.

Stereotyping in television advertising is typified by the way the sexes appear to be allocated disproportionately to different types of product and in the degree of authority attached to each sex in commercials. Typically, women were seen for many years to be associated disproportionately with commercials for domestic products set usually in the home. Men dominated non-domestic product categories and settings. Commercials have tended to use male voice-overs more often than female voice-overs. The balance was only partially redressed in respect of the latter feature in commercials for 'women's products'.

Internationally, the pattern of male predominance numerically and in terms of authority has been observed to occur in many different countries. This has remained the position even in recent years.

Women in television advertising have been frequently represented as sex-objects or because of their beauty, according to many scholars who have researched the subject. Men were seen as authority figures and advice givers, while women received advice and deferred to the more powerful male figure. These observations characterized much of the research evidence emanating from the 1970s and 1980s. Changes began to occur in the late 1980s onwards. Research started to emerge which indicated a greater presence of women in commercials for non-domestic products and a parallel downward turn in their presence in domestic product ads. More advertisements emerged featuring women in central, independent roles, assuming greater degrees of control over the immediate situation in which they were depicted and more generally over their own lives. As yet, this new pattern in gender-role portrayals has been visible in advertisements aimed at adults, while recent research has indicated that advertisements aimed at children have remained as gender-stereotyped as ever.

4 PERCEPTIONS OF GENDER ROLE PORTRAYALS

Research into the way the sexes are depicted on television has indicated that portrayals of women and men are stereotyped and repetitive, and according to some writers, lag far behind the social changes that are taking place in the world today (Butler and Paisley, 1980). It is often assumed that this stereotyping of both the roles and traits of the sexes on the screen engenders a parallel pattern of beliefs about the sexes among those who regularly watch television. The perception of gender-typed behaviours and attributes has been examined in terms of the degree to which viewers, especially children, are aware of gender-typed or stereotyped behaviours in television characterizations. Generally, the research has revealed that such images do not go unnoticed.

Some writers have envisaged a process of influence in which greater exposure *per se* to television's content results in greater television-biased responding on items of belief about the way things are in the real world (see Gerbner and Gross, 1976; Gerbner, Gross, Eleey, Jackson-Beeck, Jeffries-Fox, and Signorielli, 1977). It is assumed that mass audiences assimilate information, often incidentally, from television programmes, which may influence the way they think about the world around them. Continuous exposure to television may cultivate public beliefs about various social entities that consonant with images of these entities portrayed on television. Thus, stereotyped television portrayals (and the 'messages' they convey) concerning gender roles may give rise to stereotyped beliefs about men and women especially among heavy viewers and those individuals whose beliefs on these matters are at an early stage of development (i.e. children). As we saw in the introduction to this book, gender-role development and the adaptation of gender-appropriate attitudes and behaviours occur early in children's lives and media content may provide raw material on which youngsters formulate their ideas about the sexes.

A number of different views on the socialization of gender roles have emerged from prominent developmental theorists that have opened up the possibility of television cultivation effects on children's gender-role development by positioning theoretical accounts of gender-role learning without any direct interaction between teacher and learner. One influential cognitive-developmental view is that children learn during the first few years of life that their gender is unchangeable and are therefore motivated to value highly those attributes and behaviours culturally expected of their own gender in order to maintain self-esteem (Kohlberg, 1966). An alternative, social-learning view has asserted that children are rewarded for imitating members of their own gender and therefore attend more closely to and learn more from same-sex models (Grusec and Brinker, 1972; Mischel, 1970).

Although now an apparently theoretically feasible proposition, it is difficult in practice to isolate the relative contribution of the media to children's gender-role development. Television viewing, for instance, is so commonplace, even among pre-school children, that it is difficult to find an adequate control group who have not been exposed to this media content. As television *viewing*, rather than *non-viewing*, is the norm these days, any group of non-viewers would likely be unusual in many important respects apart from media usage and these factors might account wholly or at least in part for differences between their gender-role perceptions and those of regular television users. To get round this problem, some investigators have tested a weaker hypothesis which states that the more one watches stereotyped television content, the more likely it is that one will be affected by it in terms of stereotyped opinions or behaviours. These 'cultivation effects' are measured by comparing the beliefs of heavy and light television viewers to indicate an association between particular types of opinion and levels of television watching.

Unfortunately, this model embodies many problematical assumptions about causal relationships between what is shown on television and the formation of particular perceptions, beliefs and opinions among viewers about the world in which they live. One assumption is that 'messages' inferred from programme content profiles concerning various entities are recognized and encoded by audiences, who assimilate them into their existing knowledge structures relating to these entities. It is also assumed that heavy viewers will be more strongly influenced by television's messages than light viewers purely as a function of greater volume of exposure to them. However, measures of *amount* of viewing may not be valid and sufficient indicators of television effects, because television content and viewers' preferences for that content can vary considerably, and two heavy viewers who watch totally different kinds of programmes may hold two quite disparate sets of beliefs as a result. Relatively little research has been done on how people perceive television's images of women. Content analyses, from which inferences about television-effects are often made, may actually be poor indicators of audience perceptions however (Ceulemans and Fauconnier, 1979; Perloff, Brown and Miller, 1982). As we shall see in the sections to follow, even where direct tests of social attitudes towards women have been employed, researchers (with a few exceptions) have usually not related these reactions to specific viewing habits and preferences of individuals.

We need to know not simply *how much* television individuals watch but also *what kinds of content* they prefer to watch most often. Which particular portrayals are most salient to viewers and most likely to hold their attention? And finally, to what extent are the messages conveyed by television portrayals assimilated by viewers into their existing knowledge structures? If it is true that boys and girls learn to value most those attributes and activities which are presented by society as appropriate for their own gender, then it follows that they may also be likely to pay close attention to and show strong preference for television portrayals featuring same-sex characters.

People also learn to ascribe certain personality attributes as well as behaviours to men or to women. For example, some writers have pointed out that traits such as nurturance, dependence and passivity are typically classified as feminine, while dominance and aggression are generally considered as masculine (Bem, 1974; Rosenkrantz, Vogel, Bec, Broverman and Broverman, 1968). Furthermore, analyses of television content profiles have indicated that television portrayals tend to emphasize certain of these gender-typed characteristics in men and women (Paisley and Butler, 1980; Tuchman *et al*, 1978). What evidence is there though that traits supposedly emphasized on television are also the ones most salient to viewers? We shall now turn our attention to what is known about audience members' perceptions of the way women and men are depicted on television. We shall first look at evidence concerning children's perceptions of the sexes on television before turning to examine recent evidence on adult's perceptions.

There is plentiful evidence that both children and adults prefer same-sex characters on television and more accurately remember the appearances and actions of same-sex characters. Lyle and Hoffman (1972a) asked five-year-olds if they liked each of 13 characters appearing on the most popular children's shows. More boys than girls reported liking all 11 male characters, whereas more girls than boys reported liking each of the two female characters. The girls and boys who were interviewed were found to spend about equal amounts of time watching television.

Joy, Kimball and Zabrack (1977) showed children aged five and six years a three-minute videotape of two adults (one male and one female) engaged in dramatic action. After viewing the clip, the children were asked a series of questions including 'who did you like better – John or Mary?' Of the boys, 71 per cent chose John and 85 per cent of the girls chose Mary. This result was confirmed by Sprafkin and Liebert (1978) who found that when the theme of a television programme dealt with gender-typed content, children attended to programmes featuring a central character of their own sex more than one featuring the opposite sex.

These findings were reflected in research carried out with feature film material 20 years earlier. Maccoby and Wilson (1957) reported that 12- to 13-year-old girls and boys identified with the same-sex character in a movie. They were asked: 'which character is most like you? which part would you most like to play? which character would you most like to be like?' Ninety per cent of the girls and 84 per cent of the boys answered these questions mostly with the same-sex character from the movie.

Similar results were obtained with adults. Maccoby, Wilson and Burton (1958) found that in each of two movies, adult men spent more time watching the male character, while women spent more time watching the female character. This difference was accounted for by a time lag in shifting attention to the opposite-sex when he or she began to talk and by momentary shifts back to the same sex character while the other was talking. In other words, the time preference for the same-sex character occurred because viewers watched the same sex characters' reactions to what was being said by the opposite-sex character.

Children's perceptions of the sexes on TV

Children's perceptions of the sexes on television has been examined in relation to young viewers' observations about gender-role portrayals and gender-typed personality traits. Some researchers have also investigated the extent to which children identify with specific characters or have their attention drawn to particular character-types.

Selective attention to own sex

Two- to three-year-olds may be more responsive to female voices in certain viewing conditions, but most researchers into gender-role development recognize that slightly later, around age four to six, children are more aware of their own gender and are more interested in discovering the specific opportunities and constraints that this gender-category membership affords.

In one study of boys' and girls' selective attention to same-sex characters, preschool children aged two to five years were shown a silent colour film depicting an adult male and an adult female simultaneously carrying out a series of simple activities such as building a fire, making popcorn, playing a musical instrument and so on. The models were presented on a split-screen and the child's visual attention to each half of the picture was timed by an observer via a one-way mirror. The children themselves were differentiated according to their scores on a gender constancy test, as either being at *low* or *high* stages of gender understanding (Slaby and Frey, 1975). Both boys and girls with high levels of gender understanding devoted more attention to the same-sex model, though this result was significant only among boys. The researchers suggested that as the child becomes more aware of his or her social label, he/she then looks out for information about what is expected of people of their own gender.

Children appear to be better able to recognize same-sex characters and behaviour. Lyle and Hoffman (1972b) found that more three- to five-year-old boys than girls correctly recognized 13 out of 15 male characters tested, and more girls than boys correctly identified five female characters. Maccoby and Wilson (1957) found that after viewing a film, 12-year-old boys remembered more of the material in which only a boy was depicted. They also remembered more of the aggressive content if the boy character had been the agent of aggression. The girls remembered more of the content depicting girls alone and more of that material which depicting girl characters in interaction.

A study of children's perceptions of a small selection of 'TV mothers' revealed differences between girls and boys in the attributes to which they were most attentive. Children aged six, ten and 13 years were surveyed for their opinions about four well-known TV mothers: Mrs Ingalls of *Little House on the Prairie*, Mrs Cunningham of *Happy Days*, Edith Bunker of *All in the Family*, and Shirley Partridge of *The Partridge Family*. Girls were more likely to mention prosocial aspects of these characters than were boys. In general, however, these characters were regarded as having rather narrowly-defined personalities. As a result, many of the children did not rate them very highly. Boys, however, tended to dislike these TV mothers more than girls did (Wartella, 1980).

Identification with same-sex characters

Miller and Reeves (1976) found that when children nominated television characters as people they wanted to be like when they grow up, boys nominated only male characters while 27 per cent of the girls who nominated any character, chose male characters. This result was expected given earlier evidence of over-representation and higher status of male actors on television. In addition to the tendency to name same-sex characters, boys were likely to name more characters in general than were girls. Even so, the average numbers mentioned by either gender were low (0.81 for boys and 0.57 for girls), which does not suggest a strong preoccupation with television role models.

Commenting further on this particular study, Durkin (1985) offers a number of interpretations of its findings.

> On the one hand, a small proportion of the female population in this age group could be identifying with cross-sex TV models because of the scarcity of same-sex representatives. On the other hand, a larger proprtion have either found a same-sex model to identify with, despite these odds, or have not identified with *any* TV model. Whether it is a good or a bad thing to identify with a same-sex TV model is another (important) issue which was not the direct concern of the study. Perhaps a larger proportion of girls do not identify with TV models because they find them trivial or unrealistic. One further possibility is that among the 27 per cent of the girls who expressed ientification with opposite sex characters was a high proportion of pubertal children experiencing sexual attraction to glamorous TV stars, and their express desire to 'be like' these men could relate to social fantasies, such as joining the media set. Boys lag behind agemate girls in the onset of puberty (Tanner, 1972) and it may be less likely that these male children would express correpsonding desires yet. But note that one could invert this argument: maybe the 27 per cent were largely 'tomboyish' girls who had not yet experienced the menarche and were much less concerned about traditional femininity than their peers ... It is also conceivable that boys would be reluctant to admit to identification with female figures even if they experienced it (p. 81).

Reeves and Miller (1978) also found a tendency for children, especially boys, to identify with same-sex television characters. The identification of boys with television characters was positively related to perceptions of masculine attitudes (physical strength and activity level); girls' identification was positively related to perceptions of physical attractiveness. Reeves and Miller also found that girls were more likely to identify with male characters than boys were with female characters.

Mayes and Valentine (1979) found that young viewers tended to perceive gender-typed attributes in television cartoon characters. Whilst this study did not demonstrate cultivation effects, it does indicate that cartoon characters, who may provide role models for children, were seen to exhibit stereotypical gender-role behaviours and attributes. In this experiment, however, viewers were primed to focus on certain aspects of programme content, a feature which is not typical of ordinary viewing. To what extent do young viewers pay different amounts of attention to the presence and nature of male and female television characters when they are not given specific instructions to do so before watching a programme?

Evidence on this has emerged from a study by Sprafkin and Liebert (1976) who examined how boys and girls select and attend to male- and female-dominated scenes on television. Groups of youngsters were shown film sequences which featured female characters displaying female-appropriate behaviour, or male characters displaying male-appropriate behaviour, or males and/or females engaged in relatively less rigid gender-role portrayals. While boys selected and attended to male-focused programmes more than to female-focused programmes and attended specifically to male-dominated scenes in those programmes, precisely the opposite was true of girls who were more likely to prefer programmes or scenes that revolved around female characters and activities. Girls were no more likely to attend to male-focused programmes or scenes than were boys to attend to female-focused materials. Also boys and girls identified to the same extent with same-sex characters, and same-sex characters were named as favourites by 84 per cent of children. Elsewhere Eisenstock (1984) found, among about 240 boys and girls between the ages of 9 and 12, that identification with a counter-sterotypical female character in a television programme was greatest among boys and girls scoring high in traits conventionally said to be feminine and unrelated to scores on masculine traits.

Other research, however, has indicated that male characters on the screen may often attract greater attention from young viewers of both sexes than do female characters, and that evaluations of female characters may be especially harsh and recall of what they do or say particularly poor among female members of the audience. In a non-television study, McArthur and Eisen (1976) found that preschool boys persisted longer on a task after hearing a story about achievement by a male character than a story about a female character, although no significant trend in the opposite direction was observed for girls.

In a subsequent study that investigated differences in children's learning from male and female television newscasters, Tan, Raudy, Huff and Miles (1980) found interesting interactions between the gender of the viewer and gender of the newscaster in relation to perceived credibility and retention of the news. Groups of eight to eleven year-old children viewed one of two specially prepared 15 minute newscasts, one of which was read by a female newscaster and the other by a male newscaster. Results showed that the male newsreader was generally more effective than the female newsreader in producing retention of newscast material, and that boys remembered more of the newscast than did girls. Although children rated newsreaders of both sexes equally believable, in a test of news recall, girls remembered significantly less from the female newsreader. Tan *et al* suggest that their results may indicate something about the way boys and girls appraised male and female newscasters. While boys may have considered the role of TV newscasting to be appropriate for both men and women, girls may not have perceived this particular role as appropriate for their own sex. Girls may therefore have paid less attention to the news when it was read by a female newscaster.

Silverman-Watkins, Levi and Klein (1986) challenged the implication of gender bias on the grounds that the male newscaster had an advantage because the topics were masculine. They concocted a 12-item newscast balanced between masculine, feminine, and neutral topics with a male or female voice, and showed it to about 100 fifth, sixth, and seventh graders. The gender of the newscaster made no difference in recall, but boys and girls recalled stories linked to their gender best, and overall more children remembered the newscaster as male than female.

Young viewers' gender orientations can affect their perceptions of other areas of television. Rosenwasser, Lingenfelter and Harrington (1989) found, among about 115 pre-school and second graders, that there was a modest positive association between knowledge of non-stereotypical commercial programmes, such as *Who's the Boss?* and *The Cosby Show*, and holding non-traditional views on gender roles.

Further evidence has emerged that pre-existing gender-stereotypes among young viewers may distort their perceptions and memories for television portrayals. Drabman, Robertson, Patterson, Jarvie, Hammer, and Cordua (1982) showed pre-school and elementary school children a videotape of a male nurse and female doctor. Afterwards, the children were asked to identify photographs or names of the doctor and nurse. Reversing what they actually saw, most children up the age of 12 years, tended to select male pictures and names for the doctor and female pictures and names for the nurse. Only the oldest children (age 12 years) correctly identified the names of the doctor and nurse.

These findings have received further support from work done in the United States by Williams, La Rose and Frost (1981) and in the United Kingdom by Durkin (1983). Williams *et al* investigated the impact of a television series aimed at teaching counter-stereotyping. In one experiment they showed four segments from the prospective series to groups of children. These segments portrayed male and female characters enacting some typical role for their particular gender. The principal male character in the series was a well known actor who had formally appeared on M*A*S*H*, and was shown as a man who could mix strength and leadership with gentleness and supportiveness. Another teenage female character was shown as someone who not only possessed the usual feminine qualities but also as a person who could assume leadership and take risks in ways normally associated only with males.

Teenage boys and girls were shown these programme segments and afterwards were asked questions about how much they liked what they had seen, how much they understood what was shown and how inclined they were to emulate aspects of a particular character's behaviour. It was found that different children like and perceived different things in counter-stereotyped television portrayals.

Opinions about what they saw varied both as a function of the gender of the child and in relation to the gender of the television character in question. Boys evaluations of male and female characters from the television series indicated that the more they saw a male character in a stereotyped way, the more they liked him, whereas the more counter-stereo-typed a female character was perceived to be, the more boys liked her. The children had relatively strong factual comprehension of the television programmes, but their comprehension of the gender-role objectives of the programmes was lower than hoped for. Similarly, the desire to imitate the counter-stereotyped characters' behaviours were mixed and in some respects inconclusive.

Williams *et al* found overall a selective bias in perception of the programme materials, such that stereotypic males and non-stereotypic females seemed to be better liked and better remembered. This suggest that children may pay greater attention to masculine type behaviours, whether performed by male or female characters on the screen. On the other hand, attention to male characters behaving in a non-stereotypic fashion apparently is much weaker and may be the most difficult examples of behaviour of all to get across.

Wright, Huston, Triglio *et al* (1992) tested the hypothesis that children form separate schemata for television and real life. They asked children about nurses and police officers because they are shown frequently on TV and represent a balance of sex stereotypes. Content analyses and commentaries from professionals in these occupations revealed consistent differences between TV portrayals and real life roles. For example, nurses on TV are shown almost exclusively in hospitals, whereas in real life most nurses work in outpatient settings. Police officers on TV brandish guns frequently and are rarely shown on traffic duty, which is a major part of their jobs in real life. Second and fifth graders rated the factuality and social realism of television in general, rated reasons for viewing, and completed a checklist of programmes they usually watched. They were asked to describe the job activities of nurses or police officers, on television or in real life. Next they were asked questions about the typicality of various job activities and their sources of knowledge about and aspirations for the assigned occupation.

Children of both ages clearly differentiated their schematic knowledge about the assigned occupation on television and in real life, and most of their descriptions conformed to hypotheses about expected directions based on the content analyses. That is, nurses and police officers on television made more money, were more gender stereotyped and glamorous, and did not get hurt or sick as often as their real life counterparts. Children believed nurses and police officers in real life worked harder and had more status and excitement in their jobs than as portrayed on television. Though children could separate television information from real life information about the occupations, perceived reality still influenced their real-world beliefs, particularly for older children. Ten-year-olds who believed that entertainment television is factual and that portrayals of nurses and police officers on television are socially realistic had more 'TV-like' schemata for these jobs in real life. Children's schemata also predicted their aspirations to be nurses or police officers, especially for these jobs as they are shown on television. Moreover, aspirations were asserted most by heavy viewers of entertainment television, who also perceived television shows in general as factual (Wright, Huston, Triglio *et al*, 1992). Thus, it appears that though children form separate schemata for television and real life, these boundaries are not impermeable.

A second study tested the hypothesis that children acquire schema information about occupations from television and that they draw more of this information from factual than from fictional programmes. To control for real-life sources of knowledge, Huston *et al* chose the occupations of caterer and film director because they are information to children and balanced with respect to gender (Huston, Wright, Fitch, Wroblewski and Piemyat, 1992).

As in the first study, six- and ten-year-olds rated the factuality and social realism of television in general and completed a TV viewing checklist. Each child saw a drama and a documentary about a caterer and a film director. Stimuli were matched for occupational information portrayed, but used different formal features to convey factual or fictional status. Children's schemata about the occupational roles were measured by free response descriptions and ratings and recognition of typical job activities.

On two of these measures, children drew more occupational information from the documentaries than from the dramas, though they cited elements from both programmes more than content that was not shown at all. The reality manipulation was successful, as shown by the finding that children perceived the documentaries as more factual, socially realistic and useful for learning than the dramas. As predicted, children who rated television in general as unrealistic rated schema elements from the drama as less typical of real life jobs than the documentary elements, and this difference was larger for ten-year-olds than for five-year-olds (Huston, Wright, Fitch *et al*, 1992). Thus, children do acquire separate schemata for factual and fictional television, but even fictional TV can serve as a source of information about real life occupations.

In British research on young viewers' perceptions of counter-stereotypic role portrayals on television, Durkin (1983) investigated teenage girls' opinions about women in traditionally male roles. He conducted an experiment in which 79 pupils from a secondary school were selected to watch one of two versions of a television weather bulletin delivered by a woman forecaster. in one version, a male newsreader in the preceding news programme remarked favourably on the forecaster's new hairstyle, while in another version, this remark was edited out. The children were shown the forecast and then answered a number of questions about the forecaster herself (her qualifications, looks, dress, presentation style, experience and reliability), and about whether they would like to become a weather forecaster or newsreader themselves. The principal research question was what effect on children's opinions would the remark by the newsreader have.

Contrary to expectations, girls tended to see the forecaster as better qualified and more experienced in the version with the remark. Girls in both groups estimated the forecaster's experience as greater than boys did. This finding, suggests Durkin, may indicate that girls believe that women have to try harder. Girls also estimated the forecaster's qualifications to be slightly higher on average than did boys. Boys, saw the forecaster as slightly more experienced and qualified in the edited version. This may indicate that the flattering (though some might say 'sexist') remark made by the male newsreader reduced the level of professionalism perceived by boys.

Adults' perceptions of the sexes on TV programmes

Research on adults' perceptions of the sexes on television has investigated awareness of the relative presence of males and females on the screen and subjective ratings of the personality traits of males and females in television programmes and advertisements. These studies have sometimes revealed that viewers' subjective perceptions of the characteristics of males and females on television do not always correspond with the personality profiles of the sexes inferred in traditional content analytic research.

As an initial observation, however, issues surrounding the portrayal of women are not generally ones which are uppermost in people's minds when they discuss television (Millwood-Hargrave, 1994). Although mentions may spontaneously be made of female characters or celebrities, the issues of stereotyping or 'sexism' do not automatically enter the conversation. Women talking about television may recognize that roles assigned to their gender in programmes, as indeed in real life, are often based on assumptions about their gender. A view does seem to be emerging, nonetheless, that changes have occurred over time and cultural perceptions of male and female behaviour have modified the application of this gender divide.

In analysing adult perceptions of Saturday morning cartoons on television, Sternglanz and Serbin (1974) showed ten different videotaped cartoon shows to college undergraduates who provided subjective ratings about male and female characters in them. These viewers reported that more male than female characters appeared in the cartoons; that females were usually shown in traditional occupational roles for women; and that female characters also tended to be characterized predominantly by typically 'feminine' personal attributes (i.e. passivity, nurturance, submissiveness, dependence), whereas males were characterized by opposing 'masculine' attributes.

In a study of the perceived personality traits of male and female characters in dramatic television programmes, Peevers (1979) recruited six judges to evaluate the principal males and females in selected television dramas using Bem's Sex Role Inventory. Bem's work on psychological androgyny (1974, 1975, 1976) has presented an alternative to traditional gender-role stereotypes. Instead of conceiving of an individual as primarily masculine or feminine, as though these characteristics existed along a single continuum, the concept of androgyny allows consideration of an individual in terms of the degree to which she/he possesses both kinds of qualities. To Bem, the androgynous person is mentally healthy, able to act competently in situations which require traditional male characteristics, and also in those in which stereotypical female characteristics are adaptive. In her 1974 study, for example, Bem found that androgynous masculine males and females, as measured by the Bem Sex-Role Inventory (BSRI) (Bem, 1974), showed more independence from social pressure to conform than did participants categorized as feminine. At the same time, traditionally feminine, playful and nurtuant behaviour, was displayed to a significantly greater degree by androgynous and feminine males than by masculine males.

Peevers reported two studies conducted one year apart. In the first of these, results indicated that 85 per cent of all male characters were classified in highly masculine terms, while only 44 per cent of all ratings for females fell in the feminine range. In addition, 28 per cent of female characters' gender-role scores were in the masculine range, compared with only four per cent of male characters who had opposite sex scores. More than twice as many female characters scored in the androgynous range as did male characters (28 per cent versus 11 per cent). The second study replicated the first and indicated that males were perceived as being more stereotypical than females, thus presenting a contrast to the generally held notion that it is females who are highly and consistently stereotyped by the media.

Peevers' study indicated that the traditional male role is highly valued; so valued that it is *over* dramatized in TV programmes. The gender-role scores of many male characters were so extremely masculine that they could hardly be achieved by real people. The 'super-masculine', non-human portrayal of the male role abounded on the TV screen, presenting a continuing picture of an unattainable but supposedly desirable role model. Analysis of the female role portrayal, on the other hand, revealed that it was more diversified, more flexible, and more human, in the sense that female characters' gender-role scores fell within the limited attainable by real people. According to Peevers, these results dramatically illustrated the acceptance of greater flexibility in the female role in our society. Deviations by female characters in the direction of masculine qualities were acceptable because those qualities are valued. Conversely, male deviations from the male role remained highly unacceptable.

Viewers' perceptions of the gender-role or gender-traits of television characters, however, may depend upon the way they perceive themselves. Goff, Goff and Lehrer (1980) explored young adults' perceptions of the qualities of five well-known female characters on US television using the Bem Sex-Role Inventory and also looked at how these perceptions were related to viewers' self-ratings on the same scale. Self-perceptions turned out to have stronger associations with character perceptions than did the actual gender of respondents.

Androgynous respondents were likely to perceive television characters in androgynous terms too. Respondents who saw themselves in masculine terms, however, perceived the characters to be more feminine; while more feminine-related respondents perceived the characters in more masculine terms. These results provide evidence that the non-gender-typed (androgynous) viewer is more perceptive of the blend of masculine and feminine personality characteristics portrayed by characters perhaps because his or her own personality is perceived to consist of a similar blend.

Despite the accusations which have derived from traditional content analysis studies that television is responsible for gross gender-stereotyping, the open-ended opinions of viewers have revealed a more complex pattern of images of women as seen on television.

One recent survey which sought from viewers, their unprompted perceptions of the televised images of women found a diversity of responses among both male and female members of the audience (Atwood, Zahn and Webber, 1986). Interviewees were asked to specify a recent instance in which they had seen a woman portrayed on television in a positive way, and to cite up to three reasons for evaluating the portrayal as positive. The same procedure was then repeated for any negative portrayals that had been seen. Three-quarters of responses categorizing women on television in a positive light did so because the portrayals were seen as showing women as strong, intelligent, professional and realistic. Just one-quarter of positive portrayals were so attributes such as physical attractiveness, being nurturant or caring towards others. Viewers were much more likely to describe television portrayals of women as negative because the women were shown as weak, exploited victims, housewives, or sex objects. Having assertive, aggressive or selfish traits however were much less often likely to result in a negative evaluation of television women.

Zemach and Cohen (1986), in a study of 1,202 adult respondents in Israel, found, especially among the heavy viewers, that perceptions of the television world were stereotyped in regard to 'feminine' traits (*warmth*, *sensitivity*, *gentleness*), 'masculine' occupations (medicine, science, politics), and the roles of money management, providing for the family, and shopping for food.

Perceptions of the sexes on TV and in everyday life

Research in Britain has attempted to shed more light not only on how the sexes are seen by viewers in television, but also how these television perceptions differ from the way in which the sexes are seen in everyday life. During two weeks of programme appreciation measurement as routinely conducted by the IBA's Research Department, viewing diaries together with questionnaires were sent to representative samples of more than 600 people in each of two Independent Television regions of the United Kingdom (Yorkshire and Central Scotland). The diaries listed all programmes broadcast on the four main UK television channels during each week. Respondents gave appreciation scores for all programmes seen, thus providing a record of their viewing for the week. The questionnaire listed ten propositions about women and then precisely equivalent propositions about men, and asked respondents to say how often each proposition was true of man or of women 'as they appear on television'. On the reverse side of the sheet the same propositions were presented and respondents were asked to repeat the exercise, but for men and women 'as they actually are in real life'. The propositions were designed to reflect traits identified by previous content analysis research as typical features of female and male portrayals on television (see Gunter, 1984).

Around 500 respondents returned completed diaries and questionnaires in each region. Striking differences emerged between perceptions of men and women both on television and in real life. There were some variations as well between male and female respondents in the way women and men were perceived either on television or in real life, indicating that viewers do make subtle distinctions between the TV images of the sexes and real world appearances and characteristics. These results are set out in Tables 4.1 and 4.2. Characteristics have been listed in a normative ranking in such a way that the ones at the top of the list are those which respondents consider characterize women in real life more than men ('womanly' attributes), and work down to the bottom of the list where people apparently feel that these attributes are more characteristic of men than of women in real life ('manly' attributes).

Overall, there was not much difference between men and women respondents in the extent to which either thought that 'womanly' attributes applied to women in real life or on television. Likewise the extent to which these five more 'womanly' attributes were noticed in men, varied but little overall between real life and television. There were, however, noteworthy differences. People thought women in particular, but also men, were shown as likely to get on well if they were good looking on television, much more often than they felt applied in real life. Women respondents were less likely to say that women in real life needed to be good looking to get on, than were men. Both sexes thought television underplayed males' needs to be gentle and affectionate compared with what they considered was true in real life.

With regard to more 'manly' attributes, the overall perceptions were that they applied more to men than to women, and to a similar extent both on television and in real life. Again though, there were particular item differences; women were more likely than men to notice that women in real life might be interested in politics, and this perceived difference applied as well with regard to their perceptions of the portrayal of women's interest in politics on television.

Overall, men respondents in both these British surveys showed a slightly greater polarization in attributing characteristics to women, both on television and in real life, than did women respondents. While men again showed slightly more polarization than women in linking more male and fewer female characteristics to real life men, this did not occur in men's description of television portrayals of men. Many of the inter-respondent cross-contextual and gender-role related differences are significant and tests for these significance levels have been reported by Gunter (1984). The cross-contextual differences in particular raise an important question; for if perceivers can and do recognize that television portrayal differs from real life nature, and people are in contact with the latter, there is no need for them to infer that television portrayal is an accurate picture of real life. In short, if people recognize television is different, this may insulate them from the 'short circuits' of perception that are implied in the 'cultivation effects' theory referred to earlier.

Recent qualitative research among women in Britain has indicated that women are perceived as being featured more often in dominant roles on television (Millwood-Hargrave, 1994). This opinion was reinforced by content analysis evidence which showed that women, though out numbered in terms of total representations, fared better in major roles. Male domination of major roles was more marked in fiction programmes, whereas in factual programmes women figures more prominently.

Table 4.1. Percentages of female and male respondents who perceived each characteristic as true of women and men in real life and on TV – Yorkshire

	REAL LIFE				TELEVISION			
Those evaluated:	Women		Men		Women		Men	
Perceived by:	Women	Men	Women	Men	Women	Men	Women	Men
'Womanly' attributes:								
Likely to get on if good looking	68	82	50	46	93	92	85	85
Like to be romantically involved	91	94	94	91	96	97	95	94
Want to settle and have a family	99	97	95	94	87	91	66	70
Need to be gentle and affectionate	89	93	74	69	84	87	56	52
Could not survive with the other sex	77	76	84	77	62	73	80	75
Averages:	84.8	88.4	79.6	75.4	84.4	88.0	76.4	75.2
'Manly' attributes:								
Get on well with own sex	85	79	96	95	59	64	86	87
Successfully hold own against own sex	76	80	91	90	85	84	91	91
Interested in politics	56	42	84	82	42	31	83	77
Need a good job to justify lives	38	34	85	85	57	49	91	91
Need to feel they dominate other sex	32	40	81	75	51	51	88	81
Averages:	57.4	55.0	87.4	85.4	58.8	55.8	87.8	85.4
Difference between upper and lower averages:	27.4	33.4	-7.8	-10.0	2.56	32.2	-11.4	-10.2

Note: Survey conducted in Yorkshire ITV region; Source: Gunter, 1984

Table 4.2. Percentages of female and male respondents who perceived each characteristic as true of women and men in real life and on TV – Central Scotland

| Those evaluated: | REAL LIFE | | | | TELEVISION | | | |
| | Women | | Men | | Women | | Men | |
Perceived by:	Women	Men	Women	Men	Women	Men	Women	Men
'Womanly' attributes:								
Likely to get on if good looking	67	79	44	56	97	94	90	85
Like to be romantically involved	93	88	92	90	96	88	94	93
Want to settle and have a family	100	97	93	85	86	85	66	66
Need to be gentle and affectionate	85	84	68	61	80	83	50	51
Could not survive with the other sex	52	77	82	80	64	71	82	77
Averages:	79.4	85.0	75.8	74.4	84.6	84.2	76.4	74.4
'Manly' attributes:								
Get on well with own sex	85	76	96	95	58	55	84	81
Successfully hold own against own sex	69	69	89	88	79	86	96	92
Interested in politics	50	45	87	80	45	34	81	78
Need a good job to justify lives	49	43	87	82	49	48	93	88
Need to feel they dominate other sex	26	48	84	69	41	62	85	84
Averages:	55.8	56.2	88.6	82.8	54.4	57.0	87.8	84.7
Difference between upper and lower averages:	23.6	28.8	-12.8	-8.4	30.2	27.2	-11.4	-10.3

Note: Survey conducted in the Central Scotland ITV region; Source: Gunter, 1984

Perceptions of male and female violence on TV

We have already seen that content analysis studies of the presentation of the sexes on television have indicated pronounced stereotyping in the way women are portrayed. Women do not appear as often as men in leading roles and when they do appear they tend to fill a narrower range of roles (Butler and Paisley, 1980; Tuckman, 1978; Durkin, 1985d).

Research in the United States by Gerbner and his colleagues indicated that women tended to be less involved in violent incidents on television, but once they were involved, they were more likely to be victims of violence than perpetrators of it (Gerbner, 1972; Gerbner *et al*, 1977, 1978, 1979). In Britain, Cumberbatch, Lee, Hardy and Jones (1987) recorded a far greater involvement of men in violence than of women, both as perpetrators and victims of violence. Women were, once again, proportionately more likely than men to be featured as victims.

The profile of victimization among male and female television characters was interpreted by some researchers as a metaphor for the relative incompetence, helplessness and dependency of women in society, especially in spheres outside the home (Tuchman, 1978). Gerbner noted that 'good' female characters enjoyed a much better chance of giving than of being on the receiving end of violence (Gerbner *et al*, 1979).

Generally, leading female characters on television have been found to play good or innocent roles rather than evil or criminal roles (although this is not always true). Hence, television has tended to depict women as weaker and less able to cope effectively with problem situations, especially violent ones, most of the time. To what extent though are viewers aware of these patterns of portrayals of the sexes and to what extent is the relative prevalence of violent victimization amongst males and females on television reflected in viewers' perceptions of violent episodes?

The particular meanings supposedly conveyed about certain social groups such as women by patterns of portrayals in fictional television programmes have usually been inferred by content analysis researchers from the extent to which such groups fall victim to violence in these programmes, and depend on the validity of an assumption that viewers draw the same inferences and assimilate them into their conceptions of social reality. This may often be a questionable assumption (Gunter, 1988). Seldom have viewers' perceptions of television content been tested directly. While televised episodes which consist of male-perpetrated violence are far more *prevalent* in fictitious stories on television than are those featuring female-perpetrated violence, and while female victimization is relatively more common than male victimization, little research has been done to examine the extent to which viewers' differentiate between violent portrayals involving male and female aggressors or victims.

The significance of differential involvement of the sexes in violent television portrayals for viewers' judgements of televised violent is indicated by research with children from which physical strength emerged as the most important attribute in terms of which they discriminated between leading male and female characters (Reeves and Greenberg, 1977;

Reeves and Lometti, 1978). Thus, if male characters are generally perceived to possess greater physical strength than female characters, perhaps they might also be conceived by viewers to be better equipped to cope with a violent attack upon them. The belief that women are generally less able to defend themselves against physical attack may mediate judgements that portrayals depicting female victimization are more violent and more disturbing than are those depicting male victimization.

Gunter (1985) reported a study in which viewers' perceptions of television violence were compared across scenes in which the gender of the perpetrator or victim of violence was manipulated. Some scenes depicted a male aggressor attacking a female victim while others showed a female aggressor attacking a male victim. The scenes were taken from British and American-produced crime-drama series and American-produced science-fiction series. Each scene involved one of two forms of violence, either a fight or physical struggle, or a shooting, and each type of violence was represented equally among male-perpetrated and female-perpetrated violent incidents.

An adult viewing panel watched 12 scenes (six male-perpetrated violence, six female-perpetrated violence) and evaluated each in turn along a series of adjectival scales. Results indicated that while there were a number of fairly well-marked variations in ratings of male and female violence, the overall difference between viewers' perceptions of how 'violent' these two kinds of portrayal were seen to be was negligible. However, male violence on a female victim was perceived to be significantly more 'realistic', 'frightening', 'personally disturbing', and 'likely to disturb other people' than was a female character attacking a male victim. Scenes depicting female victims were rated as significantly less 'suitable for children', 'exciting' and 'humorous'.

Although no significant differences in the perceived seriousness of violence in male-perpetrated and female-perpetrated violent portrayals emerged over all materials, marked distinctions on this scale did occur within different programme settings, and not always in the same direction. Thus, male violence on a female victim was perceived as more 'violent' than female violence on a male victim, but only in contemporary British-produced crime-drama series. For American-produced crime-drama and science fiction portrayals, the pattern of responding on this scale was reversed. Female-perpetrated violence was perceived as significantly more violent than male-perpetrated violence. Male violence was rated as more 'realistic' than female violence across all three categories of programming. On other scales, however, such as how 'humorous', 'frightening', 'personally disturbing', 'likely to disturb people in general' or 'suitable for children' these two types of portrayal were perceived to be, no significant differences occurred except for violent episodes in contemporary British crime-drama settings. In general, male violence was rated as more serious on a variety of scales than was female violence.

While the result for violence in British settings is understandable given differences between the sexes in their perceived powerfulness, the intriguing result here is the difference in perception of violence perpetrated by male or female characters as a function of programme type. In British settings, male violence on female victims was rated as far more violent and disturbing than female violence on male victims. In American settings the reverse was true. How can these results be explained?

In the American context, content analyses had shown that violence perpetrated by male characters was far more prevalent on fictional television programmes than violence performed by females. Females, on the other hand, featured proportionately more often a victims of violence (Gerbner *et al*, 1977, 1978, 1979). Thus, viewers may have become more accustomed to seeing male aggressors than female aggressors, and female victims more so than male victims. Differential degrees of habituation or desensitization may in turn therefore occur with respect to these different types of portrayal. More unusual forms of violence may produce more extreme reactions from viewers. On this line of argument, a female attack on a male victim, being a highly unusual type of portrayal, would be expected to elicit fairly extreme responses.

A second possible explanation for the greater perceived seriousness of female violence in American drama settings might relate to attitudes toward women who engage in criminal conduct. Some writers have pointed to the basic dichotomy of women into essentially 'good' and 'bad' types (Buckhart, 1973; McGlynn *et al*, 1976). Women who conform to idealized notions of femininity–gentleness, passivity, maternity, and so on – are perceived as basically good. Any women who turns to crime or violence, however, has, in so doing, abandoned her femininity and is therefore branded as deviant and bad. Such a woman would be perceived in the most extreme and unfavourable terms.

What is more difficult to explain is why one judgmental frame of reference may be adopted in one fictional setting, while a different one is applied in another setting. One possible reason could be that the typically normative conception of women as the physically weaker sex is applied most readily in those contexts that most closely approximate the everyday reality of the viewer – in the study reported above this means in British settings. In more distant fictional locations, other rules become more salient and are applied instead.

Adults' perceptions of the sexes on TV adverts

Evidence discussed in earlier chapters has been collated to support the argument that advertising does not present a realistic view of women and their roles in society. As women have taken on a broader range of roles, controversy over the way they are depicted in advertising has heightened. Concern rests on the belief that advertising messages have the power to condition conceptions people hold about the sexes. Such messages are believed to operate to the disadvantage of women by portraying them in a very limited and stereotyped fashion. Through the clever use of imagery, the display of lifestyles and the reinforcement of particular values, advertisements communicate culturally-defined concepts such as success, status, sexuality, and what is normal or abnormal (Leymore, 1975; Williamson, 1978).

Inferences about the possible influences of advertising based purely on content analysis research neither demonstrate nor prove their existence. Profiling gender portrayals in advertising cannot by itself reveal how women (or men) respond to these explicit or implicit messages. Later chapters will review research studies which have explored the effects of gender-role portrayals on television. In this chapter, however, we are concerned with people's perceptions and attitudes relating to the advertising content itself. Thus, while content analysis may suggest that advertising projects an unrealistic or distorted series of impressions about women, do women (or men) perceive these images to be lacking in veracity? What do viewers think and feel about gender portrayals in television advertisements? Do these perceptions in turn influence viewers' attitudes towards advertised products?

Some researchers have examined viewers' direct perceptions of specific gender-role portrayals in television advertising. Scheibe (1979) had 14 male and female viewers rate a sample of 48 television commercials originally shown on-air in 1976. Judges rated the commercials using adjectival scales designed to measure the personality characteristics of the men and women portrayed. Some confirmation of earlier content analyses emerged from Scheibe's findings. Female characters in the commercials were perceived, for example, as more concerned about the appearance of their home and as more dependent on the opposite sex than were male characters. What is particularly interesting about Scheibe's findings, however, are the differences in perceptions of characters appearing in prime-time and daytime commercials. In general, female characters were perceived as less able spouses, less mature, more foolish, and less successful than male characters, but in daytime commercials the situation reversed and women were seen in a more positive light than men on similar dimensions. Scheibe concluded that, with respect to personality traits, male characters were portrayed as negatively as female characters. The real difference came with the time of day when the commercial was shown.

Sharits and Lammers (1982) extended Scheibe's findings about perceptions of male and female personalities in television commercials. Using a similar methodology, male and female business school students were asked to rate their perceptions of the roles portrayed in over 100 television advertisements. Results showed that females in the commercials were rated more favourably than men in terms of many attributes. Females were perceived to be portrayed as better spouses and parents, more mature, more attractive, more interesting and more modern than males. Little difference was found in the perceptions of male and female judges. One final interesting observation made by Sharits and Lammers was that men seemed to be increasingly filling sex-object roles in television advertisements.

Despite indications that women find the image of women as comprising an inferior class derogatory and feminist campaigns protesting against insulting and degrading portrayals of women in advertisements (Deckard, 1975), relatively little research has been conducted on how women view their portrayal in advertising. Bartos (1982) reported that female focus groups expressed strong preferences for more contemporary role portrayal, with only slight variation by work status. What variation there was suggested that the dumb and domestic stereotype was greeted with 'growing scepticism ...' (p. 16). Other research studies on consumer preference for various female portrayals in television advertising have revealed that preferences were influenced less by the respondent's attitude than by the function of the product advertised (Wortzel and Frisbie, 1974; Buchanan and Reid, 1977). Wortzel and Frisbie concluded that advertisements may portray women acceptably in household roles if the roles provided an appropriate usage environment. For personal products non-traditional roles were preferred.

An advertising agency interviewed a representative sample of women about their reactions to the way they are represented in television and magazine advertising (Foote, Cone and Belding, 1972). Only about 15 per cent of the respondents were genuinely satisfied. Most respondents (about 50 per cent) had mixed feelings, but were more negative than positive in their reactions. About 20 per cent of the interviewees were extremely resentful of female portrayals in advertisements. Although only a minority of female respondents was highly critical, this group was more articulate in voicing objections and reasons for dissatisfaction than the satisfied or mixed group. Furthermore, the strongest critics tended to be better educated and financially better off than the non- or mild critics, and thus more likely to be influential opinion leaders.

Ducker and Tucker (1977) found that attitudes toward women's role in general did not have any significant impact on perception on advertisements. A study by Lindstrom and Scimplimpaglia (1977) showed that women found that advertising suggests that they do not do important things; that their place is in the home; and that it portrays women offensively. They suggested also that both sexes would not be put off purchasing the particular product advertised. The study revealed that women, more than men, increasingly found that advertising suggests that women don't do important things, portrays women in a manner that is offensive, and complies that woman's place is in the home. Females were less likely than males to agree with the statements that advertising gives a realistic picture of men, and that it depicts women as sex-objects. The survey also examined the relationship between perceptions of gender-role portrayal and company image and buying intentions. The attitudes towards the company image showed significant differences as a function of gender. Women were more likely than men to believe that companies using offensive advertisements practised discrimination in employment, and that role portrayals in advertising were merely an extension of the company's view of women's place in society. However, with respect to buying intentions, both women and men tended to continue purchasing products, even if they were advertised in a way they considered offensive.

Although overall women were more sensitive to sex role portrayal than men, their attitudes were not excessively critical. Consistency in women's attitudes was found with respect to the statements that neither men nor women were currently portrayed in advertising and that current portrayal of women in advertising was improving. The strongest critics were better-educated, younger, upper-status women, who had rejected traditional role concepts.

Dawson replicated this study for Britain and had produced similar findings. He found that respondents were offended by the images portrayed and, using the same ad hoc attitudinal scale, reported no significant impact on purchase intentions towards a useful product. Whipple and Courtney (1980) found progressive gender-role portrayals to be at least equally preferred to, or more preferred than, traditional role portrayals. The research also showed that the unreal and exaggerated presentations of both sexes in advertisements, be they executed in either traditional or liberated styles, caused significant consumer irritation. They concluded that women were more contemporary, both in their attitudes towards themselves and toward advertisements, than their portrayals in advertising suggested.

Criticism of the role portrayal of women in British advertising takes up a similar theme. It claims that much current advertising fails to reflect a society where more than 40 per cent of the work-force is female and where more than 60 per cent of married women are known to be employed outside the home. It is also alleged to show insensitivity to the fact that the family structure is undergoing a rapid change, so that now one in every five households has a woman as its breadwinner, and very many women are independently performing roles other than those of the traditional home maker.

Hamilton, Haworth and Sardar (1982) conducted research on behalf of the Equal Opportunities Commission to investigate the ways women were portrayed in mass media advertising. The study was conducted in two stages:

1. With the help of a panel of judges, to assemble a portfolio containing both traditional and modern advertisements from the standpoint of the nature of execution of the females roles contained in them.

2. Using the Sherman Group's 'Buy Test', comparisons were made of the marketing efficiency of these types of traditional and modern advertisements for given brands in terms of their ability to fulfil the primary marketing functions of stimulating consumer interest and enhancing the likelihood of product purchase of each brand.

Both print and TV advertisements were studied. The panel of judges was recruited from advertising media and women's organizations (plus ad agency people).

Judges were asked to sort the advertisements into two categories: traditional and modern ('liberated'), then each category was further divided into what they considered 'offensive' and 'inoffensive', bearing in mind that an advertisement can depict women in a traditional role quite inoffensively. The judges also commented upon the types of evaluative scales which might be appropriate for rating attitudes to the advertisements.

The Sherman Buy-Test (c) scale was used to assess the persuasive impact of an advertisement. This instrument was able to divide the responses of a given target audience into three main categories:

(i) Those respondents who merely *recall and comprehend* the messages and content of an advertisement, but who fail to be motivated positively toward the product/brand, (*BUY-GROUP 1*);

(ii) Those respondents who, in addition to demonstrating recall and comprehension of the advertisement content, *exhibit a positive emotional or cognitive involvement* with the product/brand advertised, as a result of exposure to the advertisement *(BUY-GROUP 2)*; and

(iii) Those who, in addition to such involvement, show themselves to be *persuaded* by the advertisement and exhibit a positive orientation toward purchasing the product/brand advertised *(BUY-GROUP 3)*.

It was the latter group that was the focus of attention here.

A total of 622 personal interviews were conducted using the 'Buy Test' interviewing procedure. Four brands were investigated: Persil Automatic washing powder, Camay toilet soap, Contour Wallcoverings and the *Daily Mail* newspaper. In the case of each brand, one *traditional* and one *modern* treatment was evaluated. Interviews were conducted with women aged 16-60 from various socio-economic groups in the north and south of England. Each respondent was separately shown and interviewed as to her reactions towards one TV commercial or press advertisement only.

After exposure to the commercial, respondents first provided a description to represent as fully as possible all that they could recall seeing or hearing in the advertisement. An open-ended interviewing procedure invited them to say what they had understood to be the 'main parts or ideas' communicated by the advert. This was followed by a battery of pre-structured questions designed to determine the degree of involvement they had experienced while watching the advert. Finally, a further battery of questions was designed to measure the extent to which respondents had been *positively motivated* by the test advert and to isolate, at a diagnostic level, those specific elements within the advertisement which had contributed more significantly to any increase in the respondent's motivation to buy the advertised brand.

The characteristics of the traditional portrayals which the respondents uniformly rejected for all four advertisements were their unreality, falseness and stereotyped nature. The roles they most frequently criticized in these treatments as false were outstandingly those of typical housewife (Persil, Contour, *Daily Mail*). The rejection, however, is not of the roles of housewife or mum in themselves, but of the manner in which they were presented, for the typical housewife as seen in the modern contour treatment was a very persuasive image, and the perfect mum of the traditional *Daily Mail* treatment and the non-working woman of the traditional Persil treatment scores above average in persuasiveness.

The other side of the coin to the rejection of falseness is the attraction of realism and naturalness. This appeared explicitly as a persuasive image in the liberated Contour advertisement and the traditional Camay one, though in the latter it was heavily outweighted by the impression of falseness. However, taking all eight advertisements together, the numbers using the terms real and natural to express their perception were far lower than those using the opposite terms, unreal and false. It appears that reality is more readily noticed as a major irritant – when it is not present. The positively motivating images in the modern treatments were those of a career women (Camay, *Daily Mail*) and attractive personality (Persil, Camay), elegance (Camay, Contour, *Daily Mail*), a young modern person (Persil, Camay, Contour) and independence (Camay, Contour). The manner of portrayal, as well as the image itself, seems to be a contributory ingredient, as it is with the traditional images, for the images of independence, attractiveness and naturalness do not improve the poor performance of the modern *Daily Mail* treatment.

On the evidence here, there are two factors of the woman's portrayal in advertisements that determine its appeal and persuasiveness for the four target audiences of this study. The first is the role itself: the modern, liberated roles are much more effective than the traditional roles. The second is the manner of portrayal: the more realistic and natural it is, and the less false and stereotyped, the more effectively is the image communicated. These two factors appear to work together and have a multiplying effect so that while a traditional role portrayed realistically will be persuasive, a modern, liberated role portrayed realistically will be even more so.

As the interview programme progressed the frequency with which such terms as unreal, falseness, real and natural were used indicated a need to investigate the idea of reality as used by the respondents. The interviewers took the opportunity of post-interview discussions to explore the meaning of reality in the minds of respondents. Following extensive, albeit informal, discussions with many respondents, the research team formulated the hypothesis that, for most women, advertisements may be understood as representing a separate 'reality construct' – simultaneously related to, yet distinct from, the 'reality construct' of their daily lives.

Put simply, many women appeared to accept that advertisements, generally, will contain some element of 'unreality' and hyperbole; on this view, advertisements are to be understood as approximations to, rather than mirror-images of, daily life. The more tenuous such approximations are judged to be, however, (except perhaps in those instances when the advertisement is overtly 'unreal' almost to the point of parody) the greater the danger becomes that the advertisement will have a reduced marketing impact; it is as if the consumer distinguishes between the 'rules' of advertising and the 'rules' of reality. The 'rules' of advertising appear to allow for the use of hyperbole and exaggeration without a radical reduction in the perceived credibility of the message or its source; in those instances where such 'rules' are broken, however, and the advertisement is judged to be 'an ad-man's fantasy', the potency of the message and the credibility of the source are both seriously prejudiced.

Lysonski and Pollay (1990) studied the perceptions of female-role portrayals in television advertising among women and men in four countries: Denmark, Greece, New Zealand and the USA. Comparing attitudes in 1986 with ones surveyed in the USA in 1977, it was found that both American men and women had become more critical of advertising sexism. Women were more critical than men, although in both cases they were less inclined to intend to boycott products the advertising for which they had found to be sexist. Young adults from Denmark, Greece and New Zealand were more critical than Americans, and more inclined towards boycotts, but on average still tended to disavow boycott reactions to offensive advertisements. Individuals who were more critical were more likely to endorse boycotts. Exposure to a 30-minute consciousness-raising slide presentation about sexism in advertising increased sensitivity to the subject but did not produce any change in stated willingness to boycott advertised products or services.

DeYoung and Crane (1992) conducted a survey of attitudes towards the portrayal of women in advertisements among a sample of 175 women in a major city in eastern Canada. This study was a replication of an earlier American survey (Sciglimpaglia, Lundstrom and Vanier, 1979). A number of shifts in attitude were observed. There were two attitudes where the results were exactly the same. Over 50 per cent of respondents in both studies agreed that advertising shows women as dependent on men and at least half the women in both studies suggested that they were more sensitive to the portrayal of women in advertising.

In the Sciglimpaglia *et al* (1979) study at least six out of ten women agreed that advertising (1) suggests a women's place is in the home; (2) does not show women as they really are; (3) shows women as sex objects; and (4) infers that women do not do important things. DeYoung and Crane reported very similar results. There was a decrease over time in the percentages of women agreeing that advertising suggests a woman's place is in the home (51 per cent from 60 per cent) and that advertising suggests women do not do important things (46 per cent from 60 per cent). In addition, more than eight out of ten respondents in the earlier study (82 per cent) thought that advertising suggested women did not make important decisions, and just over six in ten (63 per cent) agreed with this view in the later survey. Sixty per cent of respondents in the earlier US study found the portrayal of women in advertising to be offensive, while 50 per cent of respondents in the later Canadian survey agreed with this viewpoint. In contrast, agreement levels increased over time in respect of the perceptions that advertising does not show women as they really are (75 per cent versus 60 per cent) and that women are shown as sex objects (80 per cent versus 60 per cent). An increase was observed in intended boycott levels for products whose advertising was found offensive to women (up from 30 per cent to 50 per cent). DeYoung and Crane asked their respondents if they believed that the portrayal of women in advertising would change for the better in the future. Over one in two (55 per cent) believed that things would improve, while over one in five (22 per cent) disagreed.

Concluding remarks

The description of gender-role portrayals on television as highly stereotyped is not consistently reinforced by the perceptions of viewers. Furthermore, the characteristics identified as typical of female or male portrayals on television by content analyses are not necessarily the ones which turn out to be the most salient to the audience.

Although audience perceptions of the sexes on television do not exhibit a consistent pattern throughout, one significant finding is that viewers do not seem to passively absorb everything they see on television. Perceptions of characters and behaviours appear to be mediated by pre-existing dispositions. Thus, boys often pay more attention to male characters than to female characters, while girls pay relatively more attention to females than do boys, although they may still be attracted to some male characters more than they are to most female characters on the screen. This, in turn, may make a difference to what children take away from a programme, such as a news broadcast. Children may feel more comfortable watching television characters or presenters behaving in a traditionally gender-stereotyped fashion.

On the question of whether viewers perceive gender-role portrayals as sexist or not, as content analysis research has indicated they are, again the findings reveal a level of sophistication among members of the audience that is so often underestimated. On some attributes audience perceptions reinforce the content descriptions of the way women and men are shown, whilst on other attributes, the two kinds of judgement do not match. One thing that has emerged from recent audience research, however, is that even if television's gender-role portrayals are seen, on some dimensions, as stereotyped, beliefs about the sexes in real life may be quite different. Perhaps overriding all of this, however, is the further observation that the issues of stereotyping or 'sexism' are not invariably (or even often) 'top-of-the-mind' matters for viewers. Thus, sex-stereotyping is not a topic which is uppermost in viewers' concerns about television, although when prompted, they can nevertheless offer considered opinions about gender-role portrayals. Such opinions may not be flattering where they perceive one sex or the other to have been unfairly or unreasonably treated. This feature of audience response has been observed particularly in connection with television advertising. Where this occurs, it could have serious implications for the marketing impact of a commercial campaign.

II
SOCIAL EFFECTS OF TELEVISION GENDER ROLE PORTRAYALS

5 EFFECTS ON CHILDREN

Research has established that children know what sex they are by between a year-and-a-half and three years of age (Money and Ehrhardt, 1972), but do they also begin to limit their life options because of a mental association between role and sex? Content analyses have indicated that one of the most prevalent areas in which gender-role stereotyping occurs on television is with respect to employment (Butler and Paisley, 1980; Downing, 1974; Tedesco, 1974). To what extent does this content influence children's perceptions of the kind of job to which they will be most suited in later life?

The career and occupational aspirations of boys and girls have been shown to differ markedly. Occupational choices among young children have been found repeatedly to reflect gender stereotypes (Dorr and Lesser, 1980). This phenomenon has a range of personal and social determinants. Even as young as age eight, boys and girls can display some awareness about occupational roles, and in particular about the status which attaches to different occupations (DeFleur, 1963; Nelson, 1963). Children's rankings of occupations in terms of prestige correlate at a high level with adults' rankings (Hansen and Caulfield, 1969; Simmons and Rosenberg, 1971).

Research has revealed that early development of awareness about the types of occupations men and women are likely to hold. Children have been found to exhibit judgements about which gender would be expected to occupy particular jobs which were strongly correlated with actual rates of gender occupancy revealed by census data (Garrett, Ein and Tremaine, 1977). Some differences have been observed in the willingness of girls and boys to project themselves into adult occupational roles. Ethnicity is a factor which makes a difference to these perceptions as well. One study found that pre-school black and white boys and girls were equally likely to project themselves into adult roles, although boys were slightly more likely to define adult roles by specific occupations (59 per cent of the boys versus 55 per cent of the girls), and girls were much more likely to define adult roles by parenthood (30 per cent of the girls versus 6 per cent of the boys) (Kirchner and Vondracek, 1973). Projections into adult roles were also more likely to occur among white children than black children.

Elsewhere, several other studies revealed clear gender stereotyping in children's occupational choices. Among three- to six-year-old boys and girls, Beuf (1974) found that 70 per cent of boys and 73 per cent of girls chose gender-stereotyped jobs for themselves, while only one boy and one girl chose non-traditional jobs. Looft (1971) reported that 76 per cent of five- and six-year-old girls questioned chose to be either teachers or nurses when they grew up. Another study found that 67 per cent of girls aged between nine and 12 years chose to be teachers, nurses, secretaries or mothers (O'Hara, 1962). These findings were corroborated by other investigators (Deutsch, 1960; Nelson, 1963). Boys also consistently nominate many more different jobs than do girls when asked what they expect to do as adults (Boynton, 1936; Siegel, 1973). Girls seem to be less able to suggest alternative occupations than are boys if told they could not pursue their first choice (Looft, 1971).

Thus, gender differences in career aspirations and occupational choice are clearly defined by young people from a fairly early age. The important question is why these differences exist and more significantly in the context of this book, what role does television play in their creation?

External influences on career or occupational choice

The choice of career or occupation to pursue can be influenced by a variety of factors which impinge upon young people in their social environment. Many adolescents have been found to mention their parents (usually the same-sex parent) as most responsible for their career choices (see Jensen and Kirchner, 1955; Pallone, Hursley and Rickard, 1973). The second source perceived as most responsible is usually someone holding the specific occupation the young person has chosen (Pallone, Rickard and Hurley, 1970).

Other studies of adolescents have described parent-child relationships and family structures as they relate to gender differences in differential motivation for occupational mobility (Douvan and Adelson, 1966; Dynes, Clark and Dinitz, 1956). According to this research, the family plays a key role in creating marked differences between boys and girls in terms of the degree of autonomy, independence and assertiveness they display. In all these areas related to occupational aspirations, girls show weaker motivation. For younger children also, similar differences in motivation between boys and girls have been identified (Lesser, 1973; Maccoby, 1966; Maccoby and Jacklin, 1974). Another interesting finding is that peers seem to be far less influential than parents and other adults in determining long-range goals such as occupational choice. Any influences that peers do exert tends to support the attitudes of adults instead of contradicting them (Douvan and Adelson, 1966; Kandel and Lesser, 1972). According to Dorr and Lesser (1980) other potential sources of influence such as schools, teachers, careers counsellors, books and catalogues are even less often cited by adolescents as significant in their career choices or occupational aspirations.

While the actual choice of career or job may be directly influenced by sources close to home, other factors may nevertheless attain a degree of importance in the provision of information about careers which young people may weigh up in reaching a decision for themselves. Some occupations would appear from the research evidence to be more visible than others to children and adolescents. Visibility of occupations in their community and within the mass media could reasonably be hypothesized to play a part at least at the level of informing young people about careers and occupations that are available.

A series of studies have indicated that television may be regarded by young people as one particular source of occupational information. In a sample of teenagers aged 13–15 years, 89 to 97 per cent mentioned television as a source of information about each of six occupations, while 7–35 per cent mentioned print media, and 6–73 per cent mentioned other people (Jeffries-Fox and Signorielli, 1979). In another survey, at least a third of black and white boys and girls aged nine to 13 years reported that most of their information about the jobs men and women have and about occupations such as police, doctors, nurses and secretaries came from television (Atkin, Greenberg and McDermott, 1979). Of course, self-attributed influences of television upon career or occupational choice may not reflect the actual significance of this medium as an influence. Nevertheless, given the extent to which television is viewed by children and adolescents it would be surprising if they picked up no information about certain occupations – especially those which are regularly featured in popular programmes.

Studies of television's influence on gender stereotyping among children have so far produced mixed results. So far there is a lack of clear evidence that television programmes or advertisements shape conventional gender roles to a significant extent. One reason for this is the difficulty of separating out the specific influences of television from other aspects of sex-role socialization. Traditional beliefs about gender roles are deeply embedded in the culture in which individuals live and more often represent the existing real-life experiences within their culture which are the primary sources of gender-role socialization. In a small number of correlational analyses, some researchers have reported no significant relationships between personal or parental estimates of children's television viewing and their gender-role perceptions, whilst others have reported significant degrees of association which have been interpreted as evidence for a television influence.

Evidence has also emerged from contrived experimental conditions that young children (aged 4–6 years) shown videos that associated previously non-gender-typed toys with either a male or female actor were more likely to choose from the same array of toys to play with those items they had seen linked with their own sex (Cobb, Stevens-Young and Goldstein, 1982). This suggests that the mere association of objects or behaviours with one gender rather than another can result in sex-typing of those objects and behaviour. Such effects may occur through audio-visual depictions and can make themselves felt among children at an early age.

General TV viewing effects

Some researchers have reported significant statistical relationships between television exposure and children's gender-role perceptions, without reference to viewing of specific types of content. Beuf (1974) conducted interviews with children of both sexes between the ages of three and six, asking them what they would like to be when they grow up. As well as specific questions about television viewing habits, each child was asked, 'What do you want to be when you grow up?' Then they were required to imagine what they would be if they were a member of the opposite sex. Thus, boys were asked, 'If you were a girl, what would you be when you grow up?' Finally, the children were engaged in a game called 'The OK Picture Game' in which they were shown several pictures, some of which were quite ordinary scenes of situations and others of which depicted something unusual or out of place, such as a five-legged cat. The interviewer explained to the children that the object of the game was to see whether a picture was 'OK' or not. Among several 'dummy' pictures were three scenes in which traditional gender roles had been reversed – a father feeding a baby, a man pouring coffee for a woman, and a female telephone-line repair person.

Results on career aspirations indicated a strong relationship between gender and envisaged future occupations for both own-gender and other-gender conditions. Boys tended to nominate traditionally 'masculine' professions such as policeman, sports star or cowboy; girls preferred quieter occupations such as nursing. While the actual jobs nominated by girls and boys were different, the tendency to stereotype career aspirations was virtually the same for both sexes. Over 70 per cent of boys and 73 per cent of the girls chose stereotypical careers for themselves. Even when asked what they would be if they were a member of the opposite sex, in nearly all cases, these youngsters selected what are normally regarded as appropriate for that gender.

Responses to pictures indicate that gender-typing increased as images moved from child-care to husband-wife roles to occupations. The children's beliefs reflected the increasing post-war trends of husbands helping around the house. However, regardless of the growing women's liberation movement, children still showed strong gender-typing with respect to occupational roles; whilst young children's gender-role perceptions measured here indicated strong stereotyping of ideas about the sexes, to what extent are they affected by television portrayals?

Beuf claims that gender stereotyping of career aspirations was more likely to occur among heavier viewers of television, but she presents no data to back up this assertion. Furthermore, Beuf's sample was small and unrepresentative of this age-band and her findings need to be replicated with other groups of children before they can be confidently accepted.

In a subsequent study, Frueh and McGhee (1975) asked children of each gender in kindergarten, second, fourth and sixth grades or their parents about television viewing, and then presented them with a projective measure of gender-role stereotyping. The latter was a paper and pencil test which examined children's choice of gender-typed toys. Strength of traditional gender-role beliefs showed a clear, positive association with amount of television viewing. Frueh and McGhee also found that boys and older children made the greatest number of traditionally gender-typed choices on the test. The conclusion of the study is that children learn about traditional gender roles from television. A number of critical questions remain unanswered however. Why were boys and older children more traditional in their attitudes? Was it their traditional attitudes that made some children heavier television viewers in the first place? What role did parents play, not only in teaching children about gender roles, but also in helping them to interpret what was seen on television? How accurate was parental monitoring of actual viewing among the youngest children? Was the sample of forty girls and forty boys representative of their age groups? Was the projective test a valid measure of children's gender role development?

In a follow-up study, McGhee (1975) and McGhee and Frueh (1980) reported further research they had conducted with the same children 15 months after their initial contact with them. On this occasion the researchers were interested to find out whether heavy television watchers (those watching 25 hours or more per week) differed from light television watchers (those watching 10 hours or less per week) among different age-groups in their adoption over time of gender-stereotyped beliefs.

McGhee (1975) reported results from two different measures of gender-role stereotyping which were related in opposite directions to the amount of television viewing claimed for children. On the basis of measures obtained from the scale used in the Freuh and McGhee study, McGhee found that lighter television viewers (but not heavier viewers had become more stereotyped in their gender-role perspections. Elsewhere, however, the validity of this scale as a measure of gender-stereotyping has been called into question and it has been claimed that it may be inadequate as such a measure with children over the age of seven years (Durkin, 1985).

With the second scale, however, gender-role stereotyping was found to be stronger among heavier television viewers. It is difficult to disentangle these findings and to know which ones are more accurate. Consistent with earlier findings, McGhee and Frueh (1980), in a further paper, reported that heavy viewers held more stereotyped perceptions than did light viewers. It also emerged, however, that the perception of male stereotypes steadily declined with increasing age among light viewers, while among heavy viewers these stereotypes were maintained with increasing age. No comparable results were obtained for stereotyped perceptions of females. The authors hypothesized that television may reinforce and maintain gender-stereotyped perceptions among heavy viewers, while light viewers, who presumably spend more time gaining experience about people other than through television, do not exhibit such strong stereotypes.

This interpretation of their results by McGhee and Frueh conveniently overlooks a serious internal problem with their study. The scale on which gender-role stereotyping was measured consisted of two sub-scales – one contained items referring to perceptions of male attributes and the other of female attributes. In fact, only responses to the male items were reported, which according to one other writer, suggests that it was perhaps only on these items that gender-role perceptions were related to television viewing (Durkin, 1985b).

Further evidence has emerged of positive relationships between increased viewing of television and more stereotyped beliefs about the sexes. Zuckerman, Singer and Singer (1980) examined variations in gender-role prejudice as a function of television viewing, demographic characteristics and family background of children. They studied 155 North American children of average age nine and a half years. In general, it was found that these children were not strongly stereotyped in their gender-role perceptions, but that where stereotyping did occur it was most evident among girls with lower IQs, who had mothers with higher educational attainment and who watched great amounts of television. The same results did not emerge among boys.

Gross and Jeffries-Fox (1978), in a panel study of 250 teenagers aged 14–17 years, found that television viewing was related to giving sexist responses to questions about the nature of men and women and how they are treated by society. Atkin and Miller (1975), in an experimental setting, found that children who viewed commercials in which females were cast in typically male occupations were more likely to say that this occupation was appropriate for women.

In another study with 11–12 year-old children, both the children's parent's gender-role perceptions were assessed along with the children's television viewing (Perloff, 1977). No significant relationship emerged between the numbers of hours per week children watched television and the degree of stereotyping in their gender-role perceptions. However, parental sexism was marginally related to stereotyping among children. Children whose mothers went out to work, for example, were less stereotyped.

The above findings were reinforced in another survey (Meyor, 1980) among 15 girls aged 6-8 and 10-12 years for whim, once again, amount of television viewing was related statistically to a range of attitudes and beliefs about the sexes. Neither personal or parental estimates of children's attitudes. A more important influence than television upon children's gender-role attitudes were the attitudes of their mothers.

Finally, in a study done by Cheles-Miller (1975) the degree of acceptance among 9–10 year-old children of traditionally gender-stereotyped beliefs about marital roles for men and women as portrayed in television commercials was found to be greater among lighter viewers of television than among heavier viewers.

Television cultivation effects

Many of the studies examining the relationship between television viewing and conceptions of gender roles have reflected the theoretical perspective of cultivation analysis that television dominates the symbolic environment of modern life. This theory posits (1) that the more time spent watching television, the more likely it is that conceptions of social reality will reflect what is seen on television, and/or (2) that television viewing contributes to the cultivation of common perspectives among otherwise diverse respondents – a phenomenon referred to as 'mainstreaming'.

Perhaps the strongest correlational evidence that television viewing influences children's gender-role attitudes so far comes from a longitudinal study of American adolescents (Morgan, 1980). Measures of television exposure (hours viewed in the 'average day'), acceptance of gender-role stereotypes and educational or occupational aspirations, were taken over the course of two years, and the method of cross-logged panel correlations was applied to the data. The results support the view that television inculcates certain gender-role views, although the effects are limited to girls. Television viewing in the first year of the study significantly mediated girls' third-year attitudes; heavy viewers were more likely than light viewers to agree that men have more ambition than women, that women are happiest raising children, and so on. There was no evidence that early degree of gender-stereotyping among girls mediated subsequent television viewing patterns. Among boys, on the other hand, television appeared to have no manifest longitudinal impact on gender-role attitudes, but existing sexism foreshadowed greater viewing at a later date. Among girls also the effects of television was greater among the middle-classes. Both lower-class females and males generally were more sexist regardless of viewing levels. These findings suggested that television viewing is most likely to have an influence among those individuals who are least stereotyped in their views.

Morgan also reported, again for girls only, a relationship between amount of television viewing in the first year of measurement and subsequent educational and occupational aspirations. Interestingly, however, the heavier viewers were the ones who two years later set their sights *higher*. This result, although predicted by Morgan on the basis of television's over-representation of professional women, runs contrary to the traditional influences reported by most other studies. Although, on balance the tone of Morgan's interpretation of his findings points to a gender-role stereotyping effect of regular television watching, in fact careful observation of the details of Morgan's study reveals that his findings are complex and difficult to explain.

Correlations between television viewing and gender-role perceptions were made at and across two points in time and were compared not only between boys and girls but also between three (high, medium and low) IQ groups. Television viewing was significantly related to sexism only among medium IQ boys and high IQ girls. No explanation is provided for the result among the boys, whilst the correlations among the girls were interpreted as evidence for television's influence, on the assumption that girls with high IQs are less likely to be sexist in the first place. Unfortunately, the small magnitude of his correlations does not provide strong evidence on which confidently to assume an effect of television (Durkin, 1985b).

A number of additional studies offer more support for the notion that TV viewing contributes to children's concepts about appropriate male and female behaviours. Rothschild (1984) found that 3rd – and 5th-grade children who watched more TV were more likely to exhibit traditional gender-role stereotypes for gender-related qualities (independence, warmth) and gender-related activities (playing sports or cooking).

Kimball (1986) examined perceptions relating to gender roles using data collected from three Canadian communities (NOTEL, UNITEL, and MULTITEL), before and after the time NOTEL received television. UNITEL had single-channel TV reception at the start of the study and MULTITEL had multiple TV channel reception. She found that in NOTEL children's perceptions relating to gender roles were less strongly sex typed before the introduction of television. Two years after the introduction of TV, however, the perceptions of these children were more gender- typed and did not differ from the perceptions relating to gender roles of the children in UNITEL and MULTITEL.

Morgan and Rothschild (1983), using data derived from the Cultural Indicators Project at the Annenberg School of Communications, University of Pennsylvania observed that of all TV's lessons, the differential portrayal of males and females may be the most stable. Year after year, even on TV men outnumber women at least three to one, and five to one on children's programmes (Gerbner and Signorielli, 1979). Women on TV were found to age faster than men, and were mainly cast in romantic or family parts. When they do work, they were usually in lower-status jobs, and they were rarely able to mix family and career with much success.

Morgan and Rothschild studied relationships between television viewing and gender-role beliefs among a sample of adolescents, taking into account also their strength of peer group affiliation. They hypothesized that TV effects would be more pronounced among young people with weaker peer group contacts. More integrated adolescents should be exposed to wider sources of influence about gender roles which might tend to counteract stereotypical TV portrayals.

Adolescents were surveyed at two points in time (T1 and T2), six months apart. TV viewing at T1 was related significantly to sexism scores six months later – the relationship was the same for males and females but stronger for those of lower SES. The TV – sexism relationship was also stronger among adolescents who named fewer friends. TV viewing at T1 was related to sexism at T2 even when controls were employed for TV sexism, SES, sex and peer group affiliation. Cable TV viewing was even more strongly linked to sexism. Thus, cable TV access did not seem to dissipate the impact of network TV – rather it appeared to exacerbate it.

Ongoing research suggested that heavy exposure to TV may cultivate conflicts between traditional gender-role and family outlooks, on the one hand, and personal aspirations on the other, particularly among teenage girls (Morgan, 1982; Morgan and Gerbner, 1982). Morgan and Rothschild's work also shed light on the question of how informal social networks and new technology intervene in adolescents' information environments. Their findings imply that the effects of TV can be suppressed by alternative information (as presumably provided by peers) but intensified by complementary media-generated information (as presumably provided by cable).

Morgan (1987) studied amount of television viewing, gender-role attitudes, and gender-role behaviour among adolescents, measured at two points in time, six months apart. The gender-role measures concerned respondents' attitudes about the gender-specific appropriateness of various household chores (cleaning the house, washing the dishes, mowing the lawn) and their own self-reported tendency to perform those chores.

Results showed that television viewing was related to adolescents' gender-role attitudes over time, but was not related to actual behaviour. The relationship between viewing and attitudes, however, was mediated by behaviour, but in different directions for boys and girls. Boys who scored high on the gender-role behaviour scale got high scores on the gender-role attitude scale, regardless of amount of viewing. Heaviest viewing boys who scored low on the behaviour scale were far less likely to express traditional gender-role attitudes; but the attitude scores of heavy viewing boys who were low on gender-typed behaviour approached the scores of boys who scored high on gender-role behaviour. This pattern for boys fits with the notion of 'mainstreaming' (Gerbner, Gross, Morgan and Signorielli, 1980, 1982) which holds that television cultivates a homogenization of outlooks among otherwise divergent groups. In other words, boys who engage in more gender-typed behaviour already have more gender-typed attitudes, and for them viewing makes no difference; boys who engage in less gender-typed behaviour also express less gender-typed attitudes, unless they are heavy viewers.

A different pattern of results emerged for girls. Girls who scored low on the sex-role behaviour scale expressed less stereotyped attitudes, regardless of viewing; it was the girls who scored high on the behaviour scale who showed a significant longitudinal association between amount of viewing and their attitudes. Thus, for girls, the tendency to engage in more gender-stereotyped behaviours creates a condition under which television's impact on attitudes is enhanced. In other words, girls whose behaviour tends to match traditional gender-roles are more vulnerable to the cultivation of traditional gender-roles attitudes by television.

Thus, the contribution of television to adolescents' attitudes about gender roles varies as a function of the degree to which their behaviour follows traditional gender-role lines. For boys, a convergence is seen of heavy viewers' attitudes, such that heavy viewers who are less likely to behave in a male-stereotyped fashion express gender-role attitudes which match those of boys whose behaviour is more gender-typed. For girls, on the other hand, the impact of television is boosted for those whose behaviour is more gender-typed. The combination of heavy viewing and gender-typed behaviour promotes more gender-typed attitudes among girls.

Repetti (1984) examined possible correlates of five- to seven-year-olds' gender stereotypes concerning toys and occupations. Measures were taken of 40 children's total TV viewing time, as well as the amount of time that the children spent viewing *educational* TV programmes, and their parents' gender-role orientations as reflected in BSRI (Bem Sex-Role Inventory) scores. No relationship was found between *total* viewing time and gender stereotyping in the children, but amount of viewing of educational TV was *negatively* correlated with stereotyping. The more educational TV a child watched, the lower his or her gender- role stereotype score, at least with respect to toys and occupations. This could reflect a deliberate avoidance of gender stereotypes in educational TV, or possible occasional interventions in this area of the medium deliberately intended to counteract traditional stereotypes; or could reflect the possibility that parents who encourage more educational TV viewing also foster less gender-typed practices in other activities at home. Repetti did report positive associations between parental gender role orientations and the children's stereotypes.

Research has shown that not only do children learn about jobs and work settings for television but that they also learn what gender that worker should be. DeFleur and Defleur (1969) found the television was an important source of occupational knowledge for children and that television portrayals often led to gender – stereotyped views of occupations. O'Bryant and Corder-Bolz (1978), in an experimental study of 67 elementary school children, found that girls were more likely than boys to exhibit stereotypes and that boys preferred jobs that were traditionally male which girls preferred jobs that were traditionally female.

Jeffries-Fox and Signorielli's (1979) examination of data from a three-year panel study revealed that television was an important source of knowledge about occupations and that many of the adolescent respondents' open-ended response revealed conceptions about occupations that were consistent with aspects of the television portrayals of these jobs; including stereotypes.

Attitudes and behaviour

Controversy over the complex and elusive relationship between attitudes and behaviour is long-standing in the social sciences. Much gender-role research (particularly research concerned with television and gender-roles) has focused on attitudinal measures, implicitly assuming that those measures have some direct or indirect behavioural consequences.

The attitude/behaviour debate has become particularly sharp in the area of gender-role research, with a slightly different focus. Recent arguments revolve not around the question of which causes which, but simply whether attitudes and behaviours are related at all. Bem's cognitive-developmental approach to sex-roles (Bem, 1981) assumes there are overlaps and parallels between gender-role traits, attitudes, and behaviours. In contrast, from a social learning perspective Spence and Helmreich (1980) argue for much less consistency, even for independence, among them.

Orlofsky, Cohen and Ramsden (1985) note that the literature provides evidence to support both perspectives. They found that while gender-role behaviours and attitudes tend to be related, the correspondence is far from perfect; gender-role behaviours cannot be 'automatically inferred' from attitudes, and vice versa. This underscores the need to take behaviour into account when examining television's contribution to gender-role attitudes. They also note that questions remain about 'the extent to which (and conditions under which) sex-role behaviours covary with sex-role traits and attitudes' (p. 379).

Signorielli and Lears (1992) examined the relationship between television viewing and gender-role attitudes/behaviours from the perspective of cultivation theory. They used a sample of fourth- and fifth grade children to examine if television viewing is related to children's attitudes and behaviours in relation to household chores that are typically viewed as 'something boys do' or 'something girls do'. The sample was equally divided into fourth and fifth graders as well as boys and girls; the racial distribution was 62 per cent white, 21 per cent black, and 14 per cent other races. There were statistically significant relationships between TV viewing and scores on an index of attitudes toward gender-stereotyped chores that maintained statistical significance under conditions of multiple controls for other relevant variables. Although viewing was not related to which chores the children actually performed, there were statistically significant relationships between attitudes, behaviours and viewing. For both the boys and girls there were moderate to strong statistically significant relationships which increased with TV viewing, between attitudes about who should do certain chores, and about whether or not the children said they did chores typically associated with the other sex.

Correlation and regression analyses revealed that TV viewing was positively related to children's attitudes toward gender-stereotyped chores. Those children who watched more television were likely to say that only girls should do those chores traditionally associated with women and that only boys should do those chores traditionally associated with men. These relationships maintained statistical significance when controlling for demographic characteristics as well as the children's specific behaviours in regard to these chores. There was no relationship between TV viewing and the children saying that they did traditional girl or boy chores.

The results also revealed that attitudes toward gender-stereotyped chores and actually doing girl or boy chores were related but gender-specific. For boys, having less stereotyped ideas about who should perform chores predicted that they would be more likely to say they did girl chores; having more stereotyped attitudes predicted that they would be likely to say they did the boy chores. Similarly, among the boys saying they did girl chores was a negative predictor of gender-stereotyped attitudes. Among the girls, however, having more gender-stereotyped attitudes was negatively related to saying they did boy chores, and saying they did boy chores indicated that they had less gender-stereotyped ideas. Moreover, television viewing seems to play a role in that the relationships between the attitude indices and the behaviour indices were stronger among those children who watched more TV.

Overall, the study revealed that among preadolescent children there was a moderate, statistically significant relationship between TV viewing and gender-stereotyped ideas about gender-related chores that maintained statistical significance under conditions of simultaneous controls for other demographic and social background members. While viewing was not related to the children's behaviours in isolation, there were statistically significant relationships between attitudes, behaviours and viewing. For both boys and girls there were moderate to strong relationships between ideas about who should do chores and whether or not the children said they did chores typically associated with the other sex. Moreover, these relationships increased in size among the boys and girls who said they watched four or more hours of TV a day.

Effects of specific programme content

One major problem with the above studies is that exposure to gender-stereotyping on television is measured purely in terms of gross viewing behaviour. It is assumed that heavy viewers will automatically see a great deal of the gender stereotyping content analysis studies have indicated is contained by television programmes. As we saw earlier, however, subjectively, viewers may not perceive portrayals and events in programmes as having the same characteristics as those described by objective coding analyses of television content. Furthermore, gross estimates of television viewing do not tell us whether viewers have actually seen programmes in which gender-role stereotyping is supposedly most commonplace. If overall television viewing does not relate to gender-role attitudes, is it because television has no effect or is it because it has more than one kind of effect, with one effect counter-balancing the other? In other words, if programmes contain stereotypical and counter-stereotypical portrayals of the sexes, are viewers' attitudes influenced by both types of portrayal in a complimentary fashion? There is correlational evidence, and as we shall see in the next section experimental evidence, that the precise influence of television on gender-role attitudes may depend on the particular kinds of portrayals viewed.

An experimental study by Tan (1979) reinforced the correlational evidence for gender-stereotyping effects of watching gender-stereotyped television portrayals under more controlled conditions of television watching. Tan found that adolescent girls fed a heavy dose of beauty advertisements were more likely than a control group of girls who did not see these advertisements to believe that being beautiful is an important female characteristic and is necessary to attract men. Twenty-three high-school girls, aged sixteen to eighteen years, viewed fifteen commercials which emphasized the desirability of sex appeal, beauty or youth (e.g. advertisements for soap, toothpaste, beauty products, etc) and thirty-three girls viewed commercials which contained no beauty messages (e.g. advertisements for dog food, soya sauce and diapers). Each girl was then asked to rank order the relative importance of ten attributes (e.g. pretty face, intelligence, sex appeal, hard-working, competence, etc) in each of four areas (career/job, wife, to be liked by men, and desirable personal attribute). The girls who saw the beauty advertisements ranked the importance of the beauty and sex-appeal qualities significantly higher than did the non-beauty advertisement group for the item 'to be liked by men' and with marginal significance in the same direction also for the item 'personally desirable'.

One British study by Gallagher (1983) describes a questionnaire survey carried out amongst a small sample of second and third-year children at a single secondary school in Northampton, and with a smaller sample of parents of some of these children. In all, the findings derive from 235 usable questionnaires from the children and 92 filled out by parents. The sample as non-representative and most families were middle class. In most instances, fathers had professional managerial or skilled occupations and many of the mothers also went out to work.

Parents were questioned on their attitudes to men and women at work, and in the family, and about their aspirations for their children. Children were given a list of fifteen concepts including such items as Men, Women, Marriage, Having an Education, Intelligence, Me, Taking Care of Children, Housework, Having a Job, Being Responsible, etc. These were presented in pairs to the children who were enquired to say how much two items belonged together. This instrument was designed to measure children's gender-role stereotyping.

Among parents, results indicated that women and men in the sample held similar attitudes towards men and women at work or in the family context in some respects, and differed in levels agreement on their attitudes. For example, both male and female respondents tended to agree that a married woman's most important task in life should be taking care of her husband and children. Both tended to disagree that if a husband and wife disagree about something, the husband should make the final decision. However, men were three times as likely as women to say that a woman, unlike a man, does not need to make a long-term career plan for her future. All parents had high educational and career aspirations for their children although occupational aspirations tended to be stronger for sons than for daughters.

From their judgements about men and women on the fifteen sex-role concepts, children showed that they perceived close relationships between women, Taking Care of Children and Housework, and between Having an Education, Intelligence, and the self-concept Me. Boys tended to perceive much more distance than did girls between the self-concept Me and concepts such as Housework, Taking Care of Children, Marriage, Showing Emotion and Being Obedient. Thus, many of the boys' and girls' perceptions indicated traditional stereotyping of gender-role beliefs.

On the relationship between television viewing and gender-role attitudes and perceptions, Gallagher correlated respondents' own estimates of amount of time spent viewing each week with questionnaire responses. She found that men and women who held more 'traditional' gender-role attitudes tended to watch more television than those who held more 'egalitarian' attitudes. However, traditional attitudes and heavier viewing were both also associated with level of education and self-perceived intelligence. Unfortunately no appropriate statistical controls were employed for these additional variables in the presence of which, the relationship between attitudes and viewing might have been weakened or reduced to non-significance.

Gallagher also reported positive relationships between 'traditional' gender-role perceptions among girls and boys and the amount of television they claimed to watch. But once again she failed to allow for other important factors such as parental attitudes which might have been explicitly or implicitly passed on to their children, or the extent to which parents shared household chores (which related independently to egalitarian perceptions amongst children).

Effects of TV advertising

Most research has concentrated on measuring relationships between boys' and girls' gender-role perceptions and television programme viewing habits. Relatively little attention has been devoted to the possible influences of gender-role portrayals in television advertisements. The small amount of research that has been carried out has tended to claim that some effects of television on gender-role stereotypes have been demonstrated (Kimball, 1986).

The limited amount of research material available, however, is far from providing a convincing demonstration of television advertising's effects on children's gender-role beliefs. It is very difficult to assess the influence of stereotyped gender-role portrayals in advertisements aimed at children, since other media sources and real life also provide sex-role models. The day-to-day example of parents, for example, provide an important primary experience for children as far as gender roles are concerned (Cumberbatch and Howitt, 1989). Gender stereotyping in television advertisements is but a small part of the total amount of gender stereotyping present in most television programmes and in real life and, consequently, their separate influence is difficult to ascertain (Kimball, 1986).

It is worth mentioning again here the research carried out by Welch *et al* (1979), who examined the gender-role cues that were conveyed through the *form* of children's toy commercials, instead of through the content. They analysed 60 toy commercials as to (1) their level of action or activity, (2) their pace (rate of change of scenes and characters), (3) their visual or camera techniques (e.g. cuts, pans, zooms, fades, dissolves, special effects) and their auditory techniques.

They found that commercials directed at boys contained highly active toys, varied scenes, high rates of camera cuts, high levels of sound effects and loud music. According to them, messages about what is distinctively 'masculine' were conveyed through a high rate of action, aggression, variation and quick shifts from one scene to another. They concluded that some of these features were probably production techniques designed to enhance the action, speed and toughness of masculine toys and may reflect conscious or unconscious gender-role stereotypes of those advertising the toys.

'Female commercials', on the contrary, featured frequent fades and background music and conveyed images of softness, gentleness and predictability. Welch *et al* argued that at the very subtle level of visual and auditory images, the stereotypes of females as quiet, soft, gentle, and inactive are supported.

Although this analysis of formal features is an interesting one and – as far as the technical findings are concerned – quite realistic, some doubt has been cast on the researchers' conclusions that the 'messages about masculine and feminine behaviour conveyed by the formal features may be more influential than the blatant stereotypes presented in the content, since they are inferential rather than clearly demonstrated

These researchers concluded from their findings that the 'messages' about masculine and feminine behaviour conveyed by these production techniques could be influential in cultivating stereotyped gender-role perceptions among young viewers. This conclusion, however, represents an inferential jump from the actual results of the study. What this study did show was that formal features of a child's toy advertisement varied according to the toy which was advertised, but this provides no direct demonstration of the effects of this material on children's perceived gender-roles.

Concluding remarks

Early research on the effects of gender-role portrayals on television on the audience's beliefs about women and men suggested a link between the two. Among children, for instance, those youngsters who were categorized as heavy viewers were found to hold stronger beliefs than did lighter viewers in what research defined as a stereotyped direction. Much of this work, however, failed to provide precise measures of what young viewers had actually watched. Further, these studies did not consider what kind of sense viewers made of the things they saw on the screen, when research evidence elsewhere has shown that viewers perceptions of the sexes on television are quite complex.

The model adopted by effects researchers has usually been one in which television is assumed to act upon a passively receptive audience. This model we now know to be over simplistic. Viewers exhibit a degree of activity in selecting what to watch on television, what to pay attention to, and what to remember of the things which pass before their eyes on the small screen. Even children respond in a selective fashion to particular characters and events or television, and their perceptions, memories and understanding of what they have seen may often be mediated by dispositions they bring with them to the viewing situation (Gunter & McAleer, 1990).

Children's informal social networks and information gleaned via their use of new technologies can play an important part in shaping children's perceptions and beliefs about gender roles. Where television depictions are consonant with the information derived from these alternative sources any television-related effects may become more influential. But when television offers a dissonant picture of the world, its effects may be overridden by other more direct sources of social information.

Even where television is implicated as having an effect on children's attitudes concerning gender-roles, it does not automatically follow that this influence will transfer to their behaviour. Gender-role behaviours cannot be automatically inferred from attitudes.

It will not be until individual differences in the psychological make-up of viewers (young and old), in their choices of what to watch, and their perception and comprehension of what they have seen on television are included in research concerned with television's effects in this context, that we can ever hope fully to understand the extent and nature of television's impact on beliefs about the sexes.

6 EFFECTS ON ADULTS

From research into the effects of television on gender-role attitudes and behaviours among children, this chapter turns to the possible influences of television on adult viewers.

The evidence linking television gender stereotyping with public attitudes and behaviours derives from two research perspectives both of which are faced with problems of methodology and theoretical interpretation of data. Some of the evidence is correlational; such studies examine the relationship between the amount of time spent with television and the degree to which viewers hold certain gender-typed attitudes or engage in gender-typed behaviours. While correlational data can offer useful indications of where relationships between variables may lie, they do not establish that one event causes another.

The second form of evidence derives from experimental studies conducted under laboratory conditions designed to facilitate the demonstration of cause-effect relationships. Under these conditions, researchers have greater control over the kinds of programmes and portrayals that are shown to and seen by groups of viewers. Problems occur, however, when attempting to generalize from television effects measured under these artificially contrived conditions of viewing to possible effects outside the laboratory under natural conditions of television exposure.

Effects of programming

Gerbner and Signorielli (1979) examined patterns of television viewing among adults and correlated them with answers to a series of questions measuring sexist attitudes. They reported positive relationships between amount of viewing and beliefs that women should stay at home and that a woman should not work if her husband can support her.

These findings were explained in terms of a television influence upon gender-role attitudes. This interpretation must be treated with caution however, since more than one explanation would be consistent with the data. Does television viewing cause sexist attitudes, or do these relationships indicate that people with sexist attitudes watch more television than less sexist people?

Volgy and Schwartz (1980) reported higher levels of sexism among adults heavily exposed to television entertainment programmes, although doubts have been cast on their results in view of the flimsy measures employed (see Hawkins and Pingree, 1982). Two years later, Ross, Anderson and Wisocki (1982) reported finding a significant relationship among college students between how they described themselves on an inventory designed to measure gender-typing and the amount of television they said they watched. Amount of gender-stereotyping in self-descriptions was positively correlated with amount of claimed viewing of programmes that had been previously rated by the researchers as strongly stereotyped in their portrayals of the sexes.

Other American researchers have suggested that the nature of television's influence on beliefs about women and men varies across different population subgroups. The relationship between television viewing and gender-stereotyping may not be a straightforward linear one in the same direction across all viewers, whereby sexism grows stronger with heavier viewing. Instead, there is evidence to suggest that television-sexism relationships work in opposite ways across different population subgroups. According to one line of argument, television cultivates a common level of sexist orientation, causing those who are less stereotyped or traditional in their beliefs about women's roles to become more so, and those who are strongly sexist in their beliefs to become less so (Gerbner and Signorielli, 1979).

Signorielli (1989) explored the image of men and women in an annual sample of prime-time network dramatic television programming, and the relationship between TV viewing and espousing sexist views of the roles of men and women in society. The analysis revealed that gender-role images over a 10–15 year period had been quite stable, traditional and conventional. Some evidence then emerged from secondary analysis of National Opinion Research Centre (NORC) General Social Surveys that TV viewing may be related to more sexist views of women's role in society. The research, conducted from the theoretical perspective of cultivation analysis, sought to ascertain if there was a relationship between TV viewing and having views of the world that are more reflective of the images seen on TV than those actually experienced.

Thus the research design consisted of two interrelated procedures: (1) message system analysis – the annual content analysis of week-long samples of prime-time and weekend-daytime network dramatic TV programmes, and (2) cultivation analysis – determining the conceptions of social reality that TV viewing tends to cultivate in different groups of viewers.

The cultivation analysis was conducted via secondary analysis of data from the 1975, 1977, 1978, 1983, 1985 and 1986 NORC General Social Surveys. The sexism hypothesis was tested by examining the relationship between TV viewing and responses to an index of sexism made up of four questions in these surveys. The index was additive in nature, summing respondents' agreement with sexist statements about woman's role in society.

The four questions (with the 'sexist' answer underlined) were:

> Do you *agree* or disagree with this statement: Women should take care of running their homes and leave running the country up to men?

Do you approve or *disapprove* of a married woman earning money in business or industry if she has a husband capable of supporting her?

If your party nominated a woman for President, would you vote for her if she were qualified for the job? Yes or No?

Tell me if you *agree* or disagree with this statement: Most men are better suited emotionally for politics than are most women.

As shown in earlier analysis (Signorielli, 1983; Gerbner and Signorielli, 1979; Signorielli, 1985) the world of US prime-time, network, dramatic TV programming was predominantly male – although the presence of women did increase significantly across the period of analysis.

Over all characters, the representation of males ranged from a low of 68 per cent to a high of 76 per cent. The largest proportion of females was 35 per cent in 1982. Among major characters, a similar pattern was found – men – 69 per cent; women – 31 per cent. Women were more family oriented, more likely to be married. Men less likely to be married, less likely to be romantically involved, more likely to be employed outside the home.

The overall picture was that TV portrayed men and women in traditional and stereotypical ways. Women were seen less often than men and could be considered in many respects as less important. When women did appear, they were usually younger than the men, more attractive and nurturing, portrayed in the context of romantic interests, home and family. They were also more likely to be victimized. If they were employed outside the home they were often cast in traditionally female occupations – nurses, secretaries, waitresses and sometimes teachers. Men were older, more powerful, and had higher prestige occupations. Turning to conceptions about gender roles, Signorielli (1989) found that heavy viewers tended to give the most sexist opinions about whether men or women, middle class, middle-aged, white or with a college education. In keeping with the notion of 'mainstreaming', there was less variation in sexism responses among heavy viewers than among light viewers.

Even in the presence of statistical controls for the effects of various demographic factors, a positive relationship survived between TV viewing and giving more sexist responses – during the 1970s and early 1980s surveys (simultaneous controls for eight demographic variables caused the viewing – sexism relationship to disappear). In more recent surveys (1983, 1985, 1986) Signorielli reported that the implementation of simultaneous controls for other variables resulted in a small, significant, but negative relationship between TV viewing and sexism, which may reflect the 'liberalization' interpretation of mainstreaming perhaps reflecting the impact of increased portrayals of dominant and successful women. Education was thought to be responsible for the negative relationships.

British research has produced less conclusive evidence of systematic relationships between television viewing and beliefs about the sexes indicative of television cultivation effects among adults. Gunter and Wober (1982) reported a study that was concerned not simply with relationships between total television viewing and beliefs about women and men, but also with the way these perceptions were associated with particular patterns of programme watching. Since different programmes may portray women and men in different ways, do individuals who watch a great deal of one type of programme hold different beliefs about each sex from individuals who watch more of another type of programme? And if such patterns relationships do exist between programme preferences and beliefs, are they to be interpreted as evidence of selective viewing or specific television influences? A further question investigated by this research related to the assumption by some writer that television cultivates sex-stereotyping as audiences assimilate traditionalist messages about the nature and roles of the sexes, conveyed explicitly or implicitly by programmes. Subjective perceptions of male and female television characters may often differ from the character profiles painted by objective content analysis. An important comparison, largely missed by most researchers, is whether viewers' perceptions of the sexes as seen on television are the same as their perceptions of the sexes in real life, and whether both sets of perceptions relate in similar ways to patterns and preferences of television viewing.

In the Gunter and Wober study diary measures of television viewing were related to questionnaire responses concerning the way women were seen first, on television and secondly, in real life. The questionnaire was in three parts. In the first part, respondents were asked to say how true or untrue it was that women on television in daily life serials (e.g. soap operas), in situation comedies, or in advertisements are portrayed as 'not being interested in politics', 'wanting at some time to be mothers', 'quarrelsome with other women', 'very interested in jobs and careers', 'very keen on romantic affairs with men', 'depending on men to help them out of trouble', and 'more likely to get on if attractive'. In the second part, respondents were required to say how true or untrue each of these items was of women in real life; and in the final part, slightly re-worded versions of these items were presented concerning the way women *ought* to lead their lives. These items were chosen to reflect common characterizations or roles portrayed by women on television which had been previously identified by content analysis studies, and which supposedly functioned to cultivate sexist stereotypes among viewers (see Lemon, 1978; Tuchman, 1978; Butler and Paisley, 1980).

From their completed viewing diaries, respondents were scored for the total number of programmes viewed during the survey week and for amount of viewing of several programme types: serious action-drama (consisting of crime-detective series and feature films), soap operas, comedy shows, and news and current affairs programmes. Respondents were then divided into light, medium and heavy viewers of television in general and of each of these programme types.

Special statistical tests were computed to assess the strength of the relationships between television viewing patterns and beliefs about women, which controlled at the same time for any differences in viewing or in perceptions that might be due to the sex, age or social class of respondents. These analyses revealed a number of significant relationships between television viewing and perceptions of women as seen on television and in real life, but only with respect of viewing of serious action-drama programming. There were no relationships between perceptions and total amount of television viewing.

Significant relationships emerged between amount of serious action-drama viewing and endorsements of how women are portrayed on television, how they appear in real life, and how they should be in real life on four attributes: 'Women as interested in jobs and careers', 'women as keen on romantic affairs with men', 'women as dependent on men to help them out of trouble' and 'women as getting on better if they are attractive'. Further significant relationships emerged between serious action-drama viewing and perceptions that 'women want to be mothers' in real life and that they 'should want to be mothers'. With respect to women as seen on television, viewing behaviour was related only to perceptions of female portrayals in daily life serials (i.e. serious dramas with a continuing story-line from one week to the next), and was unrelated to perceptions of women in situation comedies or advertisements on television.

The results showed that heavy viewers of serious action and drama programmes were significantly less likely than light viewers to perceive that women are portrayed in serious drama serials as interested in jobs and careers, keen on romantic affairs with men, dependent on men to help them, out of trouble, and as getting on if they are attractive.

There were also five attributes of real life women on which perceptions were related to amount of serious action-drama viewing. Heavy viewers of this type of programming were less likely to say that women are keen on romantic affairs. Heavy action viewers also perceived women in everyday life as less career-orientated, and less often than did light action viewers as dependent on men when in trouble and as dependent on their own attractiveness in getting on.

Further analyses revealed that viewing behaviour was also significantly related to opinions on the same five attributes concerning perceptions of how women *should be ideally* in real life. These results indicated that heavy viewers of serious action-drama programmes were less likely to agree that women should want to become mothers or that they should be interested in sexual relations as much as men. Heavy action-drama viewers were also more likely than light viewers, however, to feel that women should be interested in jobs and careers, and that they should be self-reliant when faced with problems, rather than depending on men to help them out of trouble. Heavy action-drama viewers also were less likely than were light action viewers to feel that women should get on well with other women and that women should be judged on abilities rather than looks.

Content analysis studies have, over the years, identified a number of prominent images of women on television and inferred that, through regular viewing of these, stereotyped beliefs about women are cultivated amongst the general public. The results from the present study afforded the opportunity to examine actual public perceptions of female portrayals on television *and* to see whether or not these perceptions corresponded with the 'images' of women defined through content analysis.

In serious dramas, content studies have indicated that women are portrayed mainly in domestic, familial roles, and much less often in professional career-orientated roles. Women are often shown as pre-occupied with romance and as dependent on men to help them whenever they get into trouble, especially outside the home (see Seggar and Wheeler, 1973; Lemon, 1978; Tuchman, 1978). Perceptions of women on television serials obtained from viewers by Gunter and Wober (1982), however, did not indicate strong tendencies for viewers to see women as wanting to be mothers, as pre-occupied by romance, or depending on men when in trouble. Viewers' subjective perceptions on these attributes did not coincide with the 'images' of television women identified by objective content analysis. Agreement between viewers' perceptions and objectively-coded qualities of women did occur on the item concerning women shown as interested in jobs and careers.

There was no consistent evidence across attributes of relative differences in perceptions of women on television by light and heavy viewers of serious dramas that corresponded with inferences about the cultivation of stereotyped beliefs derived from content analysis. Heavy viewers of serious action-drama actually perceived women in television serials as more independent of men rather than as less independent as would be predicted by content analysis. There was no marked relationship between amount of action-drama viewing and perceptions of television women as wanting to be mothers and settled with a family, even though content analyses have often indicated that this is the way women are shown (Tedesco, 1974; Tuchman, 1978). Heavy serious action-drama viewers were less likely than light viewers of these programmes to perceive women on television as career-orientated, and on this one item, audience perceptions actually corresponded with content analytic descriptions of the way women are portrayed (see Butler and Paisley, 1980).

Another important question is whether viewing behaviour relates to perceptions of women in real life, and also whether real-life perceptions are consistent with television perceptions of women. Gunter and Wober's study found that beliefs about women being interested in careers, being keen on romance, being dependent on men when in trouble and needing to be attractive to get on were each related to action-drama viewing for television and real-life perceptions. But how consistent in direction were these relationships?

Heavy action-drama viewers perceived women on television serials as not interested in jobs and careers more than did light-action viewers and also believed that this is the way women *are* and *should be* in real life. In addition, heavy action-drama viewers perceived women less as keen on romance on television and in reality, and believed that they should not be pre-occupied by sexual relations with men in everyday life. There was an inverse relationship between amount of serious action-drama viewing and the belief that attractiveness was an essential feature for television women to get on and that women relied heavily on their attractiveness to make progress in life. Heavy action-drama viewers also tended to believe, more than did light viewers that women should not be judged on looks alone. Finally, heavy action-drama viewers perceived women as dependent on men in television serials or in real life less than did light viewers, and believed more that women should be self-reliant. Clearly, there is consistency in the beliefs held about women as they are depicted on the television screen in certain programmes and as they appear in real life, although these beliefs do not always match the images of women on television identified by objective content analysis.

Effects of advertising

Understanding women's changing roles is essential for developing successful positioning strategies aimed at appealing to the women's market (Debevec and Iyer, 1986). Initially researchers who conducted content analyses on female images in advertising criticized advertisers for portraying women in wornout stereotypes (Belkaoui and Belkaoui, 1976); Courtney and Lockeretz, 1971; Courtney and Whipple, 1975). Although such content analysis revealed an important bias in gender-role portrayals such as depicting women as primarily homemakers, they neglected to measure and determine the precise impact of female role portrayals on advertising effectiveness.

Research has also examined the relationship between different female role portrayals and women's attitudes and preferences for advertisements (Buchanan and Reid, 1977; Duker and Tucker, 1977; Leigh, Rathens and Whitney, 1987; The Sherman Group, 1982; Wortzel and Frisbee, 1974). No consensus view emerged from this work, however. Several of these studies concluded that there was no clear preference for modern or traditional positionings when averaging over all segments of women and all tested product categories (Buchanan and Reid, 1977; Duker and Tucker, 1977; Leigh *et al*, 1987; Wortzel and Frisbee, 1974). Another study, however, supported by the US Equal Opportunities Commission did find a main effect due to positioning (The Sherman Group, 1982). This study, conducted among a representative sample of 622 women, found that a modern positioning improved advertising effectiveness among all tested product categories and across many diverse female segments.

Jaffe (1991) extended the examination of the impact of positioning on advertising effectiveness. She hypothesized that modern role portrayals depicting women with careers as well as families could enhance the effectiveness of certain kinds of advertising, in particular that for financial services.

Studies measuring the relationship between positioning (modern versus traditional female role portrayals) and a woman's own gender-role orientation (i.e. modern or traditional) on advertising effectiveness have produced more consistent conclusions (Jaffe, 1989; Jaffe and Berger, 1988; Leigh *et al*, 1987). These studies indicated that there is a significant interactive effect of positioning of female role portrayals in advertising and the gender-role orientation of women in the audience.

Using the Bem Sex-Role Inventory, Jaffe and Berger (1988) classified female respondents into two groups – those who scored higher on masculine traits and lower on feminine traits and those who scored higher on feminine traits and lower on masculine traits. They found that the high masculine/low feminine group had a higher purchase intent for products when advertised with modern female role portrayals than for those advertised with traditional feminine role models. In contrast, the high feminine/low masculine women were more responsive to traditional advertising positionings than to modern female role models.

Leigh *et al* (1987) divided a sample of women into modern versus traditional types based on a lifestyle inventory that measured gender-role orientation. They found that, for both modern and traditional women, attitudes towards the advertisements were more favourable when the role portrayed was consistent with the woman's own gender-role orientation.

Jaffe (1991) produced further evidence that women's gender-role orientations mediated the nature of their responses to advertising which used either traditional or modern gender-role depictions. A modern positioning was found to enhance responses to advertising for financial services. Across women generally, this style of advertising proved to be more appealing than one which depicted female models in traditional roles and situations. The research revealed that while a modern positioning is essential for effective communication with women who score higher in masculinity, for low masculine women there was virtually no difference in how they responded to advertising showing either modern or traditional role portrayals.

Rummel, Goodwin and Shepherd (1990) explored the effects of gender-role stereotyping in television advertising on females' self-confidence in their purchase decisions. Earlier research had shown that women were portrayed less often in authority roles (McArthur and Resko, 1971) and more often in subservient occupational roles (Dominick and Rauch, 1971) in television advertisements. It was hypothesized that, overall, for females viewing advertisements which portray men and women in stereotypic gender roles, self-efficacy (in relation to purchase decisions) would be lower than for females viewing non-stereotypic and neutral advertisements. It was also hypothesized that for males viewing advertisements which portray men and women in stereotypic and neutral advertisements, self-efficacy would be higher than for males viewing non-stereotype and neutral advertisement.

Groups of male and female undergraduate students were assigned to one of three experimental conditions. The first group was shown advertisements which portrayed men and women in stereotypical gender roles. The second group was shown advertisements which portrayed men and women in non-stereotypical sex roles and the third group was shown advertisements in which men and women occupied neutral roles. The advertisements were Australian and American.

Results showed that females felt more comfortable viewing stereotypical portrayals than did those viewing non-stereotypical portrayals. The researchers hypothesized that females may have felt uncomfortable with the non-stereotypical portrayals because they differed from advertisements they normally view. The fact that a significant difference was found in relation to female products may be explained by the socialization process. In society, females are taught that it is their role to be purchasers for goods such as clothing and kitchen products. As a result, women do in fact buy more of these types of products. Hence the reality of a stereotyped role emerges. The advertisements might therefore serve to confirm their reality. In other words, they reflect what females do in everyday life which results in an increase in their confidence ratings.

For males viewing advertisements which portrayed men and women in stereotypical gender roles, self-efficacy (in relation to all products) was significantly higher than when they viewed neutral and non-stereotypical advertisements. The level of self-efficacy was significantly higher, even in relation to all female products, for males viewing stereotypical advertisements than for males viewing neutral advertisements.

Thus, males perceived the purchase decision to be more difficult after viewing the non-stereotypical advertisement relative to males viewing the stereotypical advertisement. Yet, significantly more males in the non-stereotypical condition indicated that they could make the purchase decision with confidence. This confusion might be reflecting the changing role of males. While males perceive purchase decisions to be more difficult due to a lack of experience in the 'purchasing' role, they are willing to accept this challenge and feel confident that they are capable of doing it. Viewing non-stereotypical advertisements might serve to trigger a 'liberated' or 'non-typical' script which results in the higher percentage of males indicating that they can make a competent purchase decision.

Concluding remarks

Research on the effects of television on gender-role stereotyping among adults has explored the impact of programmes and, to a lesser extent, the impact of advertising. As with studies among children, some researchers have implicated general television viewing as a causal agent in shaping adult viewers' attitudes concerning gender roles. Other researchers have indicated that it is important to examine particular features of viewing such as the amount of viewing devoted to particular programme genres.

Much of the evidence rests on correlational surveys in which self-reported measures of viewing have been statistically linked with endorsement of attitude or belief statements concerning sex roles in different aspects of life. The association of heavier television viewing with stronger stereotyped attitudes and beliefs provided a basis for causal inferences in which television was identified as exerting an influence over viewers' perceptions of the sexes. This interpretation has emerged strongly from research carried out in the United States. In Britain, a different picture has emerged. Here, perceptions of women as they appear on television and as they appear to be in real life were found to be related to watching specific categories of programmes, most especially action-drama. Correlational evidence revealed tendencies for heavier drama viewers to hold a mixture of both stereotyped and non-stereotyped beliefs about women. This suggested a need to look more closely at specific features of programmes as they relate to portrayals of the sexes and specific beliefs which viewers hold about men and women.

In advertising, the nature of gender-role portrayals, especially as they pertain to women, may make a difference to marketing impact. However, viewers appear to be differentially sensitive to different kinds of gender-role portrayal in television commercials. Women consumers respond more positively to female role portrayals which are consistent with their own gender-role orientation. While some evidence has revealed that women are more comfortable watching stereotypical portrayals in television advertising, this finding may need to be further qualified in the light of research indicating individual differences among female viewers related to personal gender-role orientation. Women who see themselves as independent, achievement oriented and career-minded respond best to female role models of a similar kind.

7 EFFECTS ON SEXUAL RELATIONS

One of the principal ways in which gender roles can be explicitly displayed in through the depiction of human sexual behaviour. In this chapter, we turn our attention to research on the portrayal of sex and sexuality on television. In doing so, we explore what research has revealed about the depiction of normal sexual behaviour and behaviour that is generally classified as abnormal or deviant.

With the expansion of subscription television channels and use of the television set to play back video material, concern has grown about the availability of increasingly explicit sexual material. There is obvious concern about illegal forms of pornography. However, even legally transmitted material has caused growing anxiety, especially where exposure to children may occur. This concern has been fuelled by research indicating that regular exposure to certain forms of pornographic material which depicts women in narrowly stereotyped ways may cultivate unhealthy attitudes towards women among young males.

Television's treatment of sexual behaviour has been criticized at a time when young men and women are being urged to refrain from promiscuity and unprotected sex because of the threat of AIDS and the high rate of teenage pregnancy. Today, teenagers are engaging in sex at an earlier age, with more partners, and often without contraception (Courtright and Baran, 1980).

Television has been accused of allowing producers to push back the boundaries of what is acceptable (Beschloss, 1990; Polskin, 1989). Prime time dramas and movies feature explicit portrayals of sex; magazine and talk shows feature intimate conversations about impotence and orgasms; situation comedies are filled with sexual innuendo and suggestiveness (Beschloss, 1990; Franzblau, Sprofkin and Rubinstein, 1977; Hill, 1987).

There are divergent views about the use of sexually explicit materials. Consumers, producers, distributors, sex therapists and others assert that erotica is functional because it educates, stimulates and entertains (Press *et al*, 1985; Yaffe and Nelson, 1982). Moralists are concerned that sexually explicit material undermines society's values and may lead to acceptance of immoral or deviant activity (Linz and Malamuth, 1993). Some feminists argue that sexually explicit materials demean and objectify women and promote unsympathetic beliefs about and attitudes toward sexual coercion and exploitation (Brownmiller, 1975; Morgan, 1980).

Communication scholars have offered various theoretical explanations for the connection between exposure to sexual material and beliefs about and attitudes toward sexual coercion and exploitation (Burt, 1980; Malamuth, 1989; Malamuth and Briere, 1986; Zillmann and Weaver, 1989). These will be examined more fully later in this chapter. To begin with, however, what is known about the appearance of sexual behaviour on mainstream television.

Sex on mainstream TV

Initial research about sex on mainstream television began in the United States in the mid-1970s. Franzblau, Sprafkin and Rubinstein (1977) analysed 61 prime-time US network programmes from one full week in October 1975. They examined 13 categories of physical intimacy ranging from intimate behaviours (sexual intercourse) to more casual behaviours (embracing).

The behaviours which appeared most often were kissing, embracing, aggressive touching and non-aggressive touching. The most controversial acts, such as intercourse, rape and homosexual behaviour, had virtually no behavioural appearance. Only verbal references to rape and other sex crimes occurred, usually in the context of discussing crimes to be solved in dramas and crime adventure shows.

Situation comedies contained more kissing, embracing, non-aggressive touching and innuendos than any other type of programme. Variety shows also displayed frequent non-aggressive touching, but contained only moderate amounts of kissing and embracing; the most distinct feature of the variety show was that use of innuendos, particularly those without canned laughter. Drama programmes were more conservative, containing low to moderate amounts of kissing, embracing and non-aggressive touching, but almost no sexual innuendos. There was no differentiation of sexual behaviour on screen by gender of characters.

In a 1981 study, Sprafkin and Silverman (1981) found a sharp increase in the amount of sexual content in 1978-79 prime-time network programmes: 'Specifically, contextually implied intercourse increased from no weekly occurrences in 1975 to 15 in 1977 and 24 in 1978; sexual innuendos increased in frequency from about one reference per hour in 1975 to seven in 1977 and to almost 11 in 1978. Most dramatically, direct verbal references to intercourse increased from two occurrences per week in 1975 to six references in 1979 and 53 in 1978' (p. 37).

In another study, Fernandez-Collado, Greenberg, Korzenny and Atkin (1978) focused on drama series from prime-time US network television. They coded intimate sexual behaviours and found that sexual intercourse, whether shown or implied, occurred much more often between unmarried partners than between married partners on television. Nearly all sexual behaviour or references to such behaviour were heterosexual in nature and deviant forms of sexuality were rare.

Focusing specifically on afternoon soap operas, Greenberg, Abelman and Neuendorf concluded: 'Soap operas have more sexual content than do prime-time programmes, but the types of intimacies portrayed differ' (Greenberg et al, 1981, p. 88). Lowry, Love and Kirby's (1981) study of soap operas from the 1979 season found an average of more than six sexual behaviours (ie, erotic touching, implied intercourse, prostitution) per hour. And, like several earlier studies, they found more than three instances of sexual behaviour involving unmarried partners for every instance involving married partners.

Lowry and Toules (1988) replicated the 1979 study of sexual behaviours on soaps and found a substantial increase in sex between unmarried persons and a norm of promiscuous sex, with few attendant consequences. There was a generally higher rate of sexual behaviours per hour in 1987 compared with 1979, up to 7.4 behaviours per hour from 6.6. In terms of who was engaged in various forms of sexual behaviour, there was a major increase in the ratio of sexual behaviours between unmarried and married partners from 1979 to 1987. Although there was an increased amount of sexual behaviour on prime-time television, there was no major increase in soaps.

Gender differences in sexual behaviour on TV

Few of the early studies of sexual behaviour on mainstream television differentiated between genders in terms of the nature of their sexual behaviour. One exception was a study done by Silverman and her colleagues.

Following up an earlier study, Silverman, Sprafkin and Rubinstein (1979) analysed prime-time network programmes from the 1977–78 season in the USA. They found no overt portrayals of intercourse, but there were occurrences of implied intercourse, where intimate sexual behaviour was about to take place or had just happened. Touching, embracing and kissing were again the most common acts.

On this occasion, comparisons were reported between male and female characters. Females represented 32 per cent of the character population studied. Females also accounted for a greater proportion of the categories of physical kiss, physical hug, physical affectionate touching, and implied intercourse than would have been expected on the basis of their overall representation.

The most likely explanation of this is that these types of interactions are typically done heterosexually, and as the likelihood of male-female reciprocal actions increases, the male/female ratio of performers will reach one to one. Therefore, for the category of implied intercourse where, by definition, a coded instance involves a heterosexual couple, the ratio reaches an even split. In addition, females accounted for a disproportionate amount of the physical suggestiveness and references to affectionate touching.

More recently, Sapolsky and Tabarlet (1991) found that television had not diminished its portrayal of sex in an age when teenagers and adults were being urged to approach sexual intimacy with caution. Comparisons were made with an analysis by Sapolsky (1982). Network prime-time television offered viewers 15.8 instances an hour of sexual imagery or language in 1989 compared to 12.8 an hour in 1979.

Non-criminal sex acts in both years were dominated by less sensuous forms of touching, kissing and hugging. There were few instances of sexual intercourse in either programme sample: four depictions in 1979 and nine in 1989.

In accord with previous content analyses, Sapolsky and Tabarlet (1991) found that the preponderance of sexual action and language involved unmarried characters. In 1979, three out of four non-criminal sex acts featured unmarried characters; in 1989, eight in 10 characters were unmarried. Further, in each year all instances of implied or explicit intercourse portrayed unmarried partners. In 1989 only one verbal references to intercourse (out of a total of 91) occurred between a married couple.

In interactions between men and women, the male predominated as the initiator. In 1989, male characters were found to initiate two-thirds of sexual behaviour and conversation. Male characters initiated three fourths of the non-criminal sex acts in 1989. In contrast, in the 1979 season, equality of the sexes was in order. Males initiated 110 sexual acts; females precipitated an additional 111 (see Table 7.1).

Table 7.1. Frequency of sexual incidents on US television – 1989

	Gender of Initiator-Receiver	
	Male–Female	Female–Male
non-criminal sex acts	204	76
Touching	87	35
Hugging	36	9
Kissing	72	29
Implied intercourse	6	2
Explicit intercourse	3	1
Criminal sex acts	3	0
Sexual language	79	53
Sexual anatomy	15	11
Touch-hug-kiss	11	16
Intercourse	32	22
Prostitution-rape	21	4
Sexual innuendo	116	99
Atypical sex practices	9	5
Sexual responsibility	5	7
Categories combined	416	240
Rate per hour 1989	7.23	4.17

Source: Sapolsky and Tabarlet, 1991. Reproduced with permission.

Millwood-Hargave (1992) reported a content analysis of seven days evening output (6pm-midnight) on the four main UK television channels (BBC1, BBC2, ITV, Channel

4) to assess the depiction of sexual activity and nudity on British television. Out of a total of 277 programmes and 524 advertisements, 57 scenes of sexual activity were catalogued. All portrayed heterosexual sex. The most frequently occurring sexual behaviour was kissing, which was represented in over half the scenes. Just under one in four scenes depicted the coital act. Other scenes were noted to be pre-coital. There were also two scenes where sex was implied through sound though not actually seen on screen.

A further classification of sexual activity in terms of context and characterization revealed some evidence of gender differences in the depiction of sexual behaviour on British television. While over one-third of the relationships in which sexual activity occurred were established relationships, few involved married couples. This pattern is consistent with findings in North America.

Men were much more likely than women to be depicted having an extra-marital affair. Women and men, however, were equally likely to be shown engaged in sexual activity on a first date (Table 7.2).

Table 7.2. Context of sexual activity on UK television

Type of relationship	Number	%
Established married	5	9
Established non-married	15	26
Extra-marital affair: men	13	23
Extra-marital affair: women	1	2
Extra-marital affair: both	1	2
1st time pick-up by male	3	5
1st time pick up by female	3	5
1st time pick up mutual	6	11
Rape or sexual abuse	1	2
Prostitution	2	4
Other	7	12
TOTAL	57	101

Source: Millwood-Hargrave, 1992. Reproduced with permission.

There is relatively little evidence on the gender role portrayals in sexually explicit film and video materials. Some studies have shown relatively high levels of violence, others have found less violence and more sex between mutually consenting partners. Palys (1986) examined adult and 'XXX-rated' videos commercially available in Vancouver, Canada. More than 4,200 separate scenes were identified within 150 videos, of which about half could be coded for sex, aggression and/or sexual aggression.

Palys found that XXX-rated videos portrayed more egalitarian and mutually consenting sexual depictions than adult videos. For example, though in adult videos men usually played the dominant role in sexual scenes, in the XXX-rated videos men and women were depicted in the dominant role about equally often. Second, the adult videos had higher percentages of aggressive scenes and more severe and graphic forms of aggression than the XXX-rated videos and more often depicted scenes in which at least one participant did not engage in sex freely or scenes involving overt aggression. Finally, though Palys found no indication of an increase between 1979 and 1983 in non-sexual aggressive images in either type of video, the percentage of *sexual* violence appeared to have declined in X-rated materials but remained constant in adult videos. Palys found that females were more likely to be the targets of sexual violence in adult-rated videos than in X-rated videos.

A later study by Yang and Linz (1990) analysed a sample of 90 R-, X- and XXX-rated videos selected at random from a pool of more than 1,600 titles. Behaviour portrayed in these videos was classified for the presence of sex, violence, sexual violence and pro-social activity. Nearly 2,800 behavioural sequences were coded of which 52 per cent were coded as either sexual, violent, sexually violent or prosocial. Sexual behaviour was most frequently portrayed in X-rated and XXX-rated videos. Violence was most prevelant in R-rated videos. Sexually violent behaviour was infrequent in all categories. The predominant form of sexual violence overall was individual or group rape (33 per cent of such scenes) followed by exploitative and coercive sexual relations (26 per cent), and sadomasochism (19 per cent). Female and male homosexual rape was the predominant theme in around five per cent and six per cent respectively of sexually violent behaviours.

A breakdown by video type showed that in X-rated videos the predominant sexual theme was rape (either individual rape or group rape of a single female by a group of males). Exploitative and coercive sexual relations not coded as rape comprised 21 per cent of the remaining sexually violent depictions and sadomasochism an additional 21 per cent in the X-rated videos. The scenes in XXX-rated videos was exploitative and coercive sexual relations (39 per cent), followed by group rape and sadomasochism. In R-rated videos, group rape and exploitative coercive sexual relations, portrayed with nearly equal frequency, were the most frequently portrayed sexual themes. Male homosexual rape and sado-masochism, the next most frequent categories, were also portrayed with about equal frequency in R-rated videos.

Among the four types of behaviours examined here – violent, sexual, sexually violent and prosocial – the predominant behaviour in both X-rated and XXX-rated videos was sexual, while in the R-rated videos it was violence followed by prosocial behaviour. Sexually violent behaviour was infrequent but equally likely to be portrayed in R-rated, X-rated, and XXX-rated videos. When R-rated videos were compared to X- and XXX-rated types combined in a slightly more powerful staistical analysis, no difference was found.

For all three types of videos, the predominant theme in the portrayal of sexual violence was either individual rape or group rape of a single female. Further examination of sexual violence against females (female homosexual, individual, or group rape) showed no differences across R-rated and X-rated (combined) categories. A comparison of the frequency of sexual violence across year of production revealed no statistically significant increase in this type of portrayal for either R-rated or X-rated (combined) videos. Sexually violent behaviour sequences were much shorter in R-rated videos than in the others, however. There were no statistically significant changes in duration for either R-rated or X-rated (combined) videos across the years.

Computation of 'recipient/initiator' ratios indicated that females were more often the recipients than the perpetrators of violence and sexual violence in both R-rated and X-rated (combined) videos. But this ratio was different for different ratings categories. Females were more often recipients of violence in R-rated than in X-rated videos (1.89 versus 1.03) and more often the recipients of sexual violence in R-rated than in X-rated videos (4.33 versus 2.72). Finally, there was generally a greater number of violent (combined) behaviours than prosocial behaviours in both types of videos. An exception was in R-rated materials, which had more than three times as many pro-social as sexually violent behaviours.

Impact of sex on TV

What are the effects of long-term exposure to sex-laden television entertainment? According to cultivation theory, a steady diet of television influences viewers' conceptions of social reality such that heavy viewers' beliefs about the real world are shaped by the images of television (Gerbner, Gross, Jackson-Beeck, Jeffries-Fox and Signorielli, 1978). The cultivation perspective suggests that television offers a consistent, stable set of messages that serves as a common socialiser (Gerbner, Gross, Morgan and Signorielli, 1980). Further, heavy consumption of the highly repetitive messages of television can create a distorted picture of social reality (Carveth and Alexander, 1985). Accordingly, exposure to the symbolic environment of television should contribute to viewers' beliefs about the nature and frequency of sexual behaviours in the real world. Adolescents are especially susceptible to the sexual messages contained in adult television programming.

As the content analysis evidence reviewed above has indicated, television does comprise repetitive sequences of activity related to sexual behaviour. Entertainment programming emphasizes extra-marital sex and displays an apparent disregard for safe sexual practices. Thus, adolescents and teenagers who regularly watch prime-time television are offered a steady mix of marital infidelity, casual sex, the objectification of women, and exploitative relationships.

Television has, according to some writers, become an important sex educator because of both its frequent, consistent and realistic portrayals of sexuality and the lack of alternative sources for learning about sexual behaviour (Roberts, 1982). Young viewers are provided with frequent lessons of how to look and act sexy. As a consequence, television has become an important sexual socialization agent (Baran, 1976b; Courtright and Baran, 1980). In the absence of alternative sources of information, the sexual lessons young viewers derive from television foster an inaccurate image of sex that can lead to unrealistic expectations, frustration and dissatisfaction (Baran, 1976a, 1976b; Fernandez-Collado, Greenberg, Korzenny and Atkin, 1978). Documenting the specific nature of sexual portrayals on television thus becomes an important step in establishing the reality that influences the perceptions of the young viewers.

111

Little research has been conducted on the impact of portrayals of sexual behaviour on mainstream television upon audience attitudes and behaviours. Focus has instead rested upon more extreme forms of sexual portrayal than would be found ordinarily on major television channels, which would generally be classified as pornographic. This material is available either on videotape or through adult-only subscription television channels where consumers must purchase decoding equipment to be able to receive a scrambled television signal.

Concern about the impact of this kind of material has been fuelled by research indicating that exposure to particular forms of erotic imagery can result in an increase in aggressive-sexual fantasies, aggressive behaviour, acceptance of anti-female attitudes and in male aggression against females (Malamuth and Donnerstein, 1982). In extreme instances, the fusion of sex and violence is such that, among some rapists, sexual arousal is greatest in response to images of non-mutually consenting sex and even in response to non-sexual violent attacks upon female victims (Abel, Barlow, Blanchard and Guild, 1977),

Males and females have been found to exhibit different reactions to pornography. Explicit media portrayals of sexual behaviour have more generally been oriented to male consumers and have depicted women and their sexuality in distorted or exaggerated poses designed to accentuate particular anatomical characteristics and exploiting them as sexual objects (Heiman, 1977; Johnson and Goodchilds, 1973; Schmidt, Reinfeld and Weidemann-Sutor, 1970).

Even the nature of male audience response can vary with thematic elements within media portrayals of female sexuality having an important part to play. This finding is especially true of portrayals featuring violent forms of sexual behaviour. Male and female audiences can be aroused by erotic depictions of explicit sexual behaviour where the sex is mutually consenting. Rape portrayals in which the female victim is forced to have sex but nevertheless experiences involuntary orgasm has also been found to arouse male viewers more so than a portrayal in which the victim expresses only revolt and disgust (Malamuth, Heim and Feshbach, 1980). In the context of the current book, our interest in research into reactions to pornography stems from whatever this work has demonstrated about the potency of this material to shape certain stereotypes about women, among both male and female media consumers.

Effect of sexually violent stimuli

Considerable data have emerged over the past 20 years that exposure to audio-visual material depicting portrayals of rape or the blending of violent with sexual behaviour can have a profound effect on viewers' moods and attitudes towards women.

Schmidt (1975) reported both males and females rated themselves as feeling more aggressive after seeing films of sado-masochism and group rape than after seeing a film depicting romantic (non-aggressive) sex. In an important series of studies, Malamuth and his colleagues have examined the way people respond to sexual violence and its association with rape-related attitudes and behaviours. These researchers have shown that, for males, sexual responses to descriptions of sexual violence are associated with the propensity to rape, callous attitudes toward rape and victims of rape, and the simulation of sexually violent fantasies (Malamuth, 1981a, Malamuth and Check, 1981a, Malamuth, Haber and Feshbach, 1980).

Aggressive pornography has been employed in an extension of research on male aggression against females. In initial research, males retaliated against a female provoker to a higher degree after viewing aggressive pornography (a film depicting rape) than after viewing non-aggressive stimuli (a film of sexual intercourse) (Donnerstein, 1980). Furthermore, subsequent to exposure to the sexually violent film the level of male-female aggression exceeded that of male-male aggression. A later study found angered males' heightened aggression against a female target was in evidence with depictions in which the female rape victim showed extreme distress or eventually became sexually aroused (Donnerstein and Berkowitz, 1981).

By comparison, violent pornography (including portrayals of rape, sado-masochism and bondage) did not facilitate aggression between males any more than non-aggressive pornographic material, but it did promote it more than neutral material (Donnerstein, 1980; Zillmann, Bryant and Carveth, 1981; Zillmann, Bryant, Comisky and Medoff, 1981). Thus, it appears that, for angered males, violent pornography is a more powerful instigator of aggression against females than non-violent erotica and that it can facilitate aggression between males above the level found in control conditions.

Donnerstein (1980, 1983) has observed that erotic films equated for arousal but varying in aggressive content have been found to lead to differing levels of male-female aggression. When a male views a film depiction of rape and is then given an opportunity to aggress against a female annoyer, he inflicts more harm because of the female target's aggressive cue value – her association with the victim in the film. A non-violent erotic film, in contrast, lacks aggressive cues that would lower the male's inhibitions for inflicting harm against women and, therefore, male aggression against the female target is lower. It could be argued that aggressive pornography leads to more male-female aggression because a filmed portrayal of rape may be associated with greater negative affect (cf. Sapolsky and Zillmann, 1981).

The aggressive cues perspective appears to account for heightened male exposure to pornography featuring violence against women, in particular the portrayal of rape. There is also evidence to suggest that *non*-erotic stimuli featuring aggression against a female can facilitate male/female aggression. In an investigation of the independent contributions of violent and pornographic content to aggressive behaviour against women, Donnerstein (1983) found that male college students were more sexually aroused by non-violent and violent pornographic material than by a violent film. However, a violent pornographic movie was capable of enhancing aggressiveness against a female target, particularly if the male viewer had previously been angered by that person. The presence of aggressive cues and the gender of the target of aggression are central factors in this interacting rationale.

Prior arousal of anger can facilitate a predisposition to retaliate against a female annoyer and is therefore seen as interacting with the content of an erotic portrayal.

One study is particularly relevant to the issue of affective response. A film of rape with a positive outcome (the raped female became sexually aroused by her attacker) led to a greater level of retaliatory behaviour by non-angered males toward a female target than a rape culminating in a negative outcome (extreme distress) for the victim (Donnerstein and Berkowitz, 1981). The rape versions were found to be equally arousing, but no measures of affective response were obtained. It is presumed that observing a rape victim's suffering elicits less positive male response than does seeing her ultimately express pleasure. Related research has shown this to be the case: The depiction of rape with a pleasurable outcome fosters more positive affect than rape concluding with the victim experiencing disgust (Malamuth, Heim and Feshbach, 1980). In line with the arousal–affect model, the greater negative affect associated with the suffering outcome should prompt more aggressive behaviour from male viewers. The findings of Donnerstein and Berkowitz (1981), at least for non-angered subjects, are inconsistent with expectations from the two-component model. Donnerstein and Berkowitz argue that the pleaurable rape outcome stimulates more male–female aggression because it lowers males' restraints against aggression toward women.

The presence of aggressive content in erotic communications has not translated to an increment in intermale aggression when compared to non-aggressive erotica. Equally arousing and displeasing non-aggressive and aggressive pornography (sado-masochism) have been shown to elevate male–male aggression to a similar degree (Zillmann, Bryant and Carveth, 1981).

Quite apart from the obvious interest and understandable concern about effects of explicit pornographic portrayals upon the way men behave towards women, there is a broader area of concern about how such material might shape a generalized set of beliefs about women and create a less healthy climate of opinion about female sexuality. During the 1980s a series of studies emerged from Donnerstein, Malamuth, Bryant, Zillmann and their colleagues which demonstrated that violent sexual material could influence attitudes toward women. Some of this evidence will be examined below.

Impact of violent sexual material on attitudes to women

Malamuth (1984) reported three experiments in which subjects were presented first with either pornographic rape scenes in which the aggressor perceived that the assault resulted in the female victim's sexual arousal (ie, a 'positive' outcome) or with other depictions (e.g. a rape with victim abhorrence or a mutually consenting sex scene). Afterwards, all of these subjects were given a different depiction of rape and asked to indicate their perceptions of the experiences of the victim.

In two of these experiments (Malamuth, Haber and Feshbach, 1980; Malamuth and Check, 1980a) those exposed to the positive outcome version of the aggressive scenes in comparison to other subjects thought the rape victim in the second portrayal had suffered less.

The third experiment (Malamuth and Check, 1981b) revealed effects on general perceptions about women. In this experiment, male undergraduates were first classified as low versus high in terms of likelihood of raping (LR) on the basis of their responses to a questionnaire administered in a preliminary session. A laboratory session was held at a later date. In this session, subjects were randomly assigned to listen to audiotapes containing recordings of sexual activity that were systematically manipulated in their content along the dimensions of consent (women's consent versus non-consent to have sex) and outcome (women's arousal versus disgust). Later, subjects completed a questionnaire about their beliefs regarding the percentage of women, if any, who would 'enjoy' being raped. Ethical questions may be raised concerning the use of such questions since their use may perpetuate or strengthen existing beliefs in rape myths. However, the use of a debriefing session at the end of the experiment was shown to be effective at counteracting such false beliefs (Malamuth, 1984).

The results indicated a main effect of LR reports, with high LR subjects estimating much higher percentages of women enjoying being raped in comparison with low LR subjects. Whether or not the sexual behaviour was consenting or non-consenting and the nature of the women's reaction exhibited arousal or disgust also made a difference to male audience response. Within consenting portrayals, the nature of the women's reaction had no significant impact on subjects' perceptions of women's reactions to rape. However, outcome did make a difference within non-consenting (rape) depictions. Here, high LR subjects were affected by non-consenting women's arousal. For low LR subjects manipulation of outcome within non-consenting portrayals had no impact.

In a field experiment, Malamuth and Check (1981a) obtained perhaps the strongest evidence to date to suggest that depictions of sexual aggression with positive consequences can affect social perceptions and attitudes. In this investigation 271 male and female students served as subjects. Some had agreed to participate in a study ostensibly focusing on movie ratings. They watched, on two different evenings, either (1) the movies *Swept Away* and *The Getaway*, films that portray sexual aggression and suggest that such aggression may have positive consequences, or (2) sexually neutral feature-length movies. These films were viewed in theatres on campus, and two of the movies (i.e. one experimental and one control) were being shown by the university as part of the campus film programme.

Members of the classes from which subjects had been recruited, but who had not signed up for the experiment, were also used as a comparison group. The dependent measures were scales assessing Acceptance of Interpersonal Violence (AIV) against women, Rape Myth Acceptance (RMA) and beliefs in Adversarial Sexual Relations (ASB). These measures were embedded within many other items in a Sexual Attitude Survey administered to all students in classes several days after some of them (ie, those who had signed up for the experiment) had been exposed to the movies. Subjects were not aware that there was any relationship between this survey and the movies.

Results indicated that exposure to films portraying aggressive sexuality as having positive consequences significantly increased male but not female subjects' acceptance of inter-personal violence against women and tended to increased males' acceptance of rape myths. According to Malamuth (1984): 'These data demonstrated in a non-laboratory setting, not vulnerable to criticisms of laboratory artificiality and demand characteristics (Orne, 1962) that there can be relatively long-term antisocial effects for movies that portray sexual violence as having consequences' (p. 34).

The increased acceptance of aggression against women found by Malamuth and Check (1981a) occurred following exposure to movies that have been shown on national television and were clearly not X-rated pornographic films. Moreover, the primary theme of the films was not aggressive sexuality. It may be that a film that is explicitly pornographic is perceived as highly unrealistic and stimulates subjects' defenses against accepting the information conveyed uncritically. In contrast, the type of film used by these investigators may communicate more subtly false information about women's reactions to sexual aggression and thus may have a more potent effect on viewers who are not 'forewarned' by the label 'X-rated' or 'pornographic'. Linz (1985) reported that males exposed to sexually violent films were less sympathetic to a rape victim in a simulated trial (see also Linz, Donnerstein and Penrod, 1982).

Zillmann and Bryant (1984) compared the reactions of male and female undergraduates to varying dosages of pornographic material. Those who took part were invited to a weekly session in which they watched a series of film extracts either from sex films or other films not featuring sexual activity. This exercise lasted for six weeks. Some students saw only erotic films, others were fed a mixed diet of erotic and non-erotic material, and a third group saw no sexual material at all.

A few weeks after the last viewing session, the participants completed questionnaires which asked about their attitudes to sexuality, especially female sexuality. Both males and females who were fed the heavy diet of sex film material exhibited enhanced perceptions of the popularity of various forms of sexual activity. This effect was principally manifested in gross overstimates of the frequency of occurrence among the population at large of certain unusual sexual behaviours.

Of greater relevance to the theme of this book, however, were findings about effects of heavy exposure to pornography upon attitudes to rape and victims of rape. Those students who saw the greatest amount of pornographic material were more likely than other groups in this study to regard rape as a less serious offense. They tended also to recommend more lenient sentences for those accused of rape. The most surprising result, however, was that females and males were equally likely to hold these views. Zillmann and Bryant speculated that both females and males can seemingly be influenced by reported exposure to films in which women are portrayed as promiscuous and as aroused by just about any kind of sexual activity, no matter how unusual. According to these resaercers: 'Such portrayal, it seems, convinces even females of the hyper-promiscuous, accepting nature of women. What appears to be trivialized, then, is the impact of rape. The credibility of the victim's suffering during rape is being undermined' (p. 134).

In a more recent study, Perse (1994) tested two different models of the effects of sexually explicit material among college students. The first model is based on a liberal view that holds that sexually explicit materials are functional, for the most part harmless and provide fantasy and sexual stimulation (Linz and Malamuth, 1993). The second model is drawn from a feminist social responsibility view that holds that sexually explicit material objectifies and demeans women and leads those who use erotica to internalize those themes (Linz and Malamuth, 1993).

This study then, tested different connections between reasons for using sexually explicit material, exposure to erotica, and three types of hostile beliefs about women that reflect a cultural background that oppresses women (Burt, 1980). *Gender-role stereotyping* marks negativity toward non-conformity to traditional gender roles. *Sexual conservatism* refers to negativity towards nonconformity to traditional sexual behaviour. *Rape myths* are a combination of prejudiced, stereotypical and factually incorrect beliefs about rape, rape victims and rapists. These together reflect ' a climate hostile to rape victims' (Burt, 1980, p. 217).

Advocates of a liberal model of the effects of sexually explicit materials (see Linz and Malamuth, 1993; Malamuth and Billings, 1986) hold that laboratory research that connects exposure to harmful effects is not externally valid. Instead, sexual material is, for the most part, beneficial. Negative reactions to erotica are explained by individual characteristics. Analyses in various countries have found that rape has not increased any more than other violent crimes when consumption of sexually explicit materials increases (Kutchinsky, 1991).

Brannigan and Goldenberg (1987) argue that laboratory research demonstrating harmful consequences of exposure to erotica is methodologically flawed, artificial and not gener-alisable to real-world exposure. The critics explain that subjects may not typically be angered (as they are in many experiments) when they are exposed to erotica in their daily lives. Moreover, the laboratory setting offers few (if any) of the real-world sanctions to the expression of negative attitudes or behaviours; in the laboratory subjects are allowed a much more limited range of responses to sexually explicit material than they could have in the real world.

Several writers argue that sexual content is educational, therapeutic, entertaining and increases sexual pleasure. A *Newsweek* poll in the USA, for example, found that 52 per cent of the respondents believed that sexually explicit media content provides information about sex (Press *et al*, 1985). Winick's (1971) interviews with patrons of adult movies found that many men reported that they gained information about sexual practices, learned about female bodies and anatomy, and satisfied their curiosity about sexual practices. Propper (1971) reported a positive relationship between exposure to sexual material and knowledge about sex.

Although much research has focused on male erotica consumers, women also report that they derive benefits from sexual materials. Studies reveal that women read erotic romance novels for entertainment, escape, to pass time, to satisfy curiosity, to learn more about sex, as a prelude to sex or masturbation, to enhance fantasies and to relax (Coles and Shamp, 1984; Lawrence and Herold, 1988).

The liberal model also concludes that individuals interpret sexual messages differently, so that individual differences explain people's reactions to erotica (Linz and Malamuth, 1993). Attitudinal predispositions, such as sex guilt (believing that sexual thoughts are harmful) and sexual authoritarianism (less tolerance for sexual expression) lead people to label sexual content as harmful and to advocate its restriction (Kelley and Byrne, 1983).

Erotica as harmful media content

Another model that explains the relationship between sexually explicit materials and effects is based on feminist social responsibility views (Linz and Malamuth, 1993). Advocates of this model argue that sexually explicit material conveys an antifemale ideology. Erotica is seen as objectifying and dehumanizing women, portraying women as servants to men's sexual desires, denying female sexuality, and promoting sexual and social subordination of and violence toward women (Brownmiller, 1975; Lederer, 1980).

Experimental research has observed connections between exposure to erotica and several adversarial beliefs about women. Exposure to sexually explicit materials has been linked to perceptions that one's mate is less sexually attractive (Weaver, Masland and Zillmann, 1984) and to less satisfaction with one's partner's affection, physical appearance and sexual performance (Zillmann and Bryant, 1988).

Experiments also observe that exposure to erotica leads men to be more accepting of violence toward women and less sympathetic toward women's viewpoints and feelings in the sexual and non-sexual arena (Weaver, 1991b; Zillmann and Weaver, 1989). Prolonged experimental exposure to sexually explicit materials is associated with increased acceptance of violence against women (Malamuth and Check, 1981b), increased aggressive behaviour against women (Donnerstein and Berkowitz, 1981), increased acceptance of rape myths in both men and women (Malamuth and Check, 1985), and less compassion for rape victims and recommendations of lighter sentences for rapists (Zillmann and Bryant, 1982). Advocates of the feminist social responsibility model argue that these beliefs and attitudes may 'justify male dominance and female submissiveness', may be 'rape supportive', and may be associated with a 'broader acceptance of violence in non-sexual situations' (Linz and Malamuth, 1993, p. 47).

Survey research provides some limited support for this model. Malamuth and Check (1985) reported that reading men's magazines such as *Penthouse* and *Playboy* was positively related to beliefs that women enjoy being raped. Burt (1980) noted that exposure to media treatment of sexual assault was linked to acceptance of rape myths. Preston (1990) found that exposure to mainstream soft-porn magazines and X-rated videos was related to male college students holding more sex-role stereotypes. Other research, however, located no connections between exposure to sexually explicit material and several adversarial attitudes toward or beliefs about women (Demare *et al*, 1988; Padgett, Brislin-Slutz and Neal, 1989).

Researchers have offered theoretical explanations for the connection between exposure to sexually explicit material and hostile views about women and rape myth acceptance. Zillmann and Bryant (1989), for example, suggest that negative depictions of women in sexually explicit media content may become the basis for schemata or scripts about women and sexuality that direct thoughts and behaviour (Fiske and Taylor, 1984).

Social learning theory suggests that the rewards inherent in exposure to erotica make the content more likely to be learned and imitated. Malamuth and Briere (1986) suggest that erotica's effects on sexual aggression are indirect. According to their model, exposure to sexually explicit media content affects how people think about women and rape, which then influences behaviour.

The uses and gratifications perspective also holds that exposure to media content provides only part of the explanation for media effects. According to this perspective, people are active because they select media content for specific reasons. People's reasons for using media content influence attention levels, how they interpret content, how actively they use the content, and attitudinal and cognitive effects (Katz et al, 1974; Levy and Windahl, 1985; McLeod and Becker, 1974; Rubin and Perse, 1987).

Perse (1994) surveyed college undergraduates (two-thirds female) about their use of erotic or pornographic material – magazines or X-rated videos. She established respondents principal reasons for using such material and related usage data to measures of gender-role stereotyping and rape-myth beliefs concerning women. From the outset, males exhibited more stereotyped gender role beliefs than did females. To what extent, however, were these beliefs linked with reported usage of pornographic media content and the reasons for using such material.

Four categories of pornography usage motivation emerged. These were labelled Sexual Enhancement (using erotica to enhance mood or for information about sexual technique); Diversion (escape, relaxation, relief of boredom); Sexual Release (sexual fantasy and release); Substitution (as a replacement for a sexual partner). Males and females differed on two of the four motives for consuming sexually explicit material. Males were more likely to report using erotica for sexual release than were females. Males also scored higher on substitution than did females.

One of the objectives of Perse's study was to explore the feminist social responsibility model that holds that exposure to sexually explicit materials is linked to adversarial views about women. These might take the form of extreme sex-role stereotyping or hostile beliefs about women, particularly in relation to rape.

Perse found considerable support for the feminist social responsibility model. Two of the 'functional' uses of sexually explicit materials were linked to negative beliefs about women. Sexual Enhancement was directly linked to holding adversarial views about women. Males who used erotica for sexual stimulation and foreplay with their partners were more likely to report more traditional and conservative beliefs about women and sex. It was reasoned that because erotica depicted a sexist view of women (Brownmiller, 1975; Smith, 1976), use of these materials to stimulate one's female partner might cause, reinforce or grow out of views that dehumanize women and see them as objects that need to be 'turned on'.

According to Perse, although advocates of the liberal model often argue that sexual enhancement is a beneficial use of sexually oriented content, Sexual Enhancement had a significant indirect influence on Rape Myth Acceptance through its connection to gender-role stereotypes, sexual conservatism, and exposure, all significant predictors of rape myth acceptance. The use of erotica for substitution was significantly and positively related to rape myth acceptance. Although this motive was not strongly endorsed by the students in this study, using erotica as a replacement for a sexual partner was associated with greater acceptance of rape myths. Sexual Release was a significant negative predictor of rape myth acceptance, adding support for the liberal model. Using erotica for solitary fantasy and sexual release was related to lower levels of Rape Myth Acceptance. 'If this motive reflects one 'safe' approach to sex, this use of sexually explicit media content may not pose a risk for women or society' (Perse, 1994, p. 507).

Studies of media violence of a sexual nature suggest three conclusions according to Malamuth and Briere (1986): (a) Males act against female targets in the majority of the depictions (Smith, 1976); (b) although media sexual aggression has increased in the last 15 years, it is considerably lower than media non-sexual violence (Malamuth, 1986; Malamuth and Spinner, 1980; Palys, 1986; Slade, 1984; Stone, 1985; Winick, 1985); and (c) sexual aggression is often depicted quite differently from non-sexual aggression (Malamuth and Briere, 1986).

Concluding remarks

Gender roles can be displayed in many different ways. One of the most fundamental human drives is the sexual drive and the manifestation of human sexuality represents one of the key ways in which gender roles are defined. The depiction of human sexuality in the audio-visual media is therefore an important area for study in the context of gender-role socialization.

Research into depictions of sexual behaviour on mainstream television have been fairly thin on the ground. American studies during the 1970s and 1980s observed a steady growth in levels of sexual depictions on prime-time network television. Much of this behavior, however, was fairly tame; there was little, if any, evidence of explicit sexual portrayals (Franzblau *et al*, 1977; Fernandez-Collado *et al*, 1978; Silverman *et al*, 1979; Sapolsky and Tabarlet, 1991). The one significant pattern to emerge was that sexual relations tended to be shown more frequently between unmarried partners than between married partners.

Little attention was given to gender differences in sexual behavious portrayals on television. Some evidence emerged that female characters were more likely to be involved in affectionate encounters than male characters, ranging from mild physical contact to more intimate behaviour. Men were found to be initiators of sexual behaviour far more often than women on television by the late 1980s. Whereas ten years earlier both sexes had been found to be equally likely to initiate sexual contacts (Saplosky and Tabarlet, 1991). On British television, there is even less evidence about sexual behaviour portrayals. However, men were found to be more likely than women on television to have an extra-marital affair. There was no difference between the sexes in likelihood of engaging in sexual activity on a first date (Millwood-Hargrave, 1992).

Although mainstream television has delivered little fruitful evidence, the nature of images of sexuality depicted in cinema films (which might eventually be shown on television) and commercially recorded videos has attracted a great deal more attention from media scholars. Concern has arisen over the possibility that explicit portrayals of sexual behaviour which contain stereotyped images of women may cultivate socially unhealthy conceptions about female sexuality. Special focus has been directed towards explicit material in which sex is intermixed with violence and depictions show women being forced to take part of sexual activities against their will.

Violent sexual imagery has been investigated in laboratory contexts where evidence has emerged that it can shape viewers' attitudes about female sexuality, about rape and about rape victims. These images may also trigger male aggression against female targets, especially in situations where the male viewer has previously been angered and perceives certain similarities between the female victim in a film or video and a real life female target (Malamuth and Donnerstein, 1984).

Repeated studies with male undergraduates have revealed that a heavy dosage of exposure to violent erotic movies can produce a shift in attitudes so that they become more relaxed about the seriousness of rape and less sympathetic towards rape victims (see Malamuth, 1984; Linz, Donnerstein and Penrod, 1985). There is even some evidence that such material can bring about similar shifts of opinion even among female viewers (Zillmann and Bryant, 1984). Consistent results across a series of studies reinforce and add fuel to the concern which already exists about these more extreme forms of audio-visual material.

8 COUNTERING STEREOTYPES THROUGH TELEVISION

There is a tendency among mass communications researchers, which has become almost a tradition, to look only or at least primarily for the negative effects of television. This can be seen quite clearly from the vast funds and resources that have been invested in research on the impact of televised violence. And it is illustrated further in the gender-role development literature by the emphasis that is placed on television's cultivation of stereotyped beliefs about the sexes which tend to be more favourable for men than for women.

Considerably less attention and investment of research resources have been directed at exploring and developing the potential of television to contribute instrumentally and positively towards a broadening of social attitudes about the sexes. Recently, however, in a movement away from this negative tradition, several studies have emerged which have begun to explore the efficacy of television as an instrument for opening up attitudes and perceptions concerning the roles of women and men in society. There are indications from early studies that televised examples of counter-stereotyped portrayals which break away from the traditional portrayals of women and men may produce positive changes in the variety of expectations young viewers come to hold for their own and the opposite sex.

Much of the content analytic literature reviewed earlier in this book pointed to pronounced stereotyping in the way women and men were portrayed on television. Typically, men get to play a greater variety of more interesting and more powerful roles than women. In recent years, however, this pattern has begun to change. A new kind of leading female figure began to emerge during the 1980s who is independent, competent, and career-minded and is every bit as equal if not superior to the men around her (e.g. Jamie Summers in the *Bionic Woman*, Chris Cagney in *Cagney and Lacey*, Dee Dee McCall in *Hunter*, Diana Prince in *Wonder Woman*), and latterly *Murphy Brown*.

As stronger, more indrpendent and career-minded women have emerged, so too has it become more acceptable for men to show a gentle, caring side to their nature. These non-traditional role models provide alternative exemplars of a wider range of behavioural styles among both genders. What happens when television viewers, especially children, are presented with these counter-stereotype role models is an important question in the context of any discussion about television's possible influences upon gender-role conceptions.

American evidence has indicated that preschool girls seem to identify with the new breed of heroine. At the same time, it has been observed that girls of this age seem to be more assertive and aggressive than those in earlier studies conducted before such characters appeared on peak-time television (Singer and Singer, 1981). Of course, to lay responsibility for these apparent behavioural changes at the door of television is probably overshooting the mark. Broader changes on public attitudes concerning female roles in modern society, perhaps passed onto the child by his/her parents, undoubtedly play a major part in the gender-role attitudes and behaviours of young children (see Cheles-Miller, 1975; Perloff, 1977). But the role of television in influencing attitude changes which go against the traditional 'grain' ought not to be ignored.

In this chapter, we turn our attention to research concerned with the countering of traditional sex stereotypes through televised examples of alternative social roles for men and women. Although we are still concerned in a general sense with the effects of television on gender-role perceptions, the separation of research on *counter*-stereotyping effects from research on stereotyping effects has important theoretical reasons. These two kinds of effects cannot be assumed to be of the same kind. The influence of television on what are termed 'traditional' perceptions of the sexes cannot easily be differentiated from the influences of other sources of information about men and women which also typically carry traditionalist messages. Furthermore, there is every likelihood that portrayals which run counter to traditional stereotypes may not be reacted to in the same way as traditional portrayals by viewers. Their novel and unusual character may make counter-stereotyped portrayals particularly salient. On the other hand, their relative rarity may mean that the influence of counter-stereotypes and even the ability of viewers to retain them in memory, may be swamped by the overwhelming tide of traditionalism which supposedly characterizes gender-role portrayals on television (see Durkin, 1985c). Before turning to the evidence for the counter-stereotyping effects of television on gender-role portrayals, however, there are some important points to be made about different research persepctives.

As with work on gender stereotyping on television, so with counter-stereotyping studies, different approaches have been adopted by media researchers and other social scientists who have investigated this subject. Research has been conducted with adults and with children. The effects of programmes and advertisements have each been investigated. Studies have used naturalistic and contrived materials and viewing circumstances. Some researchers have measured, in fairly simplistic terms, the impact on gender-role attitudes and beliefs of exposure to specific programmes or advertising role models. Others have gone so far as to produce an elaborate educational programme involving not just television productions, but also a series of follow-up lessons, exercises and discussions.

Experimentalists have been concerned not only with the effects of viewing certain kinds of television on gender-stereotyping but have also examined the potential of television, through the portrayal of the sexes in non-traditional roles, to cultivate counter-stereotypic beliefs about men and women. It is only under the degrees of viewing control provided by experiments that the specific effects of viewing these different types of gender-role portrayal can be effectively measured. Experimental research among adult and child viewers has indicated not only that gender stereotyping on television can promote or reinforce such stereotypes, but also that counter-stereotyped portrayals can have the reverse effect.

Only the most optimistic media researcher would claim that television alone can make a difference to young viewers' gender-role conceptions and socialization. Youngsters receive information about and illustrations of gender-appropriate traits and behaviours from a variety of sources, of which television is one. Television itself may present conflicting images and messages about gender-related characteristics and roles. Television cannot be taken as a socialising agent independent of all other relevant social influences, nor can it be regarded as a source of consistent messages about gender roles.

What has emerged from the body of research on television gender-role portrayals is that the majority of such depictions emphasize stereotyped rather than counter-stereotyped characteristics and behaviours. Thus, even the best produced counter-stereotype pro-gramme faces an uphill struggle for attention and influence. Even so, the presentation of counter-stereotypes, where gender roles are concerned, can be regarded as a socially healthy objective.

Few broadcasters or media researchers involved in the production of counter-stereotyped messages would believe that their work can single-handedly re-socialize young people. Nevertheless, there are more specific, manageable and realistic goals which television can target which would result in a greater variety of gender roles being displayed. In so doing. the medium could play an important part in encouraging people to think about a wider range of potentials for each gender, and most especially for women. Indeed, the perva-siveness of traditional gender-role portrayals could to some extent play into the hands of counter-stereotype depictions. Since the latter would be quite unusual, they might also stand out more than they would otherwise. Their saliency may attract more audience attention, thus enhancing their initial impact.

Another important factor is that it should not be assumed that, if counter-stereotyped material can change young people's attitudes, traditional gender-role portrayals on tele-vision led to the establishment of sexist opinions in the first place (Durkin, 1985d). As we saw in the first chapter, gender-role stereotyping begins to be socialized early in the individual's life and is shaped by a variety of social agents.

Research with adults

One difficulty in testing the effects of media gender-role stereotyping on gender-role learning and gender-role behaviour is that of locating a control group which has never been exposed to stereotyped media portrayals. Jennings, Geis and Brown (1980) sought to overcome this problem by testing a contrast hypothesis. Rather than testing the hypothesis that stereotyped commercials depress women's self-confidence and independence of judgement, they tested the opposite of this, that commercials which *break* gender-role stereotyping raise women's self-confidence and independence of judgement. Jennings *et al* showed female college students traditional and non-traditional television commercials and found that those who saw non-traditional depictions of women subsequently expressed more career aspirations than those who saw traditional sex-stereotyped commercials. Building on these findings, the researchers investigated whether commercials could have effects, not only on the attitudes of female college students, but also on their behaviour.

Eight television commercials were devised; four showed women in traditional, dependent and subservient roles *vis-a-vis* men; the other four exactly reversed the roles within the same scenarios and showed women as dominant and men as subservient. After viewing one or the other set, viewers were questioned about the female and male roles shown. Then, half were given an Asch type conformity test. In this, they were asked to rate cartoons and were shown a set of falsified ratings supposedly supplied previously by other people. The degree to which their own opinions differed from the falsified ratings was interpreted as a measure of independence of judgement. Other participants in the experiment were asked to give a short, impromptu speech, and their degree of confidence in so doing was rated.

Those women who had seen the role-reversed commercials were more independent in their ratings of cartoons and more self-confident in giving a speech than were those who had seen the stereotyped versions. Given the absence of any similarity between the nature of the commercials and of the subsequent situations in which they were to perform, it is unlikely that the observed behavioural effects arose from the explicit content of the advertisements. Indeed the women were, it seems, unaware of the influence exercised by the commercials. Moreover, when the women were asked if they identified with the people in the commercials, all reported a low level of identification regardless of the version seen. Nevertheless, there was an apparent behavioural effect which led the authors to point to an implicit message power in the commercials, assimilated by viewers unwittingly.

Geis, Brown, Jennings (Walstedt), and Porter (1984) asserted that sex stereotypes implicitly enacted, but not explicitly articulated, in television advertisements my inhibit women's achievement aspirations. To test for this effect, groups of men and women were shown either four television advertisements in which gender-stereotyping occurred, or four ads that were exactly the same except that the gender roles in them were reversed, or no advertisements at all. Afterwards, all who took part wrote an essay imagining their lives '10 years from now'. The essays were coded for achievement and home-making themes and comparisons were made across experimental groups. The results showed that women who had viewed the traditional gender-stereotyped advertisements de-emphasized achievement in favour of homemaking, compared to men generally, and compared to women who had seen the reversed role advertisements. The reversed role ads apparently had eliminated the sex difference in net achievement focus of the essays. Those individuals who did not see any advertisements at all were indistinguishable in the essay themes they emphasized from their same sex counterparts who saw the traditional gender-role advertisements.

Research with children

Among children, counter-stereotyping effects of television sex-role portrayals have been investigated via correlational studies and experimental studies. The former have explored relationships between reported viewing patterns and preferences and children's attitudes and aspirations concerning various occupations. Experimental studies have deployed more controlled viewing conditions and compared young viewers' reactions to questions about gender-role matters following exposure to one type of televised gender-role portrayal or another.

Miller and Reeves (1976) conducted a survey of adolescent school children to assess the differential impact on gender-role beliefs of viewing programmes classified as sterotyped or non-stereotyped in the way they portrayed gender. The researchers began with the fact that objective content analyses of US television programmes had indicated that men and women are depicted differently on a number of social dimensions. For example, women are less likely than men to be employed, more likely to be married, more likely to hold jobs which are less varied and have lower status, and so on. They then located five programmes which countered this social profile, showing women in traditionally male occupations and other social roles, and measured extent of viewing of these programmes. Their results revealed a strong positive association between frequency of reported viewing of counter-stereotypical programmes and young viewers' sense that it was 'OK' for girls to aspire to the kinds of non-typical roles portrayed in these shows – school principal, police officer, park ranger and TV producer. Boys and girls were equally accepting of non-traditional aspiration as a consequence.

Ruble, Baladarn and Cooper (1981) found, among 100 four to six-year-old boys and girls, that display of a toy being played with exclusively by one or another of the genders in a commercial strongly suppressed desire to play with the toy among those of the opposite gender, and this effect occurred only among those who had reached a cognitive stage where gender is recognized as comprehensively invariant – which is thought to occur typically by about the age of five and certainly usually by the end of the sixth year; those who had yet to recognize this primarily imitated the kind of play engaged in regardless of the gender of the portrayed child.

Conversely, Dileo, Moely and Sulzer (1979) demonstrated among 120 boys and girls in nursery school, kindergarten, and the first grade that counter-normative portrayals of toy play decreased the choice of sex-typed toys, and additionally found that sex-typing was more frequent among older children and among males.

A correlational survey of American early adolescents aged 11–12 years indicated that they glean a considerable amount of occupational information from television (Wroblewski and Huston, 1987). Such young viewers were knowledgeable about occupations often shown on television even when they were not likely to have personal contact with these occupations in their everyday lives. Their awareness of television occupations contrasted sharply with their lack of knowledge about many other occupations that are not available in their everyday life experiences.

In this survey, adolescent respondents were questioned about stereotypically feminine and masculine occupations which they encountered frequently in real life, occupations often shown on television, and those infrequently encountered in real life or on television. The masculine 'television' occupations included ones in which females had been frequently portrayed in the mid-1980s.

Television occupations were regarded as more extremely gender stereotyped than real life occupations, and male participation in feminine television occupations was viewed more negatively than participation in real life feminine occupations. On the evidence of occupational prestige ratings and own aspirations, it became clear that a bias towards male occupations was heightened by television.

The results partly supported the major hypothesis that the new frequency of non-traditional occupational portrayals of women can affect the aspirations, attitudes and gender schemata of regular child viewers. Good evidence of this emerged from the self-consideration ratings. While boys showed evidence that TV is associated with polarized occupational aspirations, girls' self-consideration ratings suggested that the non-traditional portrayals in the masculine TV occupations may have altered their aspirations in the reverse manner. Girls preferred masculine TV occupations to feminine real life occupations.

In contrast to attitudes and aspirations, children's beliefs about the gender distribution in different occupations were no less traditional for TV occupations than for other occupations. In fact, one of the non-traditional occupations, private detective, was believed to be the most male-dominated with a large margin separating it from the next highest rating of male-dominance. It appears that children's beliefs about the real world may constitute part of their gender schemata which are less malleable than their attitudes and aspirations. At least for girls, the results suggest that occupational attitudes and aspirations are influenced by suggestion and demonstration, especially when such information is imparted by a very popular medium such as TV. However, the effect is not mediated by a change in occupational sex stereotypes defined by the perceived gender of actual participants.

Experimental research on the influence of non-traditional sex-role portrayals has provided some indication of a reduction in stereotyping among young viewers who have seen them. Atkin and Miller (1975), for example, showed 400 children, aged between six and ten years, a fifteen-minute videotape of children's programmes consisting of a news show, a cartoon, and several commercials. One of the commercials was for eye glasses and featured a woman modelling glasses, who, in different versions, was portrayed either as a judge, a computer programmer, or a television technician. In a fourth condition the commercial was not shown to children at all. After the television presentation, the children were given a list of jobs and asked to name which ones they thought would be suitable employment for women. Seeing the woman in the commercial as a computer programme or television technician did not affect judgements of the suitability of either of these jobs for women relative to not seeing the commercial, but seeing a female judge made children more likely to endorse this as an appropriate occupation for women (51 per cent versus 31 per cent for those who did not see this version). Girls and older children were most strongly influenced in this respect. There was also evidence of a generalization of non-traditional beliefs to other occupations. Children who saw the female judge were also more likely to think that women could be doctors. Flerx, Fidler and Rogers (1976) found that five-year-olds who saw a film depicting men and women in non-traditional roles produced significant changes in beliefs about 'working mothers', 'nurturing fathers', and the kinds of games and activities appropriate for girls and boys.

McArthur and Eisen (1976) carried out a content analysis of male and female characters in children's Saturday morning television programmes and subsequently conducted an experiment to examine the effects on children's behaviour of watching stereotyped and non-stereotyped gender-role portrayals. The content analyses revealed that males and females were portrayed in different roles on children's television, they manifested different behaviours, and their behaviours were followed by different consequences. Male characters appeared on screen more often and were more active than females.

In the experiment which followed, pre-school children were shown short videotaped vignettes which depicted an adult male and female model engaging in a number of activities. Under one condition the models behaved in ways normally associated with their sex, while in a second version they reversed their activities to perform non-sex-typical behaviours. It was found that children tended to recall and reproduce, initiatively, more of the behaviours of a same-sex than of an opposite-sex television mode. This occurred even when the same-sex model displayed behaviours normally not thought of as associated with his or her own sex. Thus, boys were more likely to remember and imitate nurturant, domestic and artistic behaviours than leadership, bravery and problem-solving activities of a television model when the former behaviours were performed by a male and the latter by a female. On the other hand, when the sex of the models performing each set of activities fit current gender-role stereotypes, so did the boys' behaviour. Similar results were obtained for girls, although their tendency to show more imitations of a same-sex model was weaker than for boys.

Davidson, Yasina and Towers (1979) showed a group of five-year-old girls one of three cartoon shows. One cartoon showed a girl in a counter-stereotyped way, successfully behaving in various traditionally male pursuits including sports and building a clubhouse. Another cartoon showed a girl in a stereotyped fashion, and the third paid no particular attention to sex roles. The reverse-stereotyped version produced significantly less gender-stereotyping of personality characteristics than the other two programmes, although as the authors admit, it is impossible to know for sure which of many differences, both related and unrelated to gender-role perceptions, among the programmes, were responsible for producing the effects.

In another study, television commercial portrayals were used to influence children's gender-role attitudes. Pingree (1978) presented seven to nine-year-olds with television commercials showing either traditional or non-traditional female characterizations. In addition, children's perceptions of the reality of the commercials were manipulated too, with instructions either that the characters were all real people or that they were all acting, or that the commercials were just like the ones seen at home (neutral). Children's perceptions of reality were successfully manipulated; children in the reality-set condition believed the commercial portrayals to be more realistic than did those in the acting-set condition, with children not given specific indications about the reality of the portrayals falling in between the latter two groups.

The overall effects of traditional and non-traditional presentations of women on attitudes were contradictory. Children who saw the commercials did not differ significantly in their attitudes towards women from a control group who saw no commercials. However, for children who received instructions about the reality of the commercials, attitudes towards women were less traditional after viewing non-traditional commercials. Non-traditional portrayals had no effect on children's attitudes towards women when no specific instructional set was provided. It seems likely that the duration of these commercials (five minutes) was too brief to effect attitude change unless something else was done to heighten their impact – such as saying that they depicted real people.

Drabman *et al* (1981) attempted to broaden young children's knowledge of which gender could be a doctor or nurse. Each of these occupations is firmly associated with a specific sex in many cultures. The researchers tried to persuade children that both career roles could actually be taken up by men or women, by showing them a videotaped film depicting a male nurse and a female doctor. In this film, special emphasis was given to their roles and occupational status through professional titles (Dr Mary Nancy and Nurse David Gregory). After viewing the film, the children were tested for their memory of the sex of the doctor and nurse, either by recognizing their names or identifying their faces in photographs. The results showed that the children often got the nurse and doctor the wrong way round, identifying the doctor as male and the nurse as female.

Similar findings emerged from another study by Cordua *et al* (1979), who also found a stronger tendency for children to identify a male nurse as a doctor and a female doctor as a nurse. Any attempts at counter-stereotyping therefore face the difficult task of reversing well-entrenched gender-role beliefs among children.

These studies indicate that even when young, pre-teenage children are shown film models in counter-stereotypical roles, they may fail to get the message. Even teenagers, who may get the point immediately upon viewing, can quickly forget the sex of two role models and exhibit memory distortions in line with normal stereotypes (Drabman *et al*, 1981).

Simply switching role models around does not guarantee that children will be to develop non-traditional gender-role perceptions. Further research has illustrated this last point. O'Bryant and Corder-Bolz (1978) showed six to 10-year-old children a number of commercials in which actresses were depicted in traditionally male jobs (e.g. pharmacist, welder, butcher, labourer). Exposure to the portrayals did not produce significant reductions in traditional gender-stereotyping of occupations. It did emerge, however, that girls who saw women in traditionally male jobs increased their reported preference for such employment. Although this kind of manipulation did not produce fundamental shifts in children's perceptions of the real world, it may have caused some of them to reconsider their own attitudes and aspirations.

In another study, Durkin and Hutchins (1984) attempted to vary the way in which counter-stereotyped portrayals of occupations were depicted to find out whether style of presentation could make a difference to their effectiveness in altering children's gender-role beliefs. In one version, non-traditional career roles were depicted in which the person doing a job happened to be of the opposite sex to that normally associated with such an occupation. In another version, the person doing the job explained why he or she had decided to go into an occupation not usually followed by their own sex. It was hypothesized by the researchers that the latter type of portrayal would be more successful in affecting the beliefs of young teenagers (aged 12–13 years).

To test his hypothesis, film examples of the above two role-portrayals were prepared together with a third film depicting traditional occupational role portrayals. These films were presented to groups of children as trial careers films which were being tested for technical quality and general usefulness to pupils thinking about possible future occupations. A further control group of same-age children saw no film.

Results showed that all the children who took part exhibited strongly traditional responses to a careers questionnaire. Some occupations were seen as being primarily for men, while others were regarded as being for women. Even when questioned about their attitudes regarding whether men or women should be trained for non-traditional occupations, responses were generally gender-stereotyped. The counter-stereotype film portrayals had no effect on children's beliefs.

Counter-stereotyping educational projects

The most elaborate and extensive study of the influence of television on gender-role stereotyping and counter-stereotyping was carried out in the Unitedi States and concerned a 13-part television series called *Freestyle*. The project was reported in two books. The first provided a detailed account of the conceptual and methodological development of the project (Williams, La Rose and Frost, 1981) and the second reported on the production process and evaluation of the television series and other educational components of the project (Johnson and Ettema, 1982). The television series was aimed at children in the nine to twelve year age range and attempted to convey a variety of counter-stereotyped lessons to young viewers. A total of 7000 children took part in the project across the United States. All children were pre- and post-tested with regard to their gender-role beliefs, attitudes and interests. As part of the formative research to develop the 13-episode *Freestyle* series, Williams *et al* (1981) showed segments designed to counter- stereotyping to more than 650 children in the fourth, fifth, and sixth grades. Factual recall was high;

recognition of interest was moderate, averaging about 50 per cent; liking for the characters was substantial; and desire to be like the characters was low. There was a lack of consistency among and between the males and females in the rating of personality traits, encouraging the authors to conclude that stereotyping among the young is not 'a general and fundamental mediator' of other responses. Comprehension and liking were enhanced when the male television characters were perceived more stereotypically; comprehension was enhanced when the female characters were perceived less stereotypically; and liking among boys was enhanced when perceiving the female characters less stereotypically – a pattern suggestive of more attention to and approval of modes of behaviour traditionally associated with maleness.

Three areas of behaviour were focused on for change in the main part of the study, children's pre-occupational activities (i.e. their interest and active involvement in activities of a mechanical or scientific nature that often lead on to specific careers later), behavioural skills (i.e. skills that children of this age begin to develop that are useful later on to the careers they decide to pursue), and adult work and family roles (including frequently stereotyped adult domestic and occupational roles). Viewing of the series took place under three different conditions. Some children viewed the programmes at school as a formal part of their curriculum and viewing was followed up by further discussion of the programmes, some children viewed in school but without further discussions, and other children were encouraged to watch the programme at home (Johnson-Ettema 1982).

Freestyle did indeed have some positive effects on the occupational aspirations, stereo-types, and attitudes of both boys and girls. Pretest measures of occupational aspirations showed that 80 per cent of the jobs boys said they would consider had male stereotypes; 56 per cent of the girls' desired jobs that had male stereotypes. Although both boys and girls expanded the number of jobs they would consider following exposure to the series, the same gender-typed trends remained.

More positive changes were found in the children's beliefs about currently existing adult roles. At the post-test, there were significant increases in children's estimates of the number of workers of the counter-stereotyped gender. Both boys' and girls' attitudes toward counter-stereotypical participation in four male – and three female-stereotyped jobs revealed a substantial degree of positive change, although girls' initial attitudes were less stereotyped and therefore changed less than boys'. Perhaps most remarkable was the finding that the net positive outcome of exposure to *Freestyle* was still evident nine months after the post-test. Subject to the right educational atmosphere being created, specially-designed counter-stereotyped television portrayals would seem to be capable of a lasting effect on how children view their role options.

The results showed that the viewing in school with follow-up discussion was the most successful condition for producing changes in beliefs and intended behaviours in a counter-stereotyped direction. The viewing in school without discussion condition produced certain changes in the same direction as the above but these were very much weaker. The viewing at home condition was the least effective.

The major changes include greater acceptance of girls who engage in athletics and mechanical activities, and who assume positions of leadership and display independence; greater acceptance of boys who engage in nurturing activities; and greater acceptance of men and women who choose non-traditional careers. Some children were tested after a delay of nine months following the end of the series. Many of the changes observed in the short term with the school viewing plus discussion condition though somewhat weaker, nevertheless persisted and remained significantly different from pre-test measures.

Attempts to study the impact of televised examples of counter-stereotyping on children in Britain have been limited. Durkin (1983) reported two experimental studies, one with primary school children and the other with secondary schoolchildren. Both attempted to facilitate changes in the gender-role beliefs of young viewers using a single programme in which examples of non-stereotypic behaviour were depicted.

The first experiment with 52 primary school children used an edition of a programme called *Rainbow*. This programme had an introductory story and subsequent sketches, cartoons and song and dance sequences amplifying the theme. The story was about a conventional family consisting of the father, mother, son and daughter, who suffer an unfortunate event when the father is made redundant. The mother goes out to work instead and the father is left to take responsibility for household chores and looking after the children.

The children were randomly split up into three groups. One group saw *Rainbow*, one saw a programme about the weather, and a third group saw no programme at all. The youngsters' gender-role beliefs were measured both before and after viewing the programme by 16 questions concerning stereotypically male occupational roles (e.g. bus driver, doctor, farm worker), stereotypically female occupational roles (e.g. shop assistant, secretary, nurse), stereotypically male domestic roles (e.g. putting up shelves, cleaning the car), and stereotypically female domestic roles (e.g. cooking, ironing, shopping). The children were asked to indicate whether a man, a woman, or both could perform these roles. The test was administered for the first time about one week before the programme was viewed, and a second time within a day of viewing.

Both boys and girls in the *Rainbow* group changed their views substantially. The *Rainbow* programme produced a short-term shift of opinion away from stereotyping. The programme seemed particularly effective in modifying children's beliefs about domestic roles. Durkin suggests that this may be because it may to some extent have alerted them to actual as opposed to stereotypical behaviour. Perhaps, many of these children already had fathers who helped with the dishes and shopping. After viewing, the children who watched *Rainbow*, may have recalled these things more readily. The programme produced less change in beliefs about occupational roles however. And this may have been because for these children, such roles were still too far distant from their own experience and concerns for already well-established stereotyping to be changed by just one television programme.

In his second experiment, Durkin attempted to modify adolescents' career beliefs with specially prepared educational films. A total of 99 children aged 12 and 13 years, participated in this exercise. They were divided into four groups. One group saw a film introducing traditional career opportunities; a second group saw a non-traditional opportunities film without any explicit attention being given in it to alternative careers for each gender (implicit counter-stereotype); a third group was shown a non-traditional opportunities film in which men and women discussed their occupations more openly (explicit counter-stereotype); and a fourth group saw no film.

The traditional film showed a male doctor, a female nurse, a male plumber and female secretary. The counter-stereotype films showed the same four occupations, but the actors were interviewed in pairs, one male and one female for each occupation. The difference between the implicit and explicit films was that in the latter more emphasis was placed on the reasons why particular actors had chosen a job not normally pursued by their gender.

Children in each group were given a list of 12 occupations consisting of four stereotypically male jobs, four stereotypically female jobs, and four 'neutral' jobs. They were asked to indicate in each case whether an occupation was 'just men's work', 'just women's work', or somewhere in between. The general finding was that children tended to rate male jobs as male, female jobs as female, and neutral jobs as neutral. There were very few differences between groups and therefore very little effect of experimental treatment. Even though the films were designed to offer career guidance, they seemed to have very little impact on children's existing stereotyped beliefs about occupations.

Concluding remarks

This chapter shifted the focus towards the part television might play in breaking down gender-related character and behaviour stereotypes. The basic idea here is that through the depiction of women or men in non-traditional roles for their own gender, gender-role stereotypes might be weakened and horizons for each gender might be broadened. Research on this topic has been carried out principally with children and teenagers. The handful of studies conducted with adults, however, have indicated that counter-stereotyped portrayals of women in television advertisements can produce short-term shifts in female viewers' perceptions of gender-appropriate roles.

Studies with very young children have also demonstrated that it is possible to encourage girls and boys to play with toys they would not automatically associate with their own gender, if appropriate counter-stereotypical role models have been seen in television commercials (Ruble *et al*, 1981; Dileo *et al,* 1979). While these fairly specific portrayals were observed to have an immediate impact, a more complicated picture has emerged from research with longer programme materials in which actors perform gender-typical or atypical behaviours. Boys and girls seem to be better able to remember the actions of a same gender actor even when that actor performs gender-atypical behaviour. Girls, however, are less likely to imitate the behaviour of a same-sex model than are boys (McArthur and Eisen, 1976).

Elsewhere, however, children were found to mix up and incorrectly recall the gender of television characters when they played counter-stereotyped roles (Cordua *et al*, 1979; Drabman *et al*, 1981). Thus, simply switching actors around so that they play gender-atypical parts does not carry any guarantees that counter-stereotyping lessons will be learned. This point underlines the need to put in perspective the potential of television to re-shape gender-role conceptions.

Elaborate attempts to produce educational programmes involving schools and course-work, of which television productions form just one part, have underlined the need to reinforce counter-stereotyped messages on television with other activities if long-term shifts in gender-role beliefs and attitudes are to be achieved (Johnson and Ettema, 1982). Even then, the changes produced by such programmes are relatively limited.

Project *Freestyle* successfully widened boys' and girls' occupational aspirations and the extent to which non-traditional jobs were considered as real options for their own gender. Television viewing, without follow-up, school-based discussion exercises, produced weaker attitude shifts than when television was used with other course work.

Drawing together the research on counter-stereotyping in gender-role socialization, the findings indicate that the intended or desired changes in conceptions and opinions do not always occur, although sometimes they do. When positive results do not materialize, however, it is important to look for reasons. A non-significant outcome does not invariably mean that television has no power to inform or shift opinions. Rather, the reason may lie with the way television material or exposure to it were produced or assessed. The strength of gender-role socialization seems to vary between genders. Traditional male roles appear to be less easy to shift than traditional female roles. This is consistent with the acknowledged rigidity of the traditional male role (Hartley, 1959; Archer, 1984).

Carefully designed studies have yielded positive results with respect to both genders. Children have been found to learn from counter-stereotyped gender portrayals on television, on both programmes and advertisements. This learning may sometimes have been aided by the distinctive and unusual quality of such portrayals. A question mark still rests over the durability of such learning. Initial counter-stereotyping images or messages on television require much repetition and reinforcement from elsewhere if they are to achieve lasting change.

9 CONCLUSION

Defining and measuring the effects of television on the public's images of women and men is a complex problem that can only be properly tackled through a multi-faceted research perspective which includes careful study of programmes, audiences, viewing behaviour, and viewers' perceptions of the things they see on television. The limitations of much of the research done so far are really to be found in the methods used. Most studies have been unidimensional, approaching the subject from one angle, employing one kind of measure and drawing conclusions which their measures do not entitle them to make. Many studies of television influence have used measures which lack any validity outside the research context or worse still are questionable even within that context. What then can be concluded from the research about the influence of television on gender-role stereotyping?

We began with a review of studies which looked at the way the sexes are depicted on the small screen. This research indicated that most television seems to be characterized by pronounced patterns of gender-stereotyping. This is manifested in a number of subtle ways. First of all, women are often numerically grossly outnumbered by men in many categories of programmes. Secondly, even in programmes where the numerical balance is restored, women appear to enjoy a much narrower range of roles than do men. Thirdly, certain personality characteristics tend to be overemphasized for women, and others for men, with the latter judged by researchers usually to possess the more favourable psychological profile.

A brief reminder of some of the main findings may be helpful at this point. In television's drama and entertainment programmes women were found to be shown less frequently than men (Dominick, 1979; Greenberg *et al*, 1980; McNeil, 1975, Tedesco, 1974; Durkin, 1985a). Some researchers have noted shifts from this predominant pattern, whereby women are featured more prominently (Seggar, 1981; Haskell, 1979). There are genre differences with males being especially prevalent in feature films and crime drama programmes (Paisley and Butler, 1980) but women fared better in soap operas and situation comedies (Katzman, 1972; Henderson, Greenberg and Atkin, 1980). The underepresentation of women is not restricted to drama and entertainment; a similar pattern has been observed in news programmes too (Cumberbatch *et al*, 1994; Thoverson, 1987).

Women on television tend to be younger than men and are picked for their physical attractiveness (Aronoff, 1974; Katzman, 1972; Long and Simon, 1974). Men are more often presented as being aggressive, competent and ready to help, while passivity and submissiveness have been noted as more frequent traits for women on television (Busby, 1974; Sternglanz and Serbin, 1974). Women have traditionally been depicted less often than men on television in occupational roles (Huston *et al*, 1992; Matelski, 1985; Seggar and Wheeler, 1973).

A small number of studies have indicated a shift towards a better balance of roles between the sexes (Haskell, 1979; Weigel and Loomis, 1981). This trend has been exemplified more by the prominence of a few leading female characters (see Reep and Dambrot, 1987), however, than by a wholesale movement in female characterizations across television (Atkin, 1991).

In advertising on television, women have been underrepresented less frequently (McArthur and Resko, 1975; Melton and Fowler, 1987; Riff *et al*, 1989) but differences have occurred in terms of gender traits and gender roles portrayed. Both men and women in advertisements have tended to be young rather than old. Female competency has tended to be limited to food, household and beauty products (O'Donnell and O'Donnell, 1978; Maracek *et al*, 1978). Men have more often been featured as central authority figures (Livingstone and Green, 1986; Furnham and Voli, 1989).

From these stereotyped patterns of male and female portrayals on television, many researchers have been tempted to infer certain effects of this content on viewers, assuming that such portrayals convey certain 'messages' to the audience about the sexes. Whilst descriptive analyses of programmes may provide interesting catalogues of gender-role portrayals on television, problems arise when statements about the effects of these portrayals are derived from them in the absence of any supporting audience research. It is one thing to classify and describe the content of television programmes, but it is quite a different matter to establish that certain 'messages' or 'meanings' supposedly conveyed by television portrayals are being apprehended by viewers and absorbed into their existing belief systems. It is essential first of all to establish that viewers are taking certain meanings from the programmes they watch and secondly, to find out if their perceptions of programmes lead them to absorb the same 'messages' as those identified by the descriptive coding schemes of some researchers. In the absence of any empirical tests of audience perceptions and comprehension of programmes, such assumptions are pure conjecture.

Conceptualizing TV influences

Turning now to a model of how television's influence might operate on viewers' beliefs about the sexes in which an audience research component is included, we find that some writers have envisaged a process of influence whereby greater exposure per se to television's 'messages' produces greater television biased responding on items of belief about the way things are in the real world (e.g. Clark, 1972; Gerbner and Gross, 1976; Gerbner et al 1977).

The evidence offered to back up this hypothesis comes from correlational surveys in which measures of how much television people say they watch are correlated with their answers to certain attitudinal statements about men and women. Heavy viewers are assumed to be more heavily exposed to stereotyped portrayals of women and men on television than are light viewers, and therefore also to hold more stereotyped beliefs about women than the latter. Significant correlations between self-reported amounts of viewing and what are designated by the researchers as gender-stereotyped answers to questions about women and men, are taken as evidence for a television influence on gender-stereotyping (e.g. Beuf, 1974; Frueh and McGhee, 1975; McGhee and Frueh, 1980). But how much faith should we have in this evidence?

The safest answer probably is that such findings must be treated with caution. First of all, reliance on self-reports of fairly generalized estimates of television viewing of the sort which characterizes correlational studies may not actually be sufficient to provide accurate measures of exposure of viewers to stereotyped portrayals. The researchers who use these measures typically assume that heavy viewing of television means heavy exposure to such content, but this does not necessarily follow. Furthermore, the descriptive evidence indicates that gender-stereotyping, though consistently present, is not always consistent in style across different types of programmes. It could be therefore that heavy viewing of certain types of television results in heavy exposure to particular kinds of stereotyping and not others. Since not all heavy viewers will watch the same programmes, it may be important to know more about what they do watch before their endorsement of particular gender-role beliefs can be meaningfully linked to what they have seen on television.

Research evidence regarding the effects of male and female representation in advertising is ambivalent. Some research indicates that gender representations affect perceptions of and attitudes towards women (Atkin, 1975; Haase, 1989; Schwarz and Kurz, 1989; Tan, 1979). Other writers, however, have suggested that advertising primarily reflects existing social norms and values and that changes in these values and norms lead to changes in advertising (Rakow, 1986; Soley and Reid, 1988). A third approach deals with the interaction between social change and advertising. Robinson (1983), for example, argued that advertising does not passively mirror norms and values, but that it actively constructs and reconstructs reality. Indeed, advertising needs to adjust to changing consumer tastes and attitudes and thus must be able to adapt to shifts in social values and roles such as, for nistance, the changing role of women in the workforce. Through reflecting these values and roles back onto society, advertising may function so as further to reinforce them.

Goffman (1979) has tried to eatablish general principles of the representation of men and women in advertising that could reflect (and possibly reinforce) certain power and role distributions. Based on case studies of American advertisements, he found support for his view that advertising reinforces traditional gender-role stereotypes of men and women. For example, camera angles and other techniques often emphasize men's size and height. Female gestures were frequently directed towards the male counterpart, emphasizing submissiveness and eagerness to be educated by him. Women more often were seen lying down, while men were shown as more active (ie, standing or walking). Men tended to be stand provocatively with their legs spread, but women cautiously with their legs pressed together. The latter observation, however, represents an image of women in advertising which has certainly seen some changes in more recent times.

Goffman (1979) also discussed typical gender differences regarding the touching of objects, and the position of hands and head. Women were seen more often softly touching objects, their hands were close to the body, and they were seen more often looking downward instead of upward or straight ahead. While Goffman considers depictions in advertising to be simply a reflection of general values in a society, some authors have argued that these non-verbal means are used intentionally by the male-dominated advertising industry to suppress and discriminate against women (Heller, 1984; Wex, 1979).

Defining what is influenced

A further issue is that of defining a gender-stereotyped belief. Researchers classify their respondents as 'sexist' on the basis of their answers to items of belief or opinion for which certain response options are pre-classified as stereotyped or non-stereotyped. But roles or characteristics deemed as most appropriate for men and women are defined by existing societal norms. These norms do not remain constant, however, but change over time, so that what is regarded as acceptable behaviour for women today is not always the same as twenty years ago. Yet researchers seldom, if ever, base their definition of gender-stereo-typing on surveys of normative social attitudes.

In dealing with questions relating to roles such as the kinds of occupations that women are best suited to, it may be relatively straightforward to distinguish between an open-minded (non-stereotypic) reply and a narrow-minded (stereotypic) one. But on questions of personality and character, it may be more problematic to make such a distinction. A descriptive study of television gender-role portrayals may conclude that women are typically shown as emotional creatures, but is this at odds with the way women are in real life? It may be shown that many women are occupied by romantic relationships, or that their lives centre on their marriages and families, but is this not true of many women in reality? Does television, across various categories of programming, play on these issues more or less than they actually occupy the attention of women and men in real life? And even if it does, we are left with the quite separate empirical question of the extent to which viewers accept or discuss television's scenarios and characterizations as conveyors of valuable lessons relevant to their own lives.

Research on viewers' perceptions of television charcters is accumulating which indicates that the way male and female actors are evaluated and described by viewers is determined by pre-existing beliefs and attitudes. Rather than being shaped by television, such beliefs and attitudes may pre-date and pre-determine preferences for and responses to television programmes (Gunter and Wober, 1982). This may occur even among young viewers. Reeves and Greenberg (1976) used multi-dimensional scaling techniques to explore the cognitive dimensions used by children in judging television characters. They found that boys focused more on physical strength and activity attributes when describing characters, while girls were more likely to emphasize physical attractiveness. Reeves and Greenberg concluded that the dimensions identified are strong predictors of the children's desires to model the social behaviour of television characters behaving stereotypically. However, what these findings could also indicate is that children come to television with already formed stereotypes and the fact that boys and girls used different terms to describe males and females, whether as seen on teleivsion or in real life, may have nothing to do directly with their experience with television gender-role portrayals.

Establishing causality

In addition to these problems, the interpretation of correlational relationships is always problematic anyway, and inferences of causal relations between sets of variables that are significantly correlated are usually fraught with ambiguity which is often extremely difficult to disentangle. The problem of causality can be tackled more effectively via experimental designs. Experiments afford the advantage of greater control over the form and content of television stimulus materials and over the level of exposure to critical portrayals among different comparison groups of viewers. These studies, however, suffer from typically small and non-representative samples, artificial conditions of viewing, and sometimes from measures of attitudinal and behavioural change which provide only poor indicators of television's capacity to produce psychological change in real life.

Furthermore, experimental studies on gender-role stereotyping or counter-stereotyping have so far demonstrated only short-term, simplistic changes in attitudes and beliefs concerning appropriate roles for each sex. They provide no conclusive proof that such effects occur in natural, everyday viewing environments and that such learning produces long-term change in the beliefs of individuals. What little experimental evidence there is of a possible long-term influence of television gender-role portrayals on viewers gender-role beliefs in the realm of counter-stereotyping has indicated that televised examples alone may not be sufficient to influence viewers' perceptions.

In attempting to fashion changes in children's gender-role beliefs through a specially produced television series, Johnson and Ettema (1982) reported that such change is dependent crucially upon further, external reinforcement of the programmes' lessons about potential non-traditional roles for girls in the form of classroom discussions and written assignments about the programmes. Of course this study was attempting to produce shifts in beliefs in a counter-stereotypic direction. It could be reasoned that in attempting to stem the tide of gender-stereotyping which pervades not only television but society in general, would require a concentrated, multi-channel approach. Where television gender-role portrayals are stereotyped, however, even single exposures whose individual effects are only short lasting, may, when repeated, add to the gender-stereotyped social conditioning process that touches practically everyone in society. Perhaps the crucial question at this point, and one which has a bearing on the value of correlational survey and laboratory experimental findings, is how to determine what is a stereotype. This is a very basic question the answer for which is seldom sought by those who investigate the gender-stereotyping effects on television.

Mediating variables

The importance of other social forces for reactions to television portrayals of the sexes was indicated in research by Williams *et al* (1981). Preconceptions about gender-appropriate traits and behaviours influenced children's ratings of male and female television actors.

Family context

Children are not simply observers of what goes on in their social environment, they also participate in it. The family is a powerful source of influence in the child's social milieu and indeed for the most part, it represents the primary source of socialization. The child's earliest impressions about gender-appropriate attributes and behaviour derive from interactions with parents. Parents activate and reinforce gender-role behaviours, which may be strongly characterized by stereotyped beliefs concerning how little girls and little boys are expected to act. The learning of gender-appropriate roles are fundamental to personal development and begin before psychologically active television viewing properly gets underway. Thus, young viewers arrive at the viewing situation with gender-role stereotypes already in place.

Day-to-day interactions with family members are likely to represent far more significant influences upon gender-role behaviour than any experiences with the mass media. Repetti (1984) found no relationship between amount of television viewing and traditional gender-role development, but did find moderately strong correlations between parental personality characteristics and gender stereotypes held by their children.

While children learn a great deal from interacting with key people in their everyday lives, television viewing may also represent an integral part of the youngsters' day-to-day routine. It has been repeatedly demonstrated that television depicts gender-role stereotypes much more often than it shows counter-stereotypes. These implicit and explicit messages about gender-appropriate traits and behaviour permeate much of television's content and feature as part of the daily viewing diet of the young child. Where these messages are consonant with the socialization practices of parents, they may serve to reinforce family cultivated gender stereotypes. In this context, although not a primary source of influence, television could supplement and reinforce what is being learned from the more immediate family environment (Greenberg, 1982). The difficulty lies in accurately identifying and measuring the extent of television's particular contribution to this complex, multi-faceted social process.

Peers

In addition to family influences, children's beliefs that their own friends and peers in real life would approve of the way a particular character behaved was found to be an important determinant of their reported intentions to imitate or 'want to be with' that character. In line with the findings of Reeves and Greenberg reported above, Williams *et al* found that gender-typed biases in character perceptions seemed to rely as much on the gender of the

142

viewer as on the sex of the character. Strength, for example, figured more prominently in the character preferences of boys than of girls. Likewise, 'good looks' was more important for girls than for boys, but also related well to the preferences of boys for female characters.

Among children and adults alike, attention to and liking for television characters may depend on whether viewers feel that their behaviour is altogether appropriate or acceptable to their particular gender, a judgement that is grounded in already well-formed opinions about gender roles. For instance, it has been observed that girls learn much less from a television news bulletin when the newscaster is a woman (Tan, Raudy, Huff & Miles 1980). And Durkin (1983) reported that young adult women tended to be much harsher in their evaluations of the reliability, qualifications, presentation skills and experience of a female weather forecaster than of a male weather forecaster. Young adult men, on the other hand, did not differ in their evaluations of the two forecasters.

Descriptive analyses of television portrayals of men and women may be relatively meaningless as indicators of the potential of television to cultivate gender-stereotyping when their schemes of programme content classification fail to take into account audience perceptions of character portrayals and social attitudinal norms which define what may currently be regarded as stereotyped or not. Research examining viewers' perceptions suggests that children's and adult's preferences for television characters and the way they behave are mediated by pre-existing beliefs concerning whether others in one's social environment are likely to approve of those characters and their behaviours. If this evidence is reliable, then the quantities of males and females shown on television (something emphasized frequently by descriptive television content research) may be considerably less important than the qualities that are portrayed for each gender, and whether these qualities are perceived to be personally or socially acceptable.

The influence of television on gender-role attitudes and beliefs does not operate in a vacuum. The assumption embodied in so much research that television acts on passively receptive viewers to shape their behavioural dispositions or outlook on life is over-simplified and fails to tell the whole story. The study of television's influence needs instead to be put into a broader social and psychological context than has characterized most research to date, and considered alongside and in relation to other factors residing within individuals and the social environment in which they live.

Willingness to change at source

Gender stereotyping in television programmes and advertising does not simply happen by accident. The tendency to use women and men in particular roles follows from decisions by producers about the part each gender is to play in a particular production. For this pattern to change requires a realization on the part of producers and directors that depicting women or men in roles other than those in which tradition normally places them will not prove to be a turn-off for the audience or a major marketing disaster.

Liberal feminists suggest that the solution to gender stereotyping may rest at source. Women need to obtain more equal positions in society, enter male-dominated fields and acquire power. This approach is recommended, too, in respect of the mass media. Meanwhile, the media can contribute to this shift in gender emphasis by portraying more women and men in non-traditional roles and by using non-sexist language (van Zoonen, 1992).

The strategies adopted by liberal feminists to achieve this end include teaching non-sexist professionalism to students in media, broadcasting and journalism, creating awareness among these professional groups in their workplace, and by lobbying media organizations to put in place affirmative action policies designed to stem the tide of sexism.

For radical feminists, playing a man's game in a man's world is not the route to change. Instead, they have adopted the strategy of creating an alternative media environment, run by women for women. The solution, for this type of feminist, lies in the creation, by women, of their own channels of communication and their own media organizations, in which women are able to exert total editorial control over content. This strategy, however, has not always worked successfully, as women fall prey to the same internal conflicts and disputes surrounding organizational management and editorial policies as do men. Such power plays are not, apparently, the preserve of male-dominated organizations (van Zoonen, 1992).

One place at which changes could be made is the script-writing stage. Here, there are opportunitites to create richer and more prominent characterizations for women. What published evidence exists on this aspect of the media production process suggests that opportunities to widen the media range of female representation tend not to be taken up. While newer producers exhibit promising gender-balancing dispositions, these disappear among more experienced counterparts, possibly as a function of economic pressures and sub-cultural, professional conditioning.

Vest (1992) investigated the manner in which changes in the characterization of women occur during the production and re-write phases of television pilots. It was hypothesized that the production and re-write process is a significant venue for restructuring of content toward traditional representation, thus limiting the portrayals of women. However, findings indicated no significant changes between the early and final versions of scripts. No support was found for the claim that changes in representation could be fouund within the production and re-write phase or that proven producers were responsible for a broadening of images during this phase.

If, as researchers exploring the production process suggest, the production and re-write process is a significant point at which story content and characterizations are restructured toward the traditional, then a discernible amount of change toward the conventional should be noted in script changes in the specific area of gender representation. In short, to the degree that the production and re-write process is responsible for the frequently documented limitations in the portrayal of women, early versions of these scripts may allow for a broader range of representation than later versions which have undergone revision under pressure to depict more conventional gender role portrayals.

To find out if such changes did seem to take place in script re-writes, Vest (1992) looked for shifts in the numerical representation of women as scripts developed. In addition, his analysis coded for centrality of female and male characters, age distribution of the sexes, and occupational roles. Scripts for more than 20 new American television series were examined.

Men were found to outnumber women in early and final versions of scripts, but there was no tendency for ratios to change across different stages of script development. There were no marked shifts either in the amount of time women and men were due to appear on screen. However, scripts by unproven producers were found to contain larger roles for women than did scripts by established producers.

Women were found in as many occupations as men. Once again, though, there were different patterns of gender representation apparent in scripts of unproven and established television producers. Unproven producers had no women in power occupations in their early scripts, but this changed by the final version. With high status producers, no women were featured as criminals in any version of their scripts. Marital status was more evident for women than for men. High status producers, however, were more likely to keep the marital status of both male and female characters unclear than were new producers.

Opportunities are available to producers to change the nature of gender role portrayals while developing television scripts. Whether or not such changes will actually occur does seem to be related with how long particular producers have been around. Longer-established producers appear to adhere to more traditional patterns of gender representation than new and unproven producers. If this is a consistent and reliable pattern of behaviour it could spell either good news or bad news for more varied gender role representation in the future. One interpretation of this finding could be that a new breed of producer is emerging which has a different view of gender representation on screen and who is prepared to experiment with non-traditional, atypical gender depictions. Alternatively, it might indicate that the longer producers have been around, the more they tend to succumb to pressures to stick to tried and tested narrative formulae and stereotyped characterizations. If television is to become a force for the cultivation of wider gender-role perceptions, and not simply a mirror of limiting stereotyped gender images, it must be hope that the first, rather than the second, interpretation holds true.

REFERENCES

Abel, G.G., Barlow, D.H., Blanchard, E. and Guild, D. (1977): 'The components of rapists' sexual arousal'. *Archives of General Psychology*, 34, 895–903.

Anastasi, A (1961). *Differential Psychology: Individual and Group Differences in Behaviour*. 3rd ed. New York: McMullan

Archer, J. (1984). 'Gender roles as developmental pathways'. *British Journal of Social Psychology*, 23, 245–256.

Atkin, C.K. (1975). *The Effects of Television Advertising on Children: Report No.2: Second Year Experimental Evidence*. Final Report, East Lansing, Michigan State University.

Atkin, C. and Miller, M.M. (1975). *Experimental effects of television advertising on children*. Paper presented at the International Communication Association convention, Chicago, April, 1975.

Atkin, C.K. Greenberg, B. and McDermott, S., (1979). 'Race and social role learning from television'. In H.S. Dordick (Ed.), *Proceedings* of the sixth Annual Telecommunications Policy Research Conference. Lexington, Mass: Lexington Books.

Atkin, D. (1991). 'The evolution of television series addressing women, 1966–1990'. *Journal of Broadcasting and Electronic Media*, 35 (4), 517–523.

Atwood, R.A., Zahn, S.B. and Webber, G. (1986). 'Perceptions of the traits of women on television'. *Journal of Broadcasting*, 30, 95–101.

Bakan, D. (1966). *The Reality of Human Existence*. Chicago, IL: Rand McNally.

Baran, S.J. (1976a). 'Sex on TV and adolescent sexual self-image'. *Journal of Broadcasting*, 20 (1), 61–68.

Baran, S.J. (1976b) 'How TV and film portrayals affect sexual satisfaction in college students'. *Journalism Quarterly*, 53 (3), 468–473.

Barcus, F.E. (1983). *Images of life on Children's Television: Sex Roles, Minorities and Families*. New York: Praeger.

Bartos, R. (1982). *The Moving Target: What Every Marketer Should Know About Women*. New York: Free Press

Belkaoui, A. and Belkaoui, J.M. (1976). 'Comparative analysis of the roles portrayed by women in print advertisements: 1958, 1970, 1972'. *Journal of Marketing Research*, 13 (2)., 168–172.

Bell, I.P. (1970). 'The double standard: Age'. *Trans-Action*, November–December, 75–80.

147

Bem, S. (1974). 'The measurement of psychological and ?'. *Journal of Consulting and androgyny Psychology*, 52, 1551–1562.

Bem, S.L. (1975). 'Sex role adaptability: One consequence of psychological and androgyny'. *Journal of Personality and Social Psychology*, 31, 634–643.

Bem, S.L. (1976). 'Probing the promise of androgyny'. In A. Kaplan and J. Bean (Eds.). *Beyond sex-role stereotypes: reading towards a psychology of androgyny*. Boston: Little, Brown.

Bem, S.L. (1981). 'Gender schema theory: A cognitive account of sex typing'. *Psychological Review*, 88, (4)., 354–364.

Benton, C.J., Hernandez, A.C., Schmit, A., Schmidt, M.D., Stone, A.J. and Werner, B. (1983). 'Is hostility linked with affiliation among males and achievement among females? A critique of Pollack and Gilligan'. *Journal of Personality and Social Psychology*, 45 (5)., 1167–1171.

Berry, G. and Mitchell-Kerman, C. (Eds.). (1982). *Television and the Socialization of the Minority Child*. New York: Academic Press.

Beuf, F.A. (1974). 'Doctor, lawyer, household drudge'. *Journal of Communication*, 24, 110–118.

Bourdeau, F., Sennott, R. and Wilson, M. (1986). *Sex Roles and Social Patterns*. New York: Praeger.

Boynton, P. (1936). 'The vocational preferences of school children'. *Journal of Genetic Psychology*, 49, 411–425

Brannigan, A. and Goldenberg, S. (1987). 'The study of aggressive pornography: The vicissitudes of relevance'. *Critical Studies in Mass Communication*, 4, 262–283.

Brettl, D.J. and Cantor, J. (1988). 'The portrayal of men and women in US television commercials: A recent content analysis and trends over 15 years'. *Sex Roles*, 18 (9/10)., 595–609.

Briere, J., Corne, S. and Runtz, M. (1984). 'The rape arousal inventory: Predicting actual and potential sexual aggression in a unversity population'. Paper presented at the annual meeting of the American Psychological Association, Toronto.

Brosius, H-B, Mundorf, N. and Staab, J.F. (1991). 'The depiction of sex roles in American and German magazine advertisements'. *International Journal of Public Opinion Research*, 3(4)., 366–383.

Broverman, I.K., Clarkson, F.E. and Rosencrantz, P.S. (1972). 'Sex-role stereotypes: A current appraisal'. *Journal of Social Issues*, 28, 59–78

Brown, J.D. and Campbell, K. (1986). 'Race and gender in music videos: The same beat but a different drummer'. *Journal of Communication*, 36 (1)., 94–106.

Bronson, C.W. (1969). 'Sex differences in the development of fearfulness: A replication'. *Psychonomic Science*, 17, 367–368.

Brownmiller, S. (1975). *Against Our Will: Men, Women and Rape*. New York: Simon and Schuster.

Beschloss, S. (1990). 'Making the rules in primetime'. *Channels*, May 7, pp. 23–27.

Buchanan, L. and Reid, L.N. (1977). 'Women role portrayals in advertising messages as stimulus cues: A preliminary investigation'. In G.E. Miracle (ed.). *Sharing for Understanding*, E. Lansing, Michigan: American Academy of Advertising.

Buckhart, K. (1973). *Women in Prison* New York: Doubleday.

Burt, M.R. (1980). 'Cultural myths and support for rape'. *Journal of Personality and Social Psychiatry* 38, 217–230.

Busby, L.J. (1975). 'Sex role research on the mass media'. *Journal of Communication*, 25, 107–131.

Butler, M and Paisley, W. (1980). *Women and the Mass Media.* New York: Human Sciences Press.

Cantor, M. (1979). 'Our days and nights on TV'. *Journal of Communication*, 29, 66–74.

Cantor, M.G. and Pingree, S. (1983). *The Soap Opera* Newbury Park, CA: Sage.

Carlson, R. (1971). 'Sex differences in ego functioning: Exploratory studies of agency and communication'. *Journal of Consulting and Clinical Psychology*, 37 (2). 267–277.

Carveth, R. and Alexander, A. (1985) 'Soap opera viewing motivations and the vultivation process'. *Journal of Broadcasting and Electronic Media*, 29(3), 259–273.

Cathey–Calvert, C. (1983). *Sexism of Sesame Street: Outdated Concepts in a Progressive Programme.* Pittsburgh: Know Inc.

Ceniti, J. and Malamuth, N.M. (1982). 'Effects of repeated exposure to sexually violent or non-violent stimuli on sexual arousal to rape and non-rape depictions'. *Behaviour Research and Therapy*, 22, 535–548.

Ceulemans, M. and Fauconnier, G. (1979). *Mass Media: The Image, Role and Social Conditions of Women.* (Report No. 84). Paris, France: United Nations Educational Scientific and Cultural Organisation.

Chappell, B. (1983). 'How women are portrayed in television commercials'. *Admap*, June, 327–331.

Cheles-Miller, P. (1975). 'Restrictions to ? roles in commercials'. *Journal of Advertising Research*, 15, 45–49.

Chulay, C. and Francis, S. (1974). 'The image of the female child on Saturday morning television commercials. ERIC (ED 095603).

Clark, C. (1972). 'Race, identification and television violence'. In G.A. Comstock, E.A. Rubinstein and J.P. Murray (Eds.). *Television and Social Behaviour: Vol. 5, Further Explorations.* Washington, D.C: US Government Printing Office.

Cobb, N.J., Stevens Long, J. and Goldstein, S. (1982). ' The influence of televised models on toy preference in children'. *Sex Roles*, 5, 1072–1080.

Coles, C.D. and Shamp, M.J. (1984). 'Some sexual, personality, and demographic characteristics of women reader of erotic romances'. *Archives of Sexual Behaviour*, 33(3)., 187–209.

Cordua, G.D., McGraw, K.O. and Drabman, R.S. (1979). ' Doctor or nurse: Children's perception of sex-typed occupations'. *Child Development*, 50, 590–593.

Courtney, A.E. and Lockeretz, S.W. (1971). 'A women's place: An analysis of the roles portrayed by women in magazine ads'. *Journal of Marketing Research*, 8(1)., 92–95.

Courtney, A.E. and Whipple, T.W. (1974). *Journal of Communication*, 24(2)., 110–118.

Courtright A.E. and Baran, S.J. (1980). 'The acquisition of sexual information by young people'. *Journalism Quarterly* 57, 107–114.

Culley, J.A. and Bennett, R. (1976). 'Selling women, selling blacks *Journal of Communication*, 26, 168–178.

Cumberbatch, G. and Howitt, D. (1989). *A Measure of Uncertainty: The Effects of the Mass Media.* (Broadcasting Standards Council Research Monograph Series). London: John Libbey and Company.

Cumberbatch, G., Lee, M., Hardy, G. and Jones, I. (1987). *The Portrayal of Violence on British Television: A Content Analysis.* Applied Psychology Division, Aston University, Birmingham, UK.

Cumberbatch, G., Maguire, A. and Woods, S. (1994). 'The Portrayal of Women on British Television – A Content Analysis'. In *BSC Research Working Paper IX: Perspectives of Women on Television.* London: Broadcasting Standards Council.

Davidson, E.S., Yasina, A. and Towers, A. (1979). 'The effects of television cartoons on sex-role stereotyping in young girls'. *Child Development*, 50, 597–600.

Davis, D.M. (1990). 'Portrayals of women in prime-time network television: Some demographic characteristics'. *Sex Roles*, 23(5/6)., 325–332.

Dawson, J.A. (1981). 'Responses to sex-role portrayals in advertising'. *Advertising Magazine*, No. 67 Spring.

Debevec, K. and Iyer, E (1986). 'Sex-roles and consumer perception of promotions, products and self: What do we know and where should we be headed'. In R.J. Lutz (Ed.). *Advances in Consumer Research*, Vol. 13. Provo, UT: Association for Consumer Research.

De Charms, R. (1976). *Enhancing Motivation Change in the Classroom.* New York: Irvington Publishers.

Deckard, B. (1975). *The Women's Movement, Political, Socio-economic and Psychological Issues.* New York: Harper & Row.

DeFleur, M.L. (1963). 'Children's knowledge of occupational roles and prestige: Preliminary report'. *Psychological Reports*, 13, 760–761.

DeFleur, M. and DeFleur, L. (1967). 'The relative contribution of television as a learning source for children's ocupational knowledge'. *American Sociological Review*, 34, 777–789.

Demare, D., Briere, J. and Lips, A.M. (1988). 'Violent pornography and self-reported likelihood of sexual aggression'. *Journal of Research in Personality*, 20, 140–153.

Deutsch, M. (1960). *Minority group and class status as related to social and personality factors in scholastic achievement.* Ithaca, N.Y. society for Applied Anthropology 32p.

De Young, S. and Crane, F.G. (1992). 'Females' attitudes toward the portrayal of women in advertising: A Canadian study'. *International Journal of Advertising*, 11, 249–255.

Dileo, J.C., Moely, B.E. and Sulzer, J.L. (1979). 'Frequency and modifiability of children's preferences for sex-typed toys, games and occupations'. *Child Study Journal*, 9(2)., 141–159.

Dispenza, J. (1975). *Advertising the American Woman.* Dayton, Ohio: Dayton Publishing.

Dohrmann, R. (1975). 'A gender profile of children's educational TV'. *Journal of Communication*, 25(4)., 56–65

Dominick, J. and Rauch, G. (1971). 'The image of women in network TV commercials'. *Journal of Broadcasting*, 16, 257–265.

Donnerstein, E. (1980). 'Aggressive erotica and violence against women'. *Journal of Personality and Social Psychology*, 39, 269–277.

Donnerstein, E. (1983): Erotica and human aggression. In R. Geen and E. Donnerstein (Eds.) Aggression: Theoretical and Empirical Reviews(Vol. 2). New York: Academic Press.

Donnerstein, E. and Berkowitz, L. (1981). 'Victim reactions to aggressive erotic films as a factor in violence against women'. *Journal of Personality and Social Psychology*, 41, 710–724.

Dorr, A. and Lesser, G.S. (1980). 'Career awareness in young children'. In M. Grewe-Portsch and G.J. Robinson (Eds.) *Women, Communication and Careers*. Munich: K.G. Saur, pp. 36–75.

Douvan, E.A.M. and Adelson, J. (1966). *The Adolescent Experience* New York: Wiley.

Dowling, G.R. (1980). 'Female role portrayal: An exploratory analysis of Australian television advertising'. *Media Information Australia*, 17, 3–7

Downing, M. (1976). 'Heroine of the daytime serial'. *Journal of Communication*, 24, 130–139.

Downs, A.C. and Abshier, G.R. (1982). 'Conceptions of physical appearance among young adolescents: The interrelationships among self-judged appearance, attractiveness stereotyping and sex-typed characteristics'. *Journal of Early Adolescence*, 2, 57–64.

Downs, A.C. and Currie, M. (1983). 'Indexing elementary school-age children's views of attractive and unattractive people: The Attitudes Towards Physical Attractiveness Scale – Intermediate Version'. *Psychological Documents*, 13, 23(MS 2579).

Downs, A.C. and Harrison, S.K. (1985). 'Embarrassing age spots or just plain ugly? Physical attractiveness stereotyping as an instrument of sexism on American television commercials'. *Sex Roles*, 13,(1/2)., 9–19.

Downs, A.C., Reagan, M.A., Garrett, C. and Kolodzy, P. (1982). 'The Attitudes Toward Physical Attractiveness Scales (ATPAS).: An index of stereotypes based on physical appearance'. *JSAS Catalogue of Selected Documents in Psychology*, 12, 44–45 (MS 2502).

Drabman, R.S., Robertson, S.J., Patterson, J.N., Jarvie, G.J., Hammer, D. and Cordua, G. (1981). 'Children's perception of media-portrayed sex roles'. *Sex Roles*, 12, 379–389.

Duker, J.M. and Tucker, L.R.Jr. (1977). 'Women's lib-ers versus independent women: A study of preferences for women's roles in advertisements'. *Journal of Marketing Research*, 14(4)., 469–475.

Durkin, K. (1983). *Sex roles and children's television*. A report to the Independent Broadcasting Authority. Social Psychology Research Unit, University of Kent, Canterbury.

Durkin, K. (1984). 'Children's accounts of sex-role stereotypes on television'. *Communication Research* 11, 341–362.

Durkin, K. (1985a). 'Television and sex-role acquisition 1: Content'. *British Journal of Social Psychology*, 24, 101–113.

Durkin, K. (1985b). 'Television and sex role acquisition 2: Effects'. *British Journal of Social Psychology*, 24, 221–222.

Durkin, K. (1985c). 'Television and sex-role acquisition 3: Counter-stereotyping'. *British Journal of Social Psychology*, 24, 211–222.

Durkin, K. (1985d). *Television, Sex Roles and Children.* Milton Keynes, UK: Open University Press

Durkin, K, and Hutchins, G. (1984). 'Challenging traditional sex-role stereotypes via careers education broadcasts: The reactions of young secondary school pupils'. *Journal of Educational Television*, 10, 25–33.

Dynes, R.R., Clarke, A.C. and Dinitz, s. (1956). 'Levels of occupational aspiration. Some aspects of family experience as a variable'. *Amrican Sociological Review*, 21, 212–215.

Eaton, B.C. and Dominick, J.R. (1991). 'Product-related programming and Children's TV: A content analysis'. *Journalism Quarterly*, 68(1)., 67–75

Eisenstock, B. (1984). 'Sex-role differences in children's identification with counter stereotypical televised portrayals'. *Sex Roles*, 10, 451–430.

Fagot, B.I. and Patterson, G.R. (1969). 'An *in vivo* analysis of reinforcing contingencies for sex-role behaviour in the preschool child'. *Development Psychology*, 1, 563–568.

Fauls, L.B. and Smith, W.D. (1956). 'Sex-role learning in 5 year olds'. *Journal of Genetic Psychology*, 89, 195–117.

Feldstein, J.H. and Feldstein, S. (1982). 'Sex differences on televised toy commercials'. *Sex Roles*, 8, 581–587.

Fernandez-Collado, C.F., Greenberg, B.S., Korzenny, F. and tkin, C.K. (1978). 'Sexual intimacy and drug use in TV series'. *Journal of Communication*, 28(3), 30–37.

Ferrante, C.L., Haynes, A.M. and Kingsley, S.M. (1988). 'Image of women in television advertising'. *Journal of Broadcasting and Electronic Media*, 32(2)., 231–237

Feshbach, N.D. (1969). 'Sex differences in children's modes of aggressive responses towards outsiders'. *The Merrill-Palmer Quarterly*, 15(3)., 249–258.

Fiske,J. (1987). *Television Culture*. London: Methuen.

Fitch, M., Huston, A.C. and Wright, J.C. (1993). 'From television forms to genre schemata. Children's perceptions of television reality'. In G. Gerry and J.K. Ashman (Eds.) *Children and Television: Images in a Changing Sociocultural World*. Newbury Park, CA: Sage, pp. 38–52.

Fiske, S.T. and Taylor, S.E. (1982). *Social Cognition*. New York: Random House.

Flerx, V., Fidler, D. and Rogers, R. (1976). 'Sex role stereotypes: Development aspects and early intervention'. *Child Development*, 47, 998–1007.

Foote, Cone and Belding (1974). *A Report on the way Women View Their Portrayal in Today's Television and Magazine Advertising*. Unpublished advertising study. New York: Foote, Cane and Belding Marketing Information Service.

Franzblau, S., Sprafkin, J.N. & Rubinstein, E.A. (1977). 'Sex on TV: A content analysis'. *Journal of Communication*, 27(2), 165–170.

Friedan, B. (1963). *The Feminine Mystique*. NY: W.W. Norton.

Freuh, T. and McGhee, P.E. (1975). 'Traditional sex-role development and amount of time spent watching television'. *Developmental Psychology*, 11, 109.

Friedan, B. (1963). *The Feminine Mystique*. NY: W.W. Norton.

Frieze, I.H., Parson, J.E., Johnson, P.B., Ruble, D.N. and Zellman, G.L. (1978). *Women and Sex roles: A social psychological perspective* New York Norton.

Furnham, A. and Bitar, N. (1993). 'The stereotyped portrayal of men and women in British television advertisements'. *Sex Roles*, 29(3/4)., 297–310

Furnham, A. and Schofield, S. (1986). 'Sex-role stereotyping in British radio advertisements'. *British Journal of Social Psychology*, 25, 165–171.

Furnham, A. and Voli, V. (1989). 'Gender stereotypes in Italian television advertisements'. *Journal of Broadcasting and Electronic Media*, 33(2)., 175–185

Gallagher, M. (1983). *Why can't a man be more like a woman?* Report on the British component of a cross-cultural study of sex-role attitudes, perceptions and television viewing. Honolulu: East, West Centre, Institute of Culture and Communication.

Garai, J.E. and Scheinfeld, A. (1963). 'Sex differences in mental and behavioural traits'. *Genetic Psychology Monographs*, 77(2)., 169–299.

Garrett, C.S., Ein, P.L. and Tremaine, L. (1977). 'The development of gender stereotyping of adult occupations in elementary school children'. *Child Development*, 48 507–512.

Geis, F.L., Brown, V., Jennings (Walstedt)., J. and Porter, N. TV commercials as achievement scripts for women'. *Sex Roles*, 10, 513–525.

Gerbner, G. (1972). 'Violence in television drama: Trends and symbolic functions'. In G.A. Comstock and E.A. Rubinstein (Eds.)., *Television and social behaviour*, Vol 1, *Content and control*. Washington, D.C: U.S., Government Printing Office.

Gerbner, G. and Gross, L. (1976). 'Living with television. The violence profile'. *Journal of Communication*, 26, 173– 199.

Gerbner, G., Gross, L., Eleey, M.E., Jackson-Beeck, M., Jeffries-Fox, S. and Signorielli, N. (1977). 'Television violence profile no. 8: The highlights'. *Journal of Communication*, 27, 171–180.

Gerbner, G., Gross, L., Jackson-Beeck, M., Jeffries-Fox, S. and Signorielli, N. (1978). 'Cultural indicators: Violence profile no. 9'. *Journal of Communication*, 28, 176–207.

Gerbner, G., Gross, L., Signorielli, N., Morgan, M. and Jackson-Beeck, M. (1979). 'The demonstration of power: Violence profile no. 10'. *Journal of Communication*, 29, 177–196.

Gerbner, G., Gross, L., Morgan, M. and Signorielli, N. (1980). 'The "mainstreaming" of America. Violence profile No. 11'. *Journal of Communication*, 30(1), 10–29.

Gerbner, G., Gross, L., Morgan, M. and Signorielli, N. (1982). 'Charting the mainstream: Television's contribution to political orientations'. *Journal of Communication*, 32, 100–127.

Gerbner, G., Gross, L., Morgan, M. and Signorielli, N. (1986). 'Living with television: The dynamics of the cultivation process'. In J. Bryant and D. Zillmann (Eds.) *Perspectives on Media Effects*. Hillsdale, NJ: Lawrence Erlbaum Associates.

Gerbner, G. and Signorielli, N. (1979). *Women and minorities in television drama: 1969–1978: Research Report.* Annenberg School of Communications, Philadelphia, in collaboration with the Seven Actors Guild, AFL–C10 October 29.

Gilly, M.C. (1988). 'Sex roles in advertising: A comparison of television advertisements in Australia, Mexico and the United States'. *Journal of Marketing*, 52(2)., 75–85.

Goff, D.H., Goff, L.D. and Lehrer, S.K. (1980). 'Sex-role portrayals of selected female television characters'. *Journal of Broadcasting*, 24, 467–475.

Goffman, E. (1979). *Gender Advertisements*. Cambridge: Harvard University Press.

Greenberg, B.S. (1982). 'Television and role socialisation: An overview'. In D. Pearl, L. Boutilet and J. Lazar (Eds.) *Television and Behaviour: Ten Years of Scientific Progress and Implications for the Eighties.* Rockville, MD: NIMH.

Greenberg, B., Richards, M. and Henderson, L. (1980). ' Trends in sex-role portrayals on television'. In B. Greenberg (Ed.)., *Life on Television*, Norwood, JJ: Ablex Press.

Gross, L. and Jeffries-Fox, S. (1978). 'What do you want to be when you grow up, little girl? In G. Tuckman, Daniels, A. and Benet, J. (Eds.) *Health and Home: Images of Women in the Mass Media.* New York: Oxford University Press.

Grusec, J.E. and Brinker, D.B. (1972). 'Reinforcement for imitation as a social learning determinant with implications for sex role development'. *Journal of Personality and Social Psychology*, 21, 149–158.

Gunter, B. (1984). *TV viewing and perceptions of men and women on TV and in real life.* London: Independent Broadcasting Authority, Research paper, September.

Gunter, B. (1985). *Dimensions of Television Violence* Aldershot, UK: Gower.

Gunter, B. and McAleer, J.L. (1990): *Children and Television: The One-Eyed Monster.* London: Routledge.

Gunter, B. and Wober, M. (1982). 'Television viewing and perceptions of women on TV and in real life'. *Current Psychological Research*, 2, 277–288.

Gutman, D. (1965). 'Women and the conception of ego-strength'. *The Merrill-Palmer Quarterly*, 11(3)., 229–240.

Haase, H. (1989). 'Werbewirkung forschung'. In P. Winterhoff-Spurk and J. Groebel (Eds.) *Empirische Medienpsychologie*, Munchen: Psychologie Verlags Union.

Hamilton, R. Haworth, B. and Sarder, N. (1982). *Adman and Eve: An Empirical Study of the Relative Marketing Effectiveness of Traditional and Modern Portrayals of Women in certain Mass Media Advertisements.* Report for Equal Opportunities Commission.

Hansen, J.C. and Caulfield, T.J. (1969). 'Parent-child occupational concepts'. *Elementary School Guidance and Counselling*, 3, 269–275

Harris, P.R. and Stobart, J. (1986). 'Sex-role stereotyping in British television advertisements at different times of the day: An extension and refinement of Manstead & McCulloch (1981). *British Journal of Social Psychology*, 25, 155–164.

Hartley, R.E. (1959). 'Sex-role pressures and the socialisation of the male child'. *Psychological Reports*, 5, 457–468.

Haskell, D. (1979). 'The depiction of women in leading roles in prime-time television'. *Journal of Broadcasting*, 23, 191–196.

Hawkins, R. and Pingree, S. (1982). 'Television's influence on social reality'. In D. Pearl, L. Bouthilet and J. Lazar (Eds.) *Television and behaviour: Ten years of scientific progress and implications for the eighties*. Rockville, Maryland, Institute of mental Health.

Head, H. (1954). 'Content analysis of television drama programmes'. *Quarterly of Film, Radio and Television*, 9, 175–194.

Heiman, J.R. (1977). 'A psychological explanation of sexual arousal patterns in females and males'. *Psychophysiology*, 14, 266–274.

Henderson, L., Greenberg, B.S. and Atkin, C.K. (1980). ' Sex differences in giving orders, making plans and needing support on television'. In B.S. Greenberg (Ed.). *Life on Television: Content Analysis of US TV Drama*. Norwood: Ablex, pp. 49–64.

Hennessee, J. and Nicholson, J. (1972). 'NOW says: TV commercials insult women'. *New York Times Magazine*, May 28, pp. 13, 48–51.

Hill, D. (1987): 'Is TV sex getting bolder?' *TV Guide*, August 8, pp. 2–5.

Hodges, K.K., Brandt, D.A. and Kline, J. (1981). 'Competence, guilt and victimization: Sex differences in ambition of causality in television dramas'. *Sex Roles,* 7, 537–546.

Holopainen, I., Kalkkinein, m.L., Rantauen, T., Sarkkimen, R. and Osterlund, M. (1984). *Good Evening, Our Main Item Tonight is...Women: A Preliminary Study on the Role of Women in Television*. Helsinki: Finnish Television Corporation.

Huston, A.C., Donnerstein, E., Fairchild, H., Feshbach, N.D., Katz, P.A., Murray, J.P., Rubinstein, E.A., Wilcox, B.G. and Zuckerman, D. (1992). *Big World, Small Screen: The Role of Television in American Society*, Lincoln: University of Nebraska Press.

Huston, A.C., Greer, D., Wright, J.C. and Welch, R. and Ross, R. (1984). 'Children's comprehension of televised formal features with masculine and feminine connotations'. *Developmental Psychology*, 20, 707–716

Jaffe, L. (1991). 'Impact of positioning and sex-role identity on women's responses to advertising'. *Journal of Advertising Research*, June/July, 57–64.

Jaffe, L. and Berger, P.D. (1988). 'Impact on purchase content of sex-role identity and product positioning'. *Psychology and Marketing*, 5(3)., 259–271.

Jeffries-Fox and Signorielli, N. (1979).

Jennings, J., Geis, F.L. and Brown, V. (1980). 'Influence of television on women's self-confidence and independent judgement'. *Journal of Personality and Social Psychology*, 38, 203–210.

Jensen, P.G. and Kirchner, w.K. (1955). 'A national answer to the question: 'Do sons follow their fathers' occupations?' *Journal of Applied Psychology*, 39, 419–421

Johnson, J. and Ettema, J.S. (1982). *Positive Images*. Beverly Hills, CA: Sage.

Johnson, P. and Goodchilds, J.D. (1973). 'Comment: Pornography, sexuality and social psychology'. *Journal of Social Issues*, 29, 231–238.

Joy, L., Kimball, M. and Zabrock, M. (1977). *Television exposure and children's aggressive behaviour*. Paper presented at the meeting of the Canadian Psychological Association, Vancouver, June.

Kandel, D.B. and Lesser, G.S. (1972). *Youth in Two Worlds: United States and Denmark*. San Francisco: Jossey-Bass.

Katz, E., Blumler, J.G. and Gurevitch, M. (1973). 'Uses and gratifications research'. *Public Opinion Quarterly*, 37, 509–523.

Katzman, N. (1972). 'Television soap operas: What's been going on anyway? *Public Opinion Quarterly*, 36, 200–212.

Kelley, K. and Byrne, D. (1983). 'Assessment of sexual responding: Arousal, affect and behaviour'. In J. Cacioppo and R. Petty (Eds.) *Social Psychology: A Sourcebook*, pp. 467–490. New York: Guilford.

Kimball, M. (1986). 'Television and sex-role attitudes'. In T.M. Williams (Ed.)., *The Impact of Television*, London: Academic Press.

Kirchner, E.P. and Vondracek, S.I. (1973). *What do you want to be when you grow up? Vocational choice in children aged three to six*. Paper presented at the Society for Research in Child Development, Philadelphia, March.

Kline, S. and Pentecost, D. (1990). 'The characterization of play: marketing children's toys'. *Play and Culture*, 3, 235–255

Knill, B.J., Peach, M., Pursey, G., Gilpin, P. and Perloff, R.M. (1981). 'Still typecast after all these years: Sex role portrayals in television advertising'. *International Journal of Women's Studies*, 4, 497–506.

Koerber, C. (1977). 'Television'. In J. King and M. Stott (Eds). *Is This Your Life? Images of Women in the Media*. London: Virago: pp. 133–142

Kohlberg, L.A. (1966). 'Cognitive developmental analysis of children's sex role concepts and attitudes'. In E. Maccoby (Ed.). *The development of sex differences. Stanford Calif.: Stanford University Press.*

Kolbe, R.H. (1990). 'Gender roles in children's television advertising: A longitudinal content analysis'. *Current Issues and Research in Advertising*, 13, 197–206.

Kuchenhoff, E. (1977). 'Die Darstellung der Frau im Fernsehen'. In. M Furlan (Ed.). 'kinder und Jugendliche im Spannungsfeld der Massunmedien. Stuttgart: Bonz Verlag.

Kutchinsky, B. (1971). 'Towards an explanation of the decrease in reported sex crimes in Copenhagen'. *Technical report of the Commission on Obscenity and Pornography*, Vol. 7. Washington DC, US Government Printing Office.

Lawrence, K. and Herold, E.S. (1988). 'Women's attitudes toward and experience with sexually explicit materials'. *Journal of Sex Research*, 24, 161–169.

Lederer, L. (1980). *Take Back the Night: Women on Pornography*. New York: William Morrow and Company.

Leigh, T.W., Rethams, A.J. and Whitney, T.R. (1987). 'Role portrayals of women in advertising. Cognitive responses and advertising effectiveness. *Journal of Advertising Research*, 27(5)., 54–62.

Lemon, J. (1977). 'Women and blacks on prime-time television'. *Journal of Communication*, 27, 70–74.

Lesser, G.S. (1973). 'Achievement motivation in women'. In D.C. McClelland (Ed.). *Human Motivation: A Book of Readings*. Morristown, N.J.: General learning Press.

Levinson, R. (1975). 'From Olive Oyl to Sweet Polly Purebread: Sex role stereotypes and televised cartoons'. *Journal of Popular Culture*, 9, 561–572.

Levy, M.R. and Windahl, S. (1985). 'The concept of audience activity'. In K.G. Rosengren, L.A. Wenner and P. Palmgreen (Eds.) *Media Gratifications Research: Current Perspectives*. pp. 109–122.

Leymore, V.L. (1975). *Hidden Myth: Structure and Symbolism in Advertising*. New York: Basic Books.

Linz, D. (1985). *Sexual Violence in the Media: Effects on male viewers and implications for society*. Unpublished doctoral dissertation, University of Wisconsin-Madison.

Linz, D., Donnerstein, E. and Penrod, S. (1984). 'The effects of multiple exposures to filmed violence against women'. *Journal of Communication*, 34(3), 130–147.

Linz, D. and Malamuth, N. (1993). *Pornography*. Newbury Park, CA: Sage.

Livingstone, S. and Green, G. (1986). 'Television advertisements and the portrayal of gender'. *British Journal of Social Psychology*, 25, 149–154.

Long, M. and Simon, R. (1974). 'The roles and statuses of women and children on family TV programmes'. *Journalism Quarterly*, 51, 107–110.

Looft, W.R. (1971). 'Sex differences in the expression of vocational aspirations by elementary school children'. *Developmental Psychology*, 5, 366.

Lovdal, L.T. (1989). 'Sex role messages in television commercials: An update'. *Sex Roles*, 21(11/12)., 715–724.

Lowry, D.T., Love, G. and Kirby, M. (1981). 'Sex on the soap operas: Patterns of intimacy'. *Journal of Communication*, 31, 90–96.

Lowry, D.T. and Towles, D.E. (1988). 'Primetime TV portrayals of sex, contraception and venereal diseases. *Journalism Quarterly*, 66, 347–352.

Lundstrom, W.J. and Sciglimpaglia, D. (1977). 'Sex role portrayals in advertising'. *Journal of Marketing,* 41(3)., 72–79.

Lyle, J. and Hoffman, H.R. (1972a). 'Children's use of television and other media'. In E.A. Rubinstein, G.A. Comstock, and J.P. Murray (Eds.) *Television and Social Behaviour, Vol. 4, Television in Day-to-Day Life: Patterns of Use*. Washington, D.C.: US Government Printing Office.

Lyle, J. and Hoffman, H.R. (1972b). 'Explorations in patterns of television viewing by pre-school-age children'. In E.A. Rubinstein, G.A. Comstock, and J.P. Murray (Eds.) *Television and Social Behaviour, Vol. 4, Television in Day-to-Day Life: Patterns of Use*. Washington, D.C.: Government Printing Office.

Lysonski, S. and Pollay, R.W. (1990). 'Advertising Sexism is forgiven, but not forgotten: Historical, cross-cultural and individual differences in criticism and purchase boycott intentions'. *International Journal of Advertising*, 9, 317–329.

Maccoby, E.E. (Ed.). '(1966). *The Development of Sex Differences* Stanford, Calif: Stanford University Press.

Maccoby, E.E. and Jacklin, C.N. (1974). *The psychology of sex differences*, Stanford, CA., Stanford University Press.

Maccoby, E.E. and Wilson, W.C. (1957). 'Identification and observational learning from films'. *Journal of Abnormal and Social Psychology*, 55, 76–87.

Macklin, M.C. and Kolbe, R.H. (1984). 'Sex role stereotyping in children's advertising: current and past trends'. *Journal of Advertising*, 13, 34–42.

Malamuth, N.M. (1981a). 'Rape fantasies as a function of exposure to violent sexual stimuli'. *Archives of Sexual Behaviour*, 10, 33–47.

Malamuth, N.M. (1981b). 'Rape proclivity among males'. *Journal of Social Issues*, 37, 138–157.

Malamuth, N.M. (1984). 'Aggression against women: Cultural and individual causes'. In N.M. Malamuth and E. Donnerstein (Eds.) *Pornography and Sexual Aggression*. Orlando, Fl: Academic Press, pp. 19–52.

Malamuth, N.M. (1986). 'Predictors of naturalistic sexual aggression'. *Journal of Personality and Social Psychology*, 50, 953–962.

Malamuth, N.M. (1989). 'Sexually violent media, thought patterns and antisocial behaviour'. In G.Comstock (Ed.). *Public Communication and Behaviour*, (Vol.2, pp. 159–204). New York: Academic Press.

Malamuth, N.M. and Billings, V. (1986). 'The functions and effects of pornography: Sexual communication versus the feminist models in light of research findings'. In J. Bryant and D. Zillmann (Eds.) *Perspectives on Media Effects*. Hillsdale, NJ: Lawrence Erlbaum Associates.

Malamuth, N.M. and Check, J.V.P. (1980). 'Penile tumescence and perceptual responses to rape as a function of victim's perceived reactions'. *Journal of Applied Social Psychology*, 10(6), 528–547.

Malamuth, N.M. and Check, J.V.P. (1981a). 'The effects of mass media exposure on acceptance of violence against women: A field experiment'. *Journal of Research in Personality*, 15, 436–446.

Malamuth, N.M. and Check, J.V.P. (1981b). *The effects of exposure to aggressive pornography: Rape proclivity, sexual arousal and beliefs in rape myths*. Paper presented at the 89th annual meeting of the American Psychological Association, Los Angeles, California, USA.

Malamuth, N.M. and Check, J.V.P. (1985). 'The effects of aggressive pornography on beliefs of rape myths: Individual differences'. *Journal of Research In Personality*, 19, 299–320.

Malamuth, N.M. and Briere, J. (1986). 'Sexual violence in the media: Indirect effects on aggression against women'. *Journal of Social Issues*, 42(3).

Malamuth, N.M. and Donnerstein, E. (1982). 'The effects of aggressive-pornographic mass media stimuli'. In L. Berkowitz (Ed.) *Advances in Experimental Social Psychology*, (vol. 15), New York: Academic Press.

Malamuth, N.M., Haber, S. and Feshbach, S. (1980). 'Testing hypotheses regarding rape: Exposure to sexual violence, sex differences, and the "normality" of reports'. *Journal of Research in Personality*, 14, 121–137.

Malamuth, N.M., Heim, M. and Feshbach, S. (1980). 'Sexual responsiveness of college students to rape depictions: Inhibitory and disinhibitory effects'. *Journal of Personality and Social Psychology*, 38, 399–408.

Malamuth, N.M. and Spinner, B. (1980). 'A longitudinal content analysis of sexal violence in the best-selling erotic magazines'. *The Journal of Sex Research*, 16(3), 226–237.

Manstead, A.R.S. and McCulloch, C. (1981). 'Sex role stereotyping in British television advertisements'. *British Journal of Social Psychology*, 20, 171–180.

Manes, A.I. and Melnyk, P. (1974). 'Televised models of female achievement'. *Journal of Applied Social Psychology*, 4, 365–374.

Maracek, J., Piliavin, J.A., Fitzsimmons, E., Krogh, E.C., Leader, E. and Trudell, B. (1976). 'women as TV experts: The voice of authority? *Journal of Communication*, 28, 159–168.

Matelski, M.G. (1985). 'Image and influence: Women in public television'. *Journalism Quarterly*, 62(1)., 147–150

Mattelart, M. (1986): *Women, Media, Crisis: Femininity and Disorder* London: Comedia.

Mayes, S.L. and Valentine, K.B. (1979). 'Sex role stereotyping in Saturday morning cartoon shows'. *Journal of Broadcasting*, 23, 41–50.

Mazzella, C., Durkin, K., Cerini, E. and Buralli, P. (1992). 'Sex role stereotyping in Australian television advertisements'. *Sex Roles*, 26(7/8)., 243–259.

McArthur, L.Z. and Eisen, S. (1976). 'Achievements of male and female storybook characters as determinants of achievement behaviour in boys and girls'. *Journal of Personality and Social Psychology*, 33, 467–473.

McArthur, L.Z. and Resko, B.G. (1975). 'The portrayal of men and women in American television commercials'. *Journal of Social Psychology*, 97, 209–220.

McClelland, D.C. (1975). *Power: The Inner Experience* New York: Irving.

McGhee, P.E. (1975). 'Television as a source of learning sex-role stereotypes'. In S. Cohen and T.J. Comiskey (Eds.) *Child Development: Contemporary perspectives*, Ithace, IL: Pencock Publishers.

McGhee, P. and Frueh, T. (1980). 'Television viewing and the learning of sex-role stereotypes'. *Sex Roles*, 2, 179–188.

McGlynn, R.P., Megas, J.C. and Benson, D.H. (1976). ' Sex and race as factors affecting the attribution of insanity in a murder trial'. *Journal of Psychology*, 93, 93–99.

McNeil, J. (1975). 'Feminism, femininity and the television shows: A content analysis'. *Journal of Broadcasting*, 19, 259–269.

Melton, G.W. and Fowler, G.L. (1987). 'Female roles in radio advertising'. *Journalism Quarterly*, 64, 145–149.

Meyer, B. (1980). 'The development of girls' sex-role attitudes'. *Child Development*, 51, 508–514.

Miles, B. (1975). *Channelling children: sex stereotyping as primetime TV*. Princeton, J.J.: Women on Words and Images.

Mischel, W. (1966). 'A social learning view of sex differences in behaviour'. In E. Maccoby (Ed.). *The development of sex differences*. Stanford, Calif.: Stanford University Press.

Miller, M. and Reeves, B. (1976). 'Dramatic TV content and children's sex-role stereotypes'. *Journal of Broadcasting*, 20, 35–50.

Millwood-Hargrave, A. (1992). *Sex and Sexuality in Broadcasting*. London; Broadcasting Standards Council and John Libbey.

Millwood-Hargrave, A. (1994). 'Attitudes towards the Portrayal of women in Broadcasting'. In *BSC Research Working Paper IX: Perspectives of Women in Television*. London: Broadcasting Standards Council.

Mischel, W. (1970). 'A social learning view of sex differences in behaviour'. In P.H. Mussen (Ed.). *Carmichael's Manual of Child Psychology*, New York: Wiley.

Money, J. and Erhardt, A.A. (1972). *Man and Woman, Boy and Girl*. Baltimore: Johns Hopkins University.

Morgan, M. (1980). *Television and role socialization*. Paper presented at the International Communication Association convention, Acapulco, Mexico.

Morgan, M. (1982). 'Television and adolescents' sex role stereotypes: A longitudinal study'. *Journal of Personality and Social Psychology*, 43, 947–955.

Morgan, M. (1987). 'Television, sex-role attitudes and sex-role behaviour'. *Journal of Early Adolescence*, 7(3)., 269–282.

Morgan, M. and Gerbner, G. (1982). 'TV professions and adolescent career choices'. In M. Schwarz (Ed.). *TV and Teens – Experts Look at the Issues*. Reading, MA: Addison-Wesley, pp. 121–126.

Morgan, M. and Rothschild, N. (1983). 'Impact of the new television technology: Cable TV, peers and sex-role cultivation in the electronic environment'. *Youth and Society*, 15(1)., 33–50.

Morgan, R. (1980). 'Theory and practice: Pornography and rape'. In L. Lederer (Ed.) *Take Back the Night: Women on Pornography*. New York: William Morrow and Company.

Morley, D. (1985). *Family Television: Cultural Power and Domestic leisure*. London: Comedia.

Morley, D. (1985). *Family television: cultural power and domestic lesiure*. London: Comedia.

Nelson, R.C. (1963). 'Knowledge and interests concerning sixteen occupations among elementary and secondary school students. *Educational and Psychological Measurement*, 23, 741–754.

Nolan, J.D., J.P. and White, M.A. (1977). 'Sex bias on children's television programmes'. *Journal of Psychology*, 96, 197–204.

O'Bryant, S.K. and Corder-Bolz, C.R. (1978). 'The effect of television on children's stereotyping of women's work roles'. *Journal of Vocational Behaviour*, 12 233–244.

O'Donnell, W.J. and O'Donnell, K.J. (1978). 'Update: sex role messages in TV commercials'. *Journal of Broadcasting*, 28, 156–158.

O'Hara, R.P. (1962). 'The roots of careers'. *Elementary School Journal*, 62, 277–280

O'Kelly, C.G. and Bloomqvist, L.E. (1976). 'Women and blacks on TV'. *Journal of Communication*, 26, 179–192.

Orlofsky, J.L., Cohen, R.S. and Ramsden, M.W. (1985). ' Relationship between sex-role attitudes and personality traits and the revised sex-role behaviour scale'. *Sex Roles*, 12, 377–391.

Orne, M. (1962). On the social psychology of the psychological experiment with particular reference to demand characteristics and their implications. *American Psychologist*, 17, 776–783.

Padgett, V.R., Brislin-Slutz, J and neal, J.A. (1989). ' Pornography, erotica and attitudes toward women: The effects of repeated exposure'. *Journal of Sex Research*, 26, 479–491.

Pallone, N.J., Hurley, R.B. and Richard, F.S. (1973). ' Further data on key influencers of occupational expectations among minority youth'. *Journal of Counselling Psychology*, 20, 484–486.

Pallone, N.J., Richard, F.S. and Hurley, R.B. (1970). ' Key influencers of occupational preference among black youths'. *Journal of Counselling Psychology*, 17, 498–501.

Palys, T.S. (1986). 'Testing the common wisdom: The social content of video pornography'. *Canadian Psychology*, 27, 22–35.

Peevers, B.H. (1979). 'Androgyny on the TV screen? An analysis of sex role portrayals'. *Sex Roles*, 5, 797–809.

Perloff, R.M. (1977). 'some antecedents of children's sex-role stereotypes'. *Psychological* 40, 436–466.

Perloff, R., Brown, J. and Miller, M. (1982). 'Mass media and sex-typing: Research perspectives and policy implications'. *International Journal of Women's Studies*, 5, 265–273.

Perse, E. (1994). 'Uses of erotica and acceptance of rape-myths'. *Communication Research*, 21(4)., 488–515.

Pierce, K. (1989). 'Sex-role stereotyping of children on television: A content analysis of the roles and attributes of child characters'. *Sociological Spectrum*, 9, 321–328.

Pingree, S. (1978). 'The effects of non-sexist television commercials and perceptions of reality on children's attitudes about women'. *Psychology of Women Quarterly*, 2, 262–276.

Pingree, S., Hawkins, R., Butler, M. and Paisley, W. (1976). 'A scale for sexism'. *Journal of Communication*, 26(4)., 193–201.

Pollack, S. and Gilligan, C. (1982). 'Image of violence in Thematic Apperception Test Stories'. *Journal of Personality and Social Psychology*, 42(1)., 159–167.

Press, A., Namuth, T., Argest, S., Gander, M., Luberow, G.C., Reese, M., Friendly, D.T. and McDaniel, A. (1985, March 18). ' The war against pornography'. *Newsweek*, pp. 58–66.

Preston, E.H. (1990). 'Pornography and the construction of gender'. In N. Signorielli and M. Morgan (Eds.) *Cultivation Analysis: New Directions in Media Effects Research*, pp. 107–122. Newbury Park, CA: Sage.

Pribram, D. (1988). *Female Spectators: Looking at Film and Television* New York: Verso.

Propper, M.M. (1971). 'Exposure to sexually oriented materials among young male prisoners'. *Technical Report to the Commission on Obscenity and Pornography* (Vol. 9). Washington DC: US Government Printing Office.

Rak, D.S. and McMullen, L.M. (1987). 'Sex-role stereotyping in television commercials: A verbal response mode and content analysis'. *Canadian Journal of Behavioural Source*, 19(1)., 25–39.

Rakow, L. (1986). 'Rethinking gender rsearch in communication'. *Journal of Communication*, 36(4)., 11–26.

Reep, D.C. and Dambrot, F.H. (1987). 'Television's professional women: working with men in the 1990s'. *Journalism Quarterly*, 64, 376–381.

Reeves, B. and Greenberg, B. (1976). 'Children's perceptions of television characters'. *Human Communication Research*, 3, 113–127.

Reeves, B. and Lometti, G. (1979). 'The dimensional structure of children's perceptions of television characters: A replication'. *Human Communication Research*, 5, 247–256.

Reeves, B. and Miller, M.M. (1978). 'A multidimensional measure of children's identification with television characters'. *Journal of Broadcasting*, 22, 71–86.

Repetti, R.C. (1984). 'Determinants of children's sex-stereotyping: Parental sex-role traits and television viewing'. *Personality and Social Psychology Bulletin*, 10, 457–468.

Riffe, D., Goldson, H., Saxton, K. and Yang-Chou, Y. (1988). 'Females and minorities in TV ads in 1987 Saturday children's programmes'. *Journalism Quarterly*, 65, 129–136.

Roberts, E. (1982). 'Television and sexual learning in childhood'. In D. Pearl, L. Bouthilet and J. Lazar (Eds.) *Television and Behaviour: Ten Years of Scientific progress and Implications for the Eighties.* Rockville, Maryland: National Institute of Mental Health.

Roberts, D.F. and Bachen, C.M. (1981). 'Mass communication effects'. *American Review of Psychology*, 32, 307–356.

Roberts, D.F. and Maccoby, N. (1985). 'Effects of mass communication'. In G. Lindzey and E. Aronson (Eds.) *Handbook of Social Psychology*, (3rd Ed.). 'New York: Random House.

Robinson, G.J. (1983). 'Changing Canadian and US magazine portrayals of women and work: Growing opportunities for choice'. In E.Wartella, D.C. Whitney and S. Windahl (Eds.) *Mass Communication Review Yearbook: Vol.4.* Beverly Hills,CA: Sage, pp. 229–250.

Rosencrantz, P., Vogel, S., Bee, H., Broverman, I. and Broverman, D. (1968). 'Sex-role stereotypes and self-concepts in college students'. *Journal of Consulting and Clinical Psychology*, 32, 287–295.

Rosenwasser, S.M., Lingenfelter, M. and Harrington, A.F. (1989). 'non-traditional gender role portrayals on television and children's gender role perceptions'. *Journal of Applied Developmental Psychology*, 10 97–105.

Rothschild, N. (1984). 'Small group affiliation as a mediating factor in the cultivation process'. In G. Melischek, K.E. Rosingren and J. Stappers (Eds.) *Cultural Indicators: An International Symposium.* Vienna: Osterreichischen Akademie der Wissenschaftten, pp. 377–387.

Rubin, A.M. and Perse, E.M. (1987). 'Audience activity and soap opera involvement: A uses and effects investigation'. *Human Communication Research*, 14, 246–268.

Ruble, D.M. Balabran, T. and Cooper, J. (1981). 'Gender constancy and the effects of sex-typed televised toy commercials'. *Child Development*, 52(2)., 667–673.

Rummel, A., Goodwin, M. and Shepherd, M. (1990). 'Self-efficacy and stereotyping in advertising: Should consumers want a change? *International Journal of Advertising*, 9, 308–316.

Sapolsky, B.S. (1982). 'Sexual acts and references on prime-time TV: A two-year look'. *Southern Speech Communication Journal*, 47, 212–226.

Sapolsky, B.S. and Tabarlet, J.L. (1991). 'Sex in prime time television: 1979 versus 1989'. *Journal of Broadcasting and Electronic Media*, 15(4), 505–516.

Sapolsky, B.S. and Zillmann, D. (1981). 'The effect of soft-core and hard-core erotica on provoked and unprovoked hostile behaviour.' *Journal of Sex Research*, 17, 319–343.

Schechtman, S.A. (1978). 'Occupational portrayal of men and women on the most frequently mentioned television shows of pre-school children'. *Resource in Education*, (ERIC Document Reproduction Service N.ED 174–156).

Scheibe, C. (1979). 'Sex roles in TV commercials'. *Journal of Advertising Research*, 19, 23–28.

Schmidt, G. (1975). 'Male–Female differences in sexual arousal and behaviour during and after exposure to sexually explicit stimuli'. In E.A. Rubinstein, R. Geen and E. Brecher (Eds.) *New Directions in Sex Research*. New York: Plenum Press.

Schneider, K.C. (1979). 'Sex roles in television commercials: new dimensions for comparison'. *Akron Business and Economic Review*, Fall, 20–24.

Schwartz, L. (1974). 'The image of women in the novels of Mme. de Souza'. *The University of Michigan Papers in Women's Studies*, I, 142–148.

Schwarz, N. and Kurz, E. (1989). 'What's in a picture? The impact of face-ism on trait attribution'. *European Journal of Social Psychology*, 19, 311–316.

Sciglimpaglia, D., Lundstrom, W.J. and Vanier, D.J. (1979). 'Women's role orientation and their attitudes toward sex role portrayals in advertising'. In J.H. Leigh and C.R. Martin, Jr. (Eds.) *Current Issues and Research in Advertising*. Ann Arbor: University of Michigan, pp. 163–175.

Schwartz, L.A. and Markham, W.T. (1985). 'Sex stereotyping in children's toy advertisements'. *Sex Roles*, 12, 157–170.

Sears, R.R. (1965). 'Development of gender role'. In F.A Beach (Ed.). *Sex and Behaviour*. New York: John Wiley and Sons.

Seggar, J.F., Hafen, J.K. and Hannonen-Gladden, H. (1981). 'Television's portrayals of minorities and women in drama and comedy drama: 1971–80'. *Journal of Broadcasting*, 25, 277–288.

Seggar, J. and Wheeler, P. (1973). 'World of work on TV: Ethnic and sex representation in TV drama'. *Journal of Broadcasting*, 17, 201–214.

Sexton, D.E. and Haberman, P. (1974). 'Women in magazine advertisements'. *Journal of Advertising Research*, 14,(4)., 41–46.

Sharits, N. and Lammers, B.H., (1983). 'Perceived attributes of models in prime-time and daytime television commercials: A person perception approach'. *Journal of Marketing Research*, 20, 64–73.

Sherman, J.A. (1971). *On the psychology of women*. Springfield, IL: Charles Thomas.

Sherman Group, The (1982). *Adman and Eve*. Unpublished study carried out for the US Equal Opportunity Commission.

Sherman, B.C. and Dominick, J.R. (1986). 'Violence and sex in music videos: TV and rock 'n' roll'. *Journal of Communication*, 36 (1)., 79–93.

Siegel, C.L.F. (1973). 'Sex differences in the occupational choices of second graders'. *Journal of Vocaitonal Behaviour*, 3, 15–19.

Signorielli, N. (1984). 'The demography of the television world'. In G. Melischeck, K.E. Rosengren, and J. Stappers (Eds.)., *Cultural Indicators: Any international symposium*. Vienna, Austria. Austrian Academy of Sciences.

Signorielli, N. (1989). 'Television and conceptions about sex roles: Maintaining conventionality and the status quo'. *Sex Roles*, 21(5/6)., 341–360.

Signorielli, N. (1991). 'Adolescents and ambivalence toward marriage: A cultivation analysis'. *Youth and Society*, 23(1)., 121–149

Signorielli, N. and Lears, M. (1992). 'Children, television and conceptions about chores: attitudes and behaviours'. *Sex Roles*, 27(3/4)., 157–170.

Silverman, L.T., Sprafkin, J.N. and Rubinstein, E.A. (1979). 'Physical content and sexual behaviour on prime-time TV'. *Journal of Communication*, 29(1), 33–43.

Silverman-Watkins, L.T., Levi, S.C. and Klein, M.A. (1986). 'Sex-stereotyping as a factor in children's comprehension of television news'. *Journalism Quarterly*, 64, 3–11.

Silverstein, A. and Silverstein, R. (1974). 'The portrayal of women in television advertising'. *Federal Communications Bar Journal*, 27, 71–78.

Simmons, R.G. and Rosenberg, M. (1971). 'Functions of children's perceptions of th stratification system'. *American Sociological Review*, 36, 235–249

Singer, J.L. and Singer, D.G. (1981). *Television, imagination and aggression: A study of preschoolers*. Hillsdale, N.J.: Lawrence Erlbaum Associates.

Slaby, R.G. and Frey, K.S. (1975). 'Development of gender constancy and selective attention to same-sex models'. *Child Development*, 40, 849–856.

Slade, J. (1984). 'Violence in the hard-core pornographic film: An historical survey'. *Journal of Communication*, 34, 148–163.

Smith, D.D. (1976). 'The social content of pornography'. *Journal of Communication*, 26, 16–23.

Smith, P.K. and Bennett, S. (1990). 'Here come the steel monsters! *Changes*, 8(2)., 97–105.

Soley, L.C. and Reid, L.N. (1988). 'Taking it off: Are models in magazine ads waering less? *Journalism Quarterly*, 65, 960–966.

Spence, J.T. and Helmreich, R.L. (1980). 'Masculine instrumentality and feminine expressiveness: Their relationships with sex role attitudes and behaviours'. *Psychology of women Quarterly*, 5, 147–163.

Spiegler, M.D. and Liebert, R.M. (1970). 'Some correlates of self-reported fear'. *Psychological Reporter*, 26, 691–695.

Silverstein, A. and Silverstein, R. (1974). 'The portrayal of women in television advertising'. *Federal Communications Bar Journal*, 27, 71–98.

Smythe, D.W. (1954). 'Reality as presented by television'. *Public Opinion Quarterly*, 18, 143–154.

Sprafkin, M. and Liebert, R.M. (1978). 'sex-typing and children's preferences'. In G. Techman, A.

Daniels and J.Benet (Eds.). *Health and Home: Images of women in the mass media* New York, Oxford University Press, 288–339.

Sprafkin, M. and Silverman, L.T. (1981). 'Update: Physically intimate and sexual behaviour on prime-time TV, 1978–1979'. *Journal of Communication*, 31(1), 34–40.

Steenland, S. (1990). *What's Wrong with the Picture? The Status of Women on Screen and Behind the Camera in Entertainment TV*. Washington, DC: National Commission on Working Women of Wider Opportunities for Women.

Stern, D.N. and Bender, E.P. (1974). 'an ethological study of children approaching a strange adult: Sex differences'. In R.C. Friedman, R.M. Richards, R.L. Vand Wiele and L.D. Stern (Eds.) *Sex Differences in Children* (New York Wiley).

Spence, J.T., Helmreich, R. and Strapp, J. (1975). 'Ratings of self and peers on sex-role attitudes and their relation to self-esteem and conception of masculinity and femininity'. *Journal of Personality and Social Psychology*, 32, 20–39.

Sternglanz, S. and Serbin, L. (1974). 'Sex role stereotyping on children's television programmes'. *Developmental Psychology*, 10, 710 715.

Streicher, H.W. (1974). 'The girls in the cartoons'. *Journal of Communication*, 24(2)., 125–129

Stone, L.E. (1985). *Child Pornography Literature: A Content Analysis*. Unpublished doctoral dissertation, International College, San Diego, CA.

Tan, A. (1979). 'TV beauty ads and role expectations of adolescent female viewers'. *Journalism Quarterly*, 56, 283–288.

Tan, A., Raudy, J., Huff, C. and Miles, J. (1980). ' Children's reactions to male and female newscasters' effectiveness and believability'. *Quarterly Journal of Speech,* 66, 201–205.

Tanner, J.M. (1972). 'Sequence, tempo and individual variation in growth and development of boys and girls aged twelve to sixteen'. In J. Kagan and R. Coles (Eds.) *Twelve to Sixteen: Early Adolescence*. New York: Norton.

Tedesco, N. (1974). 'Patterns in prime-time'. *Journal of Communication*, 74, 119–124.

Thoveron, G. (1987). *How women are Represented in Television Programmes in the EEC; Part One: Images of Women in News, Advertising, and Series and Serials*. Brussels: Commission of the European Communities.

Tuchman, G. (1978). 'The symbolic annihilation of women by the mass media'. In G. Tuchman, A. Daniels, and J. Benet, (Eds.) *Hearth and home: Images of women in the mass media*. New York: Oxford University Press.

Turner, M.E. (1974). 'Sex role attitudes and fear of success in relation to achievement behaviour in women'. *Dissertation Abstracts International*, 35, 5–B, 2451–2452.

Turow, J. (1974). 'Advising and ordering: Daytime, prime time'. *Journal of Communication*, 24, 135–141.

US Commission on Civil Rights (1977). *Window Dressing on the Set: Women and Minorities in Television*. A Report of the US Commission on Civil Rights, Washington, D.C.

Van Zoonen, L. (1992). Feminist perspectives on the media. In J. Curran and M. Gurevitch (Eds.) *Mass Media and Society*. London: Edward Arnold, pp. 33–54.

Verkateson, M. and Losco, J. (1975). 'Women in magazine ads'. *Journal of Advertising Research*, 15(5)., 49–54.

Verna, M.E. (1975). 'The female image in children's TV commercials'. *Journal of Broadcasting*, 19, 301–309.

Vernon, J.A., Williams, J.A. Jr., Phillips, T. and Wilson, J. (1990). 'media stereotyping: A comparison of the way elderly women and men are portrayed on prime-time television'. *Journal of women and Aging*, 2(4)., 55–68.

Vest, D. (1992). 'Prime-time pilots: A content analysis of changes in gender representation'. *Journal of broadcasting and Electronic Media*, 36(1)., 25–42.

Vincent, R.C. (1989). 'Clio's consciousness raised? Portrayal of women in rock videos re-examined'. *Journalism Quarterly*, 66, 155–160.

Vincent, R.C., Davis, D.K. and Boruszkowski, L.A. (1987). ' Sexism on MTV: A content analysis of rock videos'. *Journalism Quarterly*, 64, 750–755, 941.

Volgy, J.J. and Schwartz, J.E. (1980). 'TV entertainment programming and socio-political attitudes, *Journalism Quarterly*, 57, 150–155.

Wagner, L. and Banos, J.B. (1973). 'A woman's place: A follow-up analysis of the roles portrayed by women in magazine advertisements'. *Journal of Marketing Research*, 10, 213–214.

Warren, D. (1978). 'Commercial liberation: What does 'she' mean? *Journal of Communication*, 28, 169–173.

Wartella, E. (1980). 'Children's impressions of television mothers'. In M. Grewe-Partsch and G.J. Robinson (Eds.) *Women, Communication and Careers*, Munich: K.G. Saur, pp. 76–83

Weaver, J.B. (1991). 'Responding to erotica: perceptual processes and dispositional implications'. In J. Bryant and D. Zillmann (Eds.) *Responding to the Screen: Reception and Reaction Processes*. pp. 329–354. Hillsdale, NJ: Lawrence Erlbaum Associates.

Weaver, J.B., Masland, J.L. and Zillmann, D. (1984). ' Effect of erotica on young men's astethetic perception of their female partners'. *Perceptual and Motor Skills*, 58, 929–930.

Weigel, R.H. and Loomis, J.W. (1981). 'Televised models of female achievement revisited: Some progress'. *Journal of Applied Social Psychology*, 11, 58–63.

Weinberger, M. and Petroshius, S.M. (1977). *Twenty Years of Women in Magazine Advertising: An Update*. American Marketing Association.

Welch, R.L., Huston-Stein, A., Wright, J.C. and Plehal, R. (1979). 'Subtle sex-role cues in children's commercials'. *Journal of Communication*, 29 202–209.

Whipple, T.W. and Courtney, A.E. (1980). 'How to portray women in TV commercials'. *Journal of Advertising Research*, 20(2).

Wiebel, K. (1977). *Mirror, Mirror: Images of Women Reflected in popular Culture*. Garden City, N.Y.: anchor Books

Williams, F., La Rose, R. and Frost, F. (1981). *Children, television and sex-role stereotyping*. New York: Praeger.

Williams, T.M. (1986). *The Impact of Television*, London: Academic Press.

Williamson, J. (1978). *Decoding Advertisements: Ideology and Meaning in Advertising*. London: Marion Boyars.

Wilson, G.D. (1966). 'An electrodermal technique for the study of phobia'. *New England Medical Journal*, 85, 696–698.

Wilson, G.D. (1967). 'social desirability and sex differences in expressed fear'. *Behaviour Research and Therapy*, 5, 136–137.

Winick, C. (1971). 'Some observations on characteristics of patrons of adult theatres and book-stores'. In *Technical Report of the Commission on Obscenity and Pornography* (vol. 9) Washington DC: US Government Printing Office.

Winick, C. (1985). 'A content analysis of sexually explicit magazines sold in adult bookstores'. *Journal of Sex Research*, 21, 206–211.

Winick, C., Williamson, L.G., Chuzmir, S.F. and Winick, M.P. (1973). *Children's Television Commercials: A Content Analysis*. New York: Praeger.

Witkin, H. (1979). 'Socialization, culture and ecology in the development of group sex differences in cognitive style'. *Human Development*. 22(5)., 358–372.

Wortzel, L.H. and Frisbee, J.M. (1974). 'Women's role portrayal preferences in advertisements: An empirical study'. *Journal of Marketing*, 38(4)., 41–46.

Wright, J.C., Huston, A.C., Triglio, R., Fitchin, M., Smith, E.D. and pienyat, S. (1992). *Occupational portrayals on television: Children's role schemata, career aspirations and perceptions of reality*. Cited in M. Fitch, A.C. Huston and J.C. Wright, 'From Television forms to genre schemata: Children's perceptions of television reality', chapter in G.L. Berry and J.K. Asamen (Eds.) *Children and Television: Images in a Changing Sociocultural World*. Newbury Park, CA, Sage, pp. 38–52.

Wroblewski, R. and Huston, A.C. (1987). 'Televised occupational stereotypes and their effects on early adolescents: Are they changing? *Journal of Early Adolescence*, 7(3)., 283–297.

Yaffe, M. and Nelson, E.C. (Eds.) (1982). *The Influence of Pornography on Behaviour*. New York: Academic Press.

Yang, N. and Linz, D. (1990). 'Movie ratings and the content of adult videos: The sex–violence ratio'. *Journal of Communication*, 40(2), 28–42.

Zemach, T. and Cohen, A.A. (1986). 'Perception of gender equality on television and in social reality'. *Journal of Broadcasting and Electronic media*, 30(4)., 427–444.

Zillmann, D. and Bryant, J. (1984). 'Effects of message exposure to pornography'. In N.M. Malamuth and E. Donnerstein (Eds.) *Pornography and Sexual Aggression*. Orlando, Fl: Academic Press, pp. 115–138.

Zillmann, D. and Bryant, J. (1988). 'Pornography's impact on sexual satisfaction'. *Journal of Applied Social psychology*, 18, 438–453.

Zillman, D., Bryant, J. and Carveth, R.A. (1981). 'The effect of erotica featuring sado-masochism and bestiality on motivated intermale aggression'. *Personality and Social Psychology Bulletin*, 3, 153–159.

Zillman, D., Bryant, J., Comisky, P.W. and Medoff, N.J. (1981). 'excitation and hedonic valence in the effect of erotica on motivated intermale aggression'. *European Journal of Social Psychology*, 11, 233–252.

Zillmann, D. and Weaver, J.B. (1989). 'Pornography and sexual callousness toward women'. In D. Zillmann and J. Bryant (Eds.) *Pornography: Research Advances and Policy Considerations*. pp. 95–125. Hillsdale, NJ: Lawrence Erlbaum Associates.

Zuckerman, D.M., Singer, D.G. and Singer, J.L. (1980). ' Children's television viewing, racial and sex role attitudes'. *Journal of Applied Psychology*, 10, 281–294.

Subject index

Author index

Media titles available from John Libbey

Acamedia Research Monographs

Taxation and Representation: Media, Political Communication and the Poll Tax
David Deacon and Peter Golding
Hardback ISBN 0 86196 390 3

Satellite Television in Western Europe (revised edition 1992)
Richard Collins
Hardback ISBN 0 86196 203 6

Beyond the Berne Convention
Copyright, Broadcasting and the Single European Market
Vincent Porter
Hardback ISBN 0 86196 267 2

Nuclear Reactions: A Study in Public Issue Television
John Corner, Kay Richardson and Natalie Fenton
Hardback ISBN 0 86196 251 6

Transnationalization of Television in Western Europe
Preben Sepstrup
Hardback ISBN 0 86196 280 X

The People's Voice: Local Radio and Television in Europe
Nick Jankowski, Ole Prehn and James Stappers
Hardback ISBN 0 86196 322 9

Television and the Gulf War
David E. Morrison
Hardback ISBN 0 86196 341 5

Contra-Flow in Global News
Oliver Boyd Barrett and Daya Kishan Thussu
Hardback ISBN 0 86196 344 X

CNN World Report: Ted Turner's International News Coup
Don M. Flournoy
Hardback ISBN 0 86196 359 8

Small Nations: Big Neighbour
Roger de la Garde, William Gilsdorf and Ilja Wechselmann
Hardback ISBN 0 86196 343 1

European Media Research Series

The New Television in Europe
Edited by Alessandro Silj
Hardback ISBN 0 86196 361 X

Media Industry in Europe
Edited by Antonio Pilati
Paperback ISBN 0 86196 398 9

European Institute for the Media

Television and the Viewer Interest: Explorations in the responsiveness of European Broadcasters
Jeremy Mitchell and Jay G Blumler (eds)
Paperback ISBN 0 86196 440 3

Media titles available from John Libbey

Broadcasting and Audio-visual Policy in the European Single Market
Richard Collins
Hardback ISBN 0 86196 405 5

Aid for Cinematographic and Audio-visual Production In Europe
(published for the Council of Europe)
Jean-Noël Dibie
Hardback ISBN 0 86196 397 0

BBC World Service

Global Audiences: Research for Worldwide Broadcasting 1993
Edited by Graham Mytton
Paperback ISBN 0 86196 400 4

Broadcasting Standards Council Publications

A Measure of Uncertainty: The Effects of the Mass Media
Guy Cumberbatch and Dennis Howitt
Hardback ISBN 0 86196 231 1

Violence in Television Fiction: Public Opinion and Broadcasting Standards
David Docherty
Paperback ISBN 0 86196 284 2

Survivors and the Media
Ann Shearer
Paperback ISBN 0 86196 332 6

Taste and Decency in Broadcasting
Andrea Millwood Hargrave
Paperback ISBN 0 86196 331 8

A Matter of Manners? – The Limits of Broadcast Language
Edited by Andrea Millwood Hargrave
Paperback ISBN 0 86196 337 7

Sex and Sexuality in Broadcasting
Andrea Millwood Hargrave
Paperback ISBN 0 86196 393 8

Violence in Factual Television
Andrea Millwood Hargrave
Paperback ISBN 0 86196 441 1

Radio and Audience Attitudes
Andrea Millwood Hargrave
PAperback ISBN 0 86196 481 0

International Institute of Communications

Vision and Hindsight: The First 25 Years of the Internatuional Institute of Communications
Rex Winsbury and Shehina Fazal (eds)
Hardback ISBN 0 86196 449 7
Paperback ISBN 0 86196 467 5

Acamedia Textbook

Political Marketing and Communication
Philippe J. Maarek
Paperback ISBN 0 86196 377 6

Media titles available from John Libbey

UNESCO Publications

A Richer Vision: The development of ethnic minority media in Western democracies
Charles Husband (ed)
Paperback ISBN 0 86196 450 0

Video World-Wide: An International Study
Manuel Alvarado (ed)
Paperback ISBN 0 86196 143 9

University of Manchester Broadcasting Symposium

And Now for the BBC ...
Nod Miller and Rod Allen (eds)
Paperback ISBN 0 86196 318 0

It's Live – But Is It Real?
Nod Miller and Rod Allen (eds)
Paperback ISBN 0 86196 370 9

Broadcasting Enters the Marketplace
Nod Miller and Rod Allen (eds)
Paperback ISBN 0 86196 434 9

ITC Television Research Monographs

Television in Schools
Robin Moss, Christopher Jones and Barrie Gunter
Hardback ISBN 0 86196 314 8

Television: The Public's View
Barrie Gunter and Carmel McLaughlin
Hardback ISBN 0 86196 348 2

The Reactive Viewer
Barrie Gunter and Mallory Wober
Hardback ISBN 0 86196 358 X

Television: The Public's View 1992
Barrie Gunter and Paul Winstone
Hardback ISBN 0 86196 399 7

Seeing is Believing: Religion and Television in the 1990s
Barrie Gunter and Rachel Viney
Hardback ISBN 0 86196 442 X

Published in association with The Arts Council

Picture This: Media Representations of Visual Art and Artists
Philip Hayward (ed)
Paperback ISBN 0 86196 126 9

Culture, Technology and Creativity
Philip Hayward (ed)
Paperback ISBN 0 86196 266 4

Parallel Lines: Media Representations of Dance
Stephanie Jordan & Dave Allen (eds)
Paperback ISBN 0 86196 371 7

Arts TV: A History of British Arts Television
John A Walker
Paperback ISBN 0 86196 435 7

Media titles available from John Libbey

A Night in at the Opera: Media Representation of Opera
Jeremy Tambling (ed)
ISBN 0 86196 466 7

IBA Television Research Monographs

Teachers and Television:
A History of the IBA's Educational Fellowship Scheme
Josephine Langham
Hardback ISBN 0 86196 264 8

Godwatching: Viewers, Religion and Television
Michael Svennevig, Ian Haldane, Sharon Spiers and Barrie Gunter
Hardback ISBN 0 86196 198 6
Paperback ISBN 0 86196 199 4

Violence on Television: What the Viewers Think
Barrie Gunter and Mallory Wober
Hardback ISBN 0 86196 171 4
Paperback ISBN 0 86196 172 2

Home Video and the Changing Nature of Television Audience
Mark Levy and Barrie Gunter
Hardback ISBN 0 86196 175 7
Paperback ISBN 0 86196 188 9

Patterns of Teletext Use in the UK
Bradley S. Greenberg and Carolyn A. Lin
Hardback ISBN 0 86196 174 9
Paperback ISBN 0 86196 187 0

Attitudes to Broadcasting Over the Years
Barrie Gunter and Michael Svennevig
Hardback ISBN 0 86196 173 0
Paperback ISBN 0 86196 184 6

Television and Sex Role Stereotyping
Barrie Gunter
Hardback ISBN 0 86196 095 5
Paperback ISBN 0 86196 098 X

Television and the Fear of Crime
Barrie Gunter
Hardback ISBN 0 86196 118 8
Paperback ISBN 0 86196 119 6

Behind and in Front of the Screen – Television's Involvement with Family Life
Barrie Gunter and Michael Svennevig
Hardback ISBN 0 86196 123 4
Paperback ISBN 0 86196 124 2

Institute of Local Television

Citizen Television: A Local Dimension to Public Service Broadcasting
Dave Rushton (ed)
Hardback ISBN 0 86196 433 0

Reporters Sans Frontières

1995 Report
Freedom of the Press Throughout the World
Paperback ISBN 0 86196 523 X